SPANISH
QuickStart Guide®

SPANISH
QuickStart Guide®

The Simplified Beginner's Guide to Learning Essential Vocabulary, Building Practical Grammar Skills, and Mastering Conversational Spanish

Maria Block

Copyright © 2025 by ClydeBank Media LLC

All rights reserved. No part of this publication may be reproduced, distributed, or transmitted in any form or by any means, including photocopying, recording, or other electronic or mechanical methods, without the prior written permission of the publisher, except in the case of brief quotations embodied in critical reviews and certain other noncommercial uses permitted by copyright law. For permission requests, write to the publisher, addressed "Attention: Permissions Coordinator," at the address below.

ClydeBank Media LLC is not associated with any organization, product or service discussed in this book. Although the author and publisher have made every effort to ensure that the information in this book was correct at press time, the author and publisher do not assume and hereby disclaim any liability to any party for any loss, damage, or disruption caused by errors or omissions, whether such errors or omissions result from negligence, accident, or any other cause.

All trademarks, service marks, trade names, trade dress, product names and logos appearing in this publication are the property of their respective owners, including in some instances ClydeBank Media LLC. Any rights not expressly granted herein are reserved.

Trademarks: All trademarks are the property of their respective owners. The trademarks that are used are without any consent, and the publication of the trademark is without permission or backing by the trademark owner. All trademarks and brands within this book are for clarifying purposes only and are owned by the owners themselves, not affiliated with this document.

Editor: Marilyn Burkley
Cover Illustration and Design: Katie Donnachie, Copyright © 2025 by ClydeBank Media LLC
Interior Design: Liliana Guia, Katie Donnachie Copyright © 2025 by ClydeBank Media LLC

First Edition - Last Updated: July 1, 2025

ISBN-13: 9781636100913 (paperback) | 9781636100937 (hardcover) | 9781636100944 (audiobook) | 9781636100920 (eBook) | 9781636100968 (spiral-bound)

Publisher's Cataloging-In-Publication Data
(Prepared by Cassidy Cataloguing Services, Inc.)

Names: Block, Maria (Maria Ann), author.
Title: Spanish QuickStart Guide : the simplified beginner's guide to learning essential vocabulary, building practical grammar skills, and mastering conversational Spanish / Maria Block.
Other titles: Spanish Quick Start Guide
Description: [Albany, New York] : ClydeBank Media, [2025] | Series: QuickStart guides. | Bilingual. In English and Spanish. | Includes bibliographical references and index.
Identifiers: ISBN: 9781636100913 (paperback) | 9781636100937 (hardcover) | 9781636100968 (spiral-bound) | 9781636100920 (eBook) | 9781636100944 (audiobook)
Subjects: LCSH: Spanish language--Self-instruction--Handbooks, manuals, etc. | Spanish language--Vocabulary--Handbooks, manuals, etc. | Spanish language--Grammar--Handbooks, manuals, etc. | Spanish language--Conversation and phrase books--English. | LCGFT: Handbooks and manuals. | BISAC: LANGUAGE STUDY / Spanish. | LANGUAGE ARTS & DISCIPLINES / Speech & Pronunciation. | LANGUAGE ARTS & DISCIPLINES / Translating & Interpreting.
Classification: LCC: PC4112.5 .B56 2025 | DCC: 468.2421--dc23

Library of Congress Control Number: 2025935432

Author ISNI: 0000 0005 2631 4822

Ordering Information: Please visit www.clydebankmedia.com/orders or call 800-340-3069. Special discounts are available on quantity purchases by corporations, associations, and others.

Copyright © 2025
www.quickstartguides.com
All Rights Reserved

ISBN-13: 978-1-63610-091-3 (paperback)
ISBN-13: 978-1-63610-096-8 (spiral-bound)

OVER 1 MILLION READERS LOVE

QuickStart Guides

> *After reading this book, I must say that it has been one of the best decisions of my life!*
>
> — ROHIT R.

Contents

INTRODUCTION 1
 Proficiency Levels 4
 Basic Language-Learning Tips 6
 Chapter by Chapter 7
 Quick Reference to Key Grammar Concepts 9

PART I – FOUNDATIONS

| 1 | THE ESSENTIALS 13
 Alphabet and Pronunciation 14
 Numbers 20
 Months, Days, Seasons, and Dates 22
 Subject Pronouns 24
 Question Words 29
 Infinitives 32

| 2 | SPANISH–ENGLISH COMPARISONS 35
 Origins, Evolutions, and Connections 36
 The Concept of Gender 40
 More on Gender Agreement: Unknowns, Irregulars, and Adjectives ... 44

| 3 | FROM HELLO TO GOODBYE 55
 Greetings/Goodbyes 56
 Introductions and Basic Conversation 60
 More Basic Questions and Phrases 62
 Dynamic Dialogue 66

PART II – THIS IS ME

| 4 | DEFINING YOURSELF 75
 To Be or Not to Be? An Introduction to the Verb Ser 76
 Describing Yourself with the Verb Tener 80
 Birthdates and Ages Using Ser and Tener 83
 Activities Using Regular Present-Tense Verbs 84

| 5 | A DAY IN THE LIFE ... 95
- What Time Is It? ... 96
- From Sunrise to Sunset: A Typical Day ... 101
- Passing the Time ... 107
- Must Dos: Ways to Express Obligation ... 112

| 6 | LIFE WITH LOVED ONES ... 115
- My Family, Our Home: Possessive Adjectives ... 117
- Relatives and Relationships: Describing Loved Ones ... 121
- Family Fun ... 125
- Likes and Dislikes: The Verb Gustar ... 128

PART III – EVERYDAY LIFE

| 7 | WHERE I LIVE ... 139
- Mi Casa es Tu Casa ... 140
- Stepping Out ... 147
- Talking To and Describing the People You Know ... 150

| 8 | OUT AND ABOUT ... 157
- Social Spaces ... 158
- Shopping: Costs and Comparisons ... 160
- Grocery Shopping and Going Out to Eat ... 165

| 9 | COMMUNITY CONNECTIONS ... 175
- A Sense of Community ... 176
- A Trip Down Memory Lane: Describing Your Past ... 177
- Making Sense of the Past ... 188

PART IV – THE BIGGER PICTURE

| 10 | PLACES WE VISIT ... 197
- Places We've Been and Places We'll Be ... 198
- The Present Perfect ... 200
- Places I'd Like to Go and Things I'd Like to Do ... 202
- What to Pack ... 203
- Traveling To-Do List ... 208

| 11 | NAVIGATING THE UNKNOWN ... 213
- Moving from Place to Place ... 215

    Need Directions?......219
    Insider Tips: Travel Recommendations......224

| 12 | CELEBRATING CULTURAL DIVERSITY 233
    Celebrations of Spanish Language and Culture......234
    Cultural Crossroads......241
    Unity in Diversity: Embracing Our Differences......243

CONCLUSION 247
APPENDIX 251
GLOSSARY 267
ABOUT THE AUTHOR 277
ABOUT QUICKSTART GUIDES 279
INDEX 281

To my teachers

From the professors who saw my potential and encouraged me to reach for more, to the Spanish speakers who have welcomed me with open arms into their language and culture, I couldn't have achieved any of this without you.

To my students

Thank you for challenging me, inspiring me, and shaping me into the teacher that I am today. While I might have taught you a thing or two about Spanish, you have taught me so much about life, and have inspired me to pursue my dreams. I hope you will never let anyone convince you that you are capable of anything less than incredible things.

BEFORE YOU START READING, DOWNLOAD YOUR FREE DIGITAL ASSETS!

- Preterite vs. Imperfect Workbook
- Gender Agreement Workbook
- 12 Irregular Present Tense Verbs Workbook
- Ser vs. Estar Workbook

TWO WAYS TO ACCESS YOUR FREE DIGITAL ASSETS

Use the camera app on your mobile phone to scan the QR code or visit the link below and instantly access your Digital Assets.

go.quickstartguides.com/spanish

Introduction

Welcome to *Spanish QuickStart Guide*! I am beyond thrilled that you have chosen this book, and I truly hope that it will be a source of inspiration as well as a useful tool for you on your language-learning journey.

Like many of you, I took Spanish as a high school student. I took it mostly because I needed the language credits to graduate, but I also hoped to actually learn some of the language. Unfortunately, I found Spanish class to be pretty difficult and overwhelming. I felt as if many students around me were picking up what we were learning, but for some reason everything was going over my head. I spent two years in a Spanish classroom reciting grammar exercises from a textbook out loud but not really knowing what I was saying or doing; I was just trying my best to act like I knew what was going on so that none of my classmates would think I was stupid. I wasn't *completely* unsuccessful in Spanish class; I learned lots of vocabulary, and I could conjugate verbs into many tenses. Besides that, though, I had no real working knowledge of the language.

Coincidentally, as I was finishing up my second and last required year of Spanish, a family friend told me about an opportunity that would allow me to go to Mexico and live with a host family for a month during the summer while I attended Spanish immersion classes. As a teenager, I was ready to spread my wings and get out of my tiny hometown in South Dakota, so I gladly accepted the opportunity. (More than anything, I just wanted to go anywhere, and I saw this as a ticket out of the place I no longer wanted to be.) I figured I knew enough Spanish to get by, and I wasn't opposed to trying to learn more of the language, so off to Mexico I went.

When I arrived, it took me about two minutes to realize that I did not know any Spanish at all. When people spoke to me, I didn't understand a word they said. I also wasn't able to put together sentences well enough to even remotely attempt to communicate my ideas. The real world of Spanish was a lot different than the fill-in-the-blank textbook exercises I was used to doing. I realized this month abroad was going to be quite different than I had originally imagined.

Over the next month, I spent about six to eight hours a day taking Spanish immersion lessons. The rest of my time was spent on outings that would immerse me even more into the language. To my surprise, I was learning basic Spanish pretty quickly. I was able to take the little bit of Spanish I knew from high school and combine it with what I was learning in class, and it all started to come together for me. Being able to experience the language in a realistic setting helped me put everything together in a way that my high school Spanish classes had not. During that one month, I did not become an expert user of the language, but I learned enough to have basic conversations, which felt very encouraging.

When I returned home to finish up my high school studies, I got two jobs: one at a Mexican restaurant and one at the multicultural center in my hometown. I started using my Spanish to communicate with coworkers at the restaurant and families who came to use resources offered by the multicultural center. The more I practiced, the better I got, and I continued to learn more and more Spanish. (Not to mention that I was now one of the best students in my Spanish III high school class! The version of me who had struggled in Spanish three months before would never have believed I would one day be able to say that.) I took advantage of every opportunity I could to practice my Spanish. One of my coworkers even convinced me to tutor his whole family so that they could learn English. Looking back, I think that was the moment when I first started falling in love with language education.

Anxious to learn more, I returned to Mexico upon graduating from high school. I went there with no plan other than to continue learning the language and figure out what path I wanted to take in life, because I knew that no matter what I decided, it was going to involve Spanish. I continued to take Spanish immersion classes. I also tutored English for Spanish speakers, attended culinary classes, and even got to perform on national TV with a dance group that I took dance classes with. I had discovered a new appreciation for life. Because I took a chance at learning a second language, I was able to discover a whole new world. My Spanish enabled me to live in another country and connect with a whole new culture and people I would never have connected with otherwise. I gained a new level of respect for anyone who learns another language and/or moves to another country. My time in Mexico wasn't always easy. There were many difficult moments as I attempted to learn how to navigate a new language and culture all at the young age of eighteen, but I believe that's what made me the person that I am today.

After my time in Mexico, I continued to expose myself to the language in every way I could. I began earning my bachelor's degree in Spanish education at South Dakota State University. During my studies, I also did an internship with social services, volunteered at an immigration detention center to serve as an interpreter for pro bono immigration lawyers, and did what I could to help Spanish speakers in my community. Toward the end of my studies,

I moved to Houston, Texas, to complete my student teaching requirement. Upon graduating, I continued to work as a Spanish teacher for the next seven years while also earning my master's degree in Spanish at Sam Houston State University. I taught many levels of Spanish to students in the Houston area, including high school Spanish I and II for native and non-native speakers of Spanish, Spanish III, and AP Spanish Language and Culture. I now work as an instructional designer for a local community college, and I assist professors with designing courses that are engaging and help students gain the real-world skills I was missing in my high school Spanish classes. On top of my day job, I am an adjunct professor of Spanish and am really enjoying the opportunity to teach at the college level. I have learned so much about the Spanish language over the past ten-plus years, and I continue to learn more each day.

I fully recognize that my journey to learn Spanish came from a place of privilege. Not everyone is able to move to another country to learn the language, to pay for language immersion courses, or even to attend college. However, my experiences have heavily influenced the way I teach Spanish. I did not want my students to ever feel overwhelmed and incapable like I did when I took Spanish in high school. I realized that the way we are taught language is often based on outdated practices. Also, the way you and I learn Spanish is not the same as the way a young child does, who is able to *absorb* the language (more on that later). You can't just surround yourself with Spanish and pick it all up; you need many concepts explained to you. I have found that many textbooks focus so much on grammar that the context part of it gets lost in the background, which keeps us from understanding how a concept functions in real life. Although it is not easy to balance grammar and context, this book aims to provide you with a more effective balance. I have found that learners are more successful in learning the language when it is presented in a way that more accurately reflects the real-world use of the language and is presented in comprehensible bits and pieces that connect with one another.

I don't believe that language learning should feel hard or impossible. It isn't easy, but it definitely can be done. You will find many books on the market today claiming that you can learn Spanish in time frames such as thirty days or six weeks. The reality is, you can learn (some) Spanish in that time frame, but you won't have mastered every Spanish language concept. I am writing this book with beginners in mind. It is going to present language concepts to you in a real-life context and break down the grammar in a way that is more digestible. This book is intended to serve as a tool that you will use on your language-learning journey. It will give you tips, strategies, and the foundational information you need to get yourself going with everyday Spanish.

I also want to be sure to acknowledge that everyone learns differently. I hope that the way I present the information to you will be easy to understand. Some of you may understand a concept the first time you read it. Others may need to go back and review the concept again and again until it sticks. We are all on different journeys in terms of what we want to be able to do with Spanish, and we are all coming from different places. Please use this book in the way that works best for you, and remember that a book will never replace the learning that you can get from a trip abroad or a conversation class with a fluent speaker of Spanish. This book will not replace your use of other ways to continue to expose yourself to the language (more on this later also). However, I truly hope that it will make learning Spanish more accessible to people who want to learn, and that it will give you the confidence to continue your journey of learning Spanish—and maybe also an interest in various Spanish-speaking cultures. Though this is not a history book, I have included occasional cultural points throughout the text, to note some worthwhile information about various cultures from various time periods that use the Spanish language. It's my belief that a true mastery of a language will include at least some measure of education about the history of the countries that speak that language—even if it's not always a cheerful one.

Proficiency Levels

We often hear people say that someone "knows" or "doesn't know" a language. However, it's a bit more complex than that, as language fluency is on a spectrum. Many organizations have taken the time to create their own descriptions of this spectrum, to help learners identify their proficiency level. As to how many sublevels are within each level, it depends on what organization you get your information from. One such organization is the ACTFL (American Council on the Teaching of Foreign Languages); it has created descriptions of each language fluency level and sublevel, and I often show this information to my students, since I am a foreign language teacher. Despite the varying descriptions that are promoted, I think it's safe to say we can agree that there are at least three main levels of language proficiency: beginner, intermediate, and advanced. For simplification purposes I am not going to break it down into sublevels, but I will generally describe the three overall levels of language proficiency.

Beginner: Typically, a beginner can identify words that they have explicitly learned. For example, when you listen or read in Spanish, you will be able to pick out words and/or phrases that you have learned, but you likely won't understand every single detail; however, by focusing on key words you understand, you should be able to grasp the overall topic. You will depend on short sentences or words that you have memorized to communicate about everyday topics. The speech that you form will mainly be based on language formulas you have learned. It may feel robotic at times, but that is all part of the process of building your fluency.

Intermediate: You will be able to communicate about everyday topics by combining various language concepts you have learned to express yourself in a more fluid way. You are able to navigate simple unrehearsed everyday tasks in the language, such as engaging in a friendly conversation with someone you just met, or asking for directions or how to do something. Although your grammar is still developing, you can form sentences or strings of sentences to communicate thoughts and ideas in a way that is not as formulaic as that of a beginner.

Advanced: You will be able to communicate about a wide range of topics, from everyday concepts to the more abstract. You will be able to easily communicate about the past, present, future, etc., and move from one verb tense to another with ease. You can navigate unexpected situations in the language. You are also able to form paragraphs. You can communicate with native speakers of the language with ease, and you don't have to pause often to gather your thoughts before expressing yourself.

In this book, I will be focusing on building a beginner proficiency level. We will focus on learning high-frequency vocabulary, and I will draw your attention to basic grammar patterns in the language. Even if you are not completely new to Spanish, this book will still be a useful tool for review and freshening up on concepts that might need reinforcement. I also want to mention that it is normal to have skills at varying levels of proficiency. For example, reading and writing have always been much easier for me in Spanish than speaking and listening. These loose proficiency descriptions (beginner, intermediate, advanced) are provided to help you form realistic expectations for the language-learning process and can also be used to self-identify your language proficiency as you progress along this journey. Just remember that it is completely normal that certain language skills will be stronger than others.

Basic Language-Learning Tips

Learning a language takes lots of work, which is why I highly recommend that you find some additional ways to practice and reinforce what you'll be learning in this book. Below are some tips for ways to incorporate more of the Spanish language into your daily life.

- » Listen to the radio, a podcast, or songs in Spanish (lyricstraining.com is a fun way to practice listening comprehension with songs).

- » Watch movies or series in Spanish with Spanish subtitles. (If you are listening in English and putting the subtitles in Spanish, this won't help your listening comprehension. I especially recommend watching something you have seen before so that you can connect what you already know to the language you're hearing and reading in Spanish.)

- » Practice speaking Spanish with a friend or neighbor.

- » When you go to a restaurant with Spanish speakers, ask if you can practice ordering in Spanish.

- » Download a language-learning app (such as Duolingo) or game (such as LingoClip) to your phone for extra practice.

- » Practice conjugating verbs (conjuguemos.com is a great website for practicing online).

- » Find a website that lets you sign up for virtual conversation practice with native Spanish speakers.

- » Try picking up a Spanish newspaper or magazine to practice reading.

- » Practice journaling about everyday topics in Spanish to challenge yourself and see what you can come up with.

Chapter by Chapter

- **PART I - Foundations**

- **Chapter 1:** "The Essentials" introduces some building blocks essential to any language, such as the alphabet, pronunciation, numbers, and question words. This chapter also explores subject pronouns and common verbs, two topics that will be continuously built on throughout the book.

- **Chapter 2:** "Spanish–English Comparisons" commences our exploration of the main similarities and differences between Spanish and English. Related topics include cognates, a brief history of the Spanish language, and one of the most notable language differences for English speakers learning Spanish: gender agreement.

- **Chapter 3:** "From Hello to Goodbye" introduces practical and common conversational words and phrases. From formal to informal greetings to expressing fundamental needs and asking questions, this chapter serves as a toolkit to jump-start your Spanish communication. It's a crucial stepping stone to fluency.

- **PART II - This Is Me**

- **Chapter 4:** "Defining Yourself" emphasizes self-expression with a focus on two fundamental verbs, *ser* and *tener*, which can be used to express personal characteristics. Additionally, this chapter introduces the present tense, which will enable you to articulate actions that reflect who you are as a person.

- **Chapter 5:** "A Day in the Life" further builds on the previous chapter's self-expression, explaining what you need to express information about your daily life. This involves going deeper into the present tense, as well as common irregular verb patterns.

- **Chapter 6:** "Life with Loved Ones" expands from self-expression to cover family life, enabling you to describe the people closest to you. This chapter reinforces the present tense through descriptions of the actions of those around you. It also teaches how to express possession, make comparisons, and express likes and dislikes to enrich your descriptions of yourself and others.

- **PART III - Everyday Life**

  - **Chapter 7:** "Where I Live" embarks on an exploration of the spaces we inhabit and navigate in our daily lives. It highlights the vocabulary related to describing a home and teaches location-related descriptions and the present progressive tense to express ongoing activities in the here and now. This chapter also covers vocabulary related to running errands and engaging in activities in the community, and focuses on the complexities of the verbs *ser* and *estar* to describe our surroundings and events taking place around us.

  - **Chapter 8:** "Out and About" continues to build around the topic of navigating our daily surroundings, specifically beyond the confines of our home. It covers vocabulary and communication related to places we visit with friends, making social plans, and getting around.

  - **Chapter 9:** "Community Connections" is about community life and delves into the past tense, which enables communication of the impact the past has had on cultures and communities. This chapter also introduces cultural vocabulary, providing the terminology needed to properly express cultural contexts. It intertwines the expression of feelings with past events, so you can express the impact of past events on our communities today.

- **PART IV - The Bigger Picture**

  - **Chapter 10:** "Places We Visit" broadens further to help describe places we have visited or hope to visit in the future. It covers preparation for travel with vocabulary related to weather, geography, and clothing. (For those interested in further exploration of this topic, the appendix provides additional language instruction related to travel.)

  - **Chapter 11:** "Navigating the Unknown" covers practical matters of transportation and getting from place to place, including phrases and basic commands used to give or ask for directions and effectively communicate needs and preferences.

» **Chapter 12:** "Celebrating Cultural Diversity" wraps up the book, and the broader topic of the world outside our homes, with an exploration of cultural diversity in the Spanish-speaking world. A discussion of common cultural celebrations and Spanish speakers' influence on the arts serves as a vehicle for a comprehension check on reading, listening to, and understanding Spanish.

Quick Reference to Key Grammar Concepts

Subject pronouns	Ch. 1, p. 24
Infinitive verbs	Ch. 1, p. 32
Definite/indefinite articles	Ch. 2, p. 41
Gender agreement	Ch. 2, p. 40
Singular vs. plural words	Ch. 2, p. 42
Demonstrative adjectives/pronouns	Ch. 2, p. 49
Regular present tense conjugation	Ch. 4, p. 84
Regular present tense reflexive verbs	Ch. 5, p. 103
Possessive adjectives	Ch. 6, p. 117
The verb *gustar*	Ch. 6, p. 128
Indirect object pronouns	Ch. 6, p. 130; Ch. 11, p. 225
The present progressive tense	Ch. 7, p. 145
The near future tense: ir + a + infinitive	Ch. 7, p. 148
Ser vs. *estar*	Ch. 7, p. 151
The conditional tense	Ch. 8, p. 170
Past tense: preterite vs. imperfect	Ch. 9, p. 178
The present perfect tense	Ch. 10, p. 200
Two-verb constructions	Ch. 11, p. 223

Irregular present tense stem-changing verbs:	
Costar (o-ue)	Ch. 8, p. 163
Jugar (u-ue)	Ch. 5, p. 111
Pedir (e-i)	Ch. 8, p. 161
Preferir (e-ie)	Ch. 8, p. 161
Querer (e-ie)	Ch. 8, p. 160
Recomendar (e-ie)	Ch. 8, p. 169
Sentirse (e-ie)	Ch. 6, p. 127
Other irregular present tense verbs:	
Conducir	Ch. 11, p. 216
Conocer	Ch. 7, p. 151
Dar	Ch. 5, p. 110
Decir	Ch. 11, p. 227
Estar	Ch. 7, p. 143
Hacer	Ch. 5, p. 108
Ir	Ch. 5, p. 109
Reunirse	Ch. 6, p. 126
Saber	Ch. 7, p. 151
Salir	Ch. 5, p. 108; Ch. 8, p. 159
Ser	Ch. 4, p. 77
Tener	Ch. 4, p. 81
Venir	Ch. 8, p. 168

PART I

FOUNDATIONS

In part 1, we will focus on establishing some of the building blocks essential to preparing you to really expand your language proficiency in parts II, III, and IV. These first few chapters will focus on basics such as pronunciation and accumulating essential Spanish vocabulary. We will look at some of the major grammar concepts of Spanish, so you can get a feel for the overall structure of the language. You will also learn some basic conversation so that you can start engaging in everyday uses of the language!

| 1 |
The Essentials

If you've ever shopped for a fun but educational toy for a baby or a toddler, you might have noticed that these toys usually focus on teaching the building blocks of language, such as the alphabet, or how to count. Although adult language learners don't need to spend years familiarizing themselves with the basic concepts of letters and numbers and how they form building blocks of communication and literacy, the principles of language learning are similar no matter the age—which means starting with the simple stuff when learning a language that is new to you.

In this chapter, we will be covering essential building blocks that form a foundation of knowledge in Spanish. This does include letters and numbers, but we'll be adding some other essentials that will come into play in later chapters. Question words, for example, will help us get basic information; pronouns (he, she, they, etc.) will help us communicate who we are talking to or about; and finally, common verbs (actions) will allow us to put our ideas into action. All these components of language will play a part as you continue through the book and your Spanish language-learning journey.

Chapter Overview

By the end of this chapter, you will be able to do the following:
- » Listen to the alphabet in Spanish and practice reciting it.
- » Make comparisons of English versus Spanish pronunciation.
- » Identify numbers in Spanish.
- » Express months, days, seasons, and dates in Spanish.
- » Identify subject pronouns and understand how they are used.
- » Identify question words in Spanish and learn some basic questions.
- » Categorize infinitive verbs in Spanish (e.g., "to read," "to learn," "to be").

Alphabet and Pronunciation

In table 1.1, you will see the Spanish alphabet with the English phonetic pronunciation of each letter.

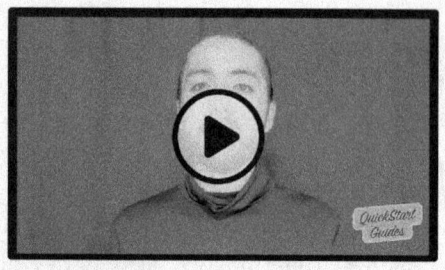

In this recording, you will hear how Daniel from Mexico pronounces each letter of the Spanish alphabet. Use this recording to practice listening to and repeating the pronunciations of each letter.

To watch the QuickClip, use the camera on your mobile phone to scan the QR code or visit the link below.

www.quickclips.io/spanish-1

table 1.1

LETTER	PRONUNCIATION	LETTER	PRONUNCIATION
A	ah	Ñ	EN-yeh
B	beh	O	oh
C	seh	P	peh
D	deh	Q	koo
E	eh	R	EH-reh
F	EH-feh	S	EH-seh
G	heh	T	teh
H	AH-cheh	U	oo
I	Ee	V	beh
J	HOH-tah	W	DOH-bleh-beh
K	Kah	X	EH-kees
L	EH-leh	Y	ee-REE-eh-gah
M	EH-meh	Z	SEH-tah
N	EH-neh		

Pronouncing the alphabet.

Note that the pronunciations in table 1.1 are how you would say the letter by itself, if you were spelling something out loud in Spanish; the pronunciation of the letters when they're within a word is covered in table 1.2.

Now that you have heard the alphabet, practice spelling your first and last name out loud.

You've gone through how to recite these letters individually in Spanish; now look at table 1.2, which illustrates the sounds those letters make when they are found in Spanish words.

In this clip, Arantza from Mexico says each letter of the Spanish alphabet along with a word in Spanish that contains that letter (table 1.2).

#2

To watch the QuickClip, use the camera on your mobile phone to scan the QR code or visit the link below.

or www.quickclips.io/spanish-2

table 1.2

LETTER	SPANISH WORD WITH ENGLISH PHONETIC SPELLING	ENGLISH TRANSLATION
A	amigo – ah-MEE-go	friend
B	barco – BAR-koh	boat
C	casa – KAH-sah	house
D	dinero – dee-NEH-ro	money
E	escape – es-KAH-peh	escape
F	familia – fah-MEE-lyah	family
G	gato – GAH-toh	cat
H	hola – OH-lah	hello
I	isla – EES-lah	island

| 1 | The Essentials   15

LETTER	SPANISH WORD WITH ENGLISH PHONETIC SPELLING	ENGLISH TRANSLATION
J	jirafa – hee-RAH-fah	giraffe
K	kiwi – KEE-wee	kiwi
L	león – laeh-OWN	lion
M	manzana – mahn-SAH-nah	apple
N	naranja – nah-RAHN-hah	orange
Ñ	niño – NEE-nyoh	child
O	oficina – oh-fee-SEE-nah	office
P	pájaro – PAH-hah-roh	bird
Q	queso – KAY-soh	cheese
R	ropa – ROH-pah	clothing
S	sol – SOHL	sun
T	taco – TAH-koh	taco
U	uva – OO-vah	grape
V	vino – VEE-noh	wine
W	wifi – WEE-fee	Wi-Fi
X	xilófono – see-LOH-foh-noh	xylophone
Y	yogur – yo-GOOR	yogurt
Z	zapato – sah-PAH-toh	shoe

Pronouncing letter sounds within words.

As I will mention many times throughout this book, there are twenty-one official Spanish-speaking countries. This speaks to the fact that Spanish is an incredibly diverse language, and we will explore many components of it that differ based on location. One of these that I want to be sure to mention is the concept of accents. You have probably come in contact with English speakers from different areas, and you've likely noticed that the way they pronounce certain sounds can vary slightly. This same concept applies to Spanish. Above, I have instructed you on the general pronunciation rules of the Spanish language, but be aware that what I have taught you can sound slightly different depending on the birthplace of the Spanish speakers that you encounter. This is a normal phenomenon in any language, and it can make comprehension trickier for new users of the language. Actors and comedians are often able to imitate different accents, but the general population is not skilled at that. Do not expect yourself to be able to immediately and flawlessly pronounce sounds in Spanish that are new to you, and don't be surprised if the accents of some Spanish speakers are easier for you to understand than others. I personally take a while to adjust to different accents, and that can be a very humbling experience for someone who considers herself an advanced user of the language. If you're interested in this topic, I encourage you to do an online search to find video examples of different accents in Spanish so you can start to expose yourself to them, especially if you expect to come in contact with Spanish speakers from lots of different areas.

Additional Sounds

There are a few letters/sounds that are not officially part of the alphabet but that are often taught as if they were, because of their centrality to the language.

ch: This letter combination works just as it does in English, such as with the Spanish word *nachos*.

ll: The double *l* in Spanish makes a sound like the English *y*, as in the Spanish word *quesadilla*. In parts of Argentina and Uruguay, you will sometimes hear the double *l* pronounced as an English "sh" sound.

rr: When you see two of the letter *r*, you're supposed to roll your tongue to pronounce them in Spanish. But don't worry if you can't do this; just do your best! Plenty of people whose first language is English can't do it at first, because it's not a sound used in our native language, so many of us just need to practice it. It's the key difference between, for example, *caro* (expensive) and *carro* (car). The double *r* is what technically distinguishes the two words from one another.

ü: This letter is not seen very often in the Spanish language, but it is worth mentioning. The two dots above the letter *u* form what is called a *diaeresis*. A few Spanish words you might come across with this letter are *bilingüe* (bilingual), *pingüino* (penguin), and *vergüenza* (shame). Look at the Spanish word *guitarra* (guitar), for example; the *u* is silent in this word. It is pronounced "gee-TAH-rrah." If that word had a *ü*, it would be pronounced "gwee-TAH-rrah." Essentially, the *ü* signals that we should pronounce the *u* and not treat it as if it were silent. Therefore, *bilingüe* would be pronounced bee-LEAN-gweh, *pingüino* would be peen-GWEE-noh, and *vergüenza* would be behr-GWEN-sah.

 Need some help learning how to roll your tongue? Look up YouTube videos for some guided practice. This is how I eventually learned to roll my tongue, as I was unable to do it for quite a while. I watched some YouTube videos and practiced every morning in the car during my commute to work, and I eventually got it!

Las vocales – The Vowels

Considering that vowels can cause some confusion at first for English speakers, it is worth taking some time to focus more on these letters and their sounds. Table 1.3 shows the pronunciation of vowels.

#3

In this clip, Mónica from Colombia pronounces the vowels from the alphabet, as well as a word that uses each vowel in table 1.3, so you can really focus on these particular sounds.

 To watch the QuickClip, use the camera on your mobile phone to scan the QR code or visit the link below.

 or www.quickclips.io/spanish-3

table 1.3

VOWEL	ENGLISH PHONETIC PRONUNCIATION	SPANISH WORD USING THE VOWEL WITH ENGLISH PHONETIC SPELLING	ENGLISH TRANSLATION
A	ah	manzana – man-SAH-nah	apple
E	eh	elefante – eh-leh-FAHN-teh	elephant
I	ee	identificación – ee-den-tee-fee-kah-SYOHN	identification
O	oh	ojo – OH-hoh	eye
U	oo	uniforme – oo-nee-FOR-meh	uniform

Pronunciation of vowels

Vowels can be challenging to learn, because when spoken on its own, the letter *e* in Spanish is pronounced exactly like we would say the individual letter *a* in the English alphabet. The letter *i* in Spanish when spoken on its own is pronounced exactly like the individual English letter *e* in English. Be patient with yourself, as these tricky vowel differences will take some practice!

You will notice that some words in Spanish have an accent mark written above one of the letters. In Spanish, only the vowels can have this type of accent mark: á, é, í, ó, and ú. It's written on certain words to indicate that stress needs to be put on that syllable of the word when it's being said out loud. Listen again to the audio recording of the alphabet and vowels, but this time focus on the stress of the words with accent marks, and you will hear how the native speaker puts emphasis on that part of the word.

There are a few other letters that I would like to draw your attention to, because they can take extra time to get used to. Figure 1.1 introduces two of them.

fig. 1.1

grande
big

chica
small

» *B* and *V*: In Spanish, these letters have the same sound; they are both pronounced like a *B* in English. Since you cannot distinguish between the two letters when saying them out loud, a lot of people will say *b grande* and *v chica* to differentiate them. So think of the *b* as the *grande*, or big one, because it's taller than the letter *v*, which is *chica*, or small, because it's shorter.

| 1 | The Essentials

» *G*: In Spanish, this letter can make two different sounds. When it is followed by *e* or *i*, it makes a sound like the English *h*. For example, the Spanish word *gente* is pronounced "HEN-teh." Otherwise, the letter is pronounced as a hard *g*, such as in the word *guacamole*.

» *H*: In Spanish, this letter is usually silent. For example, think of the Spanish word *hola*. Basically, when you see the letter *h*, pretend it isn't there (unless it is preceded by a *c*, in which case you pronounce it as mentioned previously, e.g., *nachos*).

» *J*: In Spanish, this letter makes the sound of an *h* in English. For example, think of the Spanish name *José*.

» *Ñ*: This letter with the tilde on top makes an *n* sound, but your tongue will make slightly longer contact with the roof of your mouth, so it will end up sounding similar to an English "ny" sound. Think of the Spanish word *jalapeño*.

» *QU*: These two letters together make a sound like the English letter *k*, as in the words *queso* or *quesadilla*.

» *Z* and *S*: These two letters both make an English *s* sound. However, in some areas of Spain, they are pronounced somewhat like the "th" sound in English.

When in doubt about a pronunciation, try to think of Spanish words you already know, and apply those sounds to new words you come across in the language. This will help pronunciation of new words come more easily.

Numbers

Table 1.4 is a chart to help you learn the numbers 1 to 100. As you can see, the words for numbers from 0 to 15 don't follow any sort of repetitive pattern, so those must be memorized. However, once you get to the 16–19 range, you'll start to see a pattern. The root of those numbers, *dieci*, comes from the number *diez* (10) and the *i* makes the sound of the Spanish word *y* (and), so essentially you are saying *ten and* another number. The number 18, for example, is made up of ten and eight, hence *dieciocho*.

table 1.4

NUMBER	WORD	NUMBER	WORD
0	cero	19	diecinueve
1	uno	20	veinte
2	dos	21	veintiuno
3	tres	22	veintidós
4	cuatro	23	veintitrés
5	cinco	24	veinticuatro
6	seis	25	veinticinco
7	siete	26	veintiséis
8	ocho	27	veintisiete
9	nueve	28	veintiocho
10	diez	29	veintinueve
11	once	30	treinta
12	doce	40	cuarenta
13	trece	50	cincuenta
14	catorce	60	sesenta
15	quince	70	setenta
16	dieciséis	80	ochenta
17	diecisiete	90	noventa
18	dieciocho	100	cien

When we get to the twenties, there is also a pattern. Because *veinte* is 20, at 21 the root changes to *veinti* (which is like combining the words *veinte* + *y* in Spanish) and then we combine that with the numbers 1 through 9. So, for example, when you say *veintinueve*, you are basically saying *twenty and nine*.

The chart does not include every number from 30 to 100. These numbers follow a pattern similar to what we use for the twenties. Starting with 30, you will follow the pattern below:

tens place number + y + ones place number

So, for example, if you are trying to say the number 34 in Spanish, you will start with the tens place number, which is treinta; the second word will be *y*, and then in the ones place you will put *cuatro*. Together that will be *treinta y cuatro*, which is literally *thirty and four*. Below are a few additional examples showing this process:

45	cuarenta y cinco (you're literally saying forty and five)
58	cincuenta y ocho (literally fifty and eight)
99	noventa y nueve (literally ninety and nine)

Do you notice how the Spanish words for 60 and 70 are almost exactly the same except for the third letter? The way I remember them is that with 60, the third letter is an *s*, which comes before the letter *t* in the alphabet, which is the third letter in 70. Since 60 numerically comes before 70, it correlates with *s* being before *t* in the alphabet.

Months, Days, Seasons, and Dates

Let's take a look at months, days of the week, seasons, and how to write dates in Spanish. I like to include this information alongside numbers because we often use numbers while communicating about the calendar.

Los días de la semana – The Days of the Week

On the traditional Spanish calendar, the first day of the week is Monday, rather than Sunday, which is typically shown first on American calendars. Another big difference from English is that days and months are not capitalized in Spanish. See figure 1.2 for a visual of the days of the week on a Spanish calendar.

fig. 1.2

Los meses y las estaciones – The Months and Seasons

In figure 1.3 you will find the seasons as well as the months of the year in Spanish. You will notice that a lot of the month names look similar to those we have in English.

PRIMAVERA	VERANO	OTOÑO	INVIERNO

marzo abril mayo	junio julio agosto	septiembre octubre noviembre	diciembre enero febrero

fig. 1.3

To remember the Spanish words for seasons, I use correlations. For spring I think about a pasta primavera dish, which is typically made with fresh vegetables. Spring, or *primavera*, is a time when many plants start to grow, so to me those two things correlate. We typically spend more time inside in the winter, so I use the word *in* to remember *invierno*. Verano looks a lot like invierno but without the "in," so to me it makes sense that *verano* and *invierno* are essentially opposites of one another. Lastly, *otoño* sounds like it has the word *tone* in it, and fall is when the leaves change tone, or color.

Las fechas – Dates

In addition to specific seasons and months, there are some useful words related to dates in Spanish, which help readers and speakers more clearly express the time frame they are referring to.

hoy	today
ayer	yesterday
anteayer	the day before yesterday
mañana	tomorrow
en la mañana	in the morning; and yes, you can say mañana en la mañana: tomorrow in the morning
el próximo (día/mes/año)	next (day/month/year)
la próxima (semana)	next (week)
el (mes/año) pasado	last (month/year)
la (semana) pasada	last (week)

| 1 | The Essentials

NOTE: Do you notice how the word for "next" in Spanish can be *próximo* or *próxima* and the word for "last" can be *pasado* or *pasada* depending on the word that follows it? We will be talking about this phenomenon more in depth in the next chapter.

Here are some examples of how dates are communicated in Spanish:

Hoy es lunes.	Today is Monday.
Ayer fue domingo.	Yesterday was Sunday.
Mañana es martes.	Tomorrow is Tuesday.
Hoy es el cuatro de mayo.	Today is May 4.
La próxima semana es mi cumpleaños.	Next week is my birthday.
El mes pasado fue mi cumpleaños.	Last month was my birthday.
Durante el mes de julio es el verano.	During the month of July, it is summer.

It's also worth mentioning that official dates in Spanish are written as day/month/year. For example, my birthdate in English is written 2/18/1994, but in Spanish it would be 18/2/1994. If you have a passport, you will notice that your birthdate is written in this format.

Subject Pronouns

Subject pronouns are used to communicate who we are talking about (or directly addressing) when we speak. In English, these are words like "I," "he," "she," "we," "they," and both plural and singular forms of "you." This book covers the Spanish equivalent of all those words, which are a crucial building block for learning the language. After all, we need to be able to express who we are talking to or about before we can get to the next step, which is adding action verbs to describe what those people are doing.

In table 1.5 you will see all the subject pronouns we will be working with in Spanish. The order they are in is not random. This order of subject pronouns will be important later when we get to ***verb conjugation***—the process of changing the form of a verb to show a change in person, number, tense, and so on. (For example, the difference between "I was" and "I am," or "I walk" and "she walks.") Because so much of learning a language properly depends on conjugation, it is very important that we learn the subject pronouns in this arrangement. I highly recommend memorizing the exact layout of table 1.5 and the placement of the subject pronouns. Table 1.6 breaks down the meaning of these pronouns.

table 1.5

| SUBJECT PRONOUNS ||
SINGULAR	PLURAL
yo	nosotros nosotras
tú	vosotros vosotras
él ella usted (Ud.)	ellos ellas ustedes (Uds.)

table 1.6

| SUBJECT PRONOUNS ||
SINGULAR	PLURAL
yo = I	nosotros = we (m.) nosotras = we (f.)
tú = you (informal)	vosotros = you plural (m.) (informal) vosotras = you plural (f.) (informal)
él = he ella = she usted (Ud.) = you (formal)	ellos = they (m.) ellas = they (f.) ustedes (Uds.) = you plural (formal)

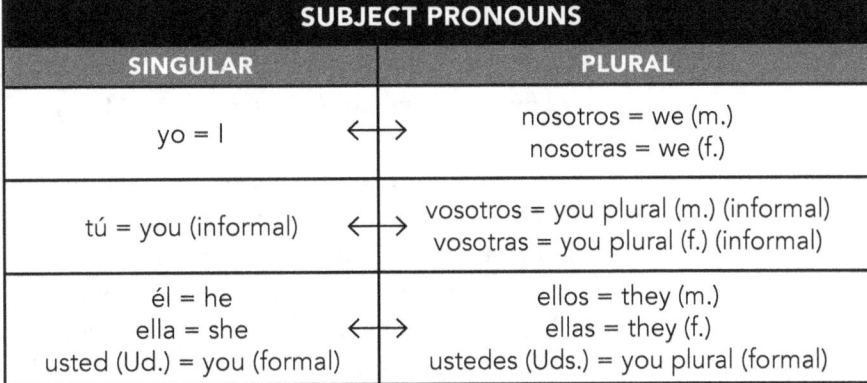

We will be focusing on the "ustedes" form, rather than the "vosotros/vosotras" form, in this book.

As you can see in table 1.6, the subject pronouns in Spanish are as follows:

yo	I
tú	you (informal)
él	he
ella	she
usted	you (formal)
nosotros	we (if the group is all men, or a mix of men and women)
nosotras	we (if the group is all women)
vosotros	you all/you plural (informal) (if the group is all men, or a mix of men and women)
vosotras	you all/you plural (informal) (if the group is all women)

ellos	they (if the group is all men, or a mix of men and women)
ellas	they (if the group is all women)
ustedes	you all/you plural (formal)

I'll refer to this chart a few times throughout this section of the chapter as we get further into subject pronouns.

If you are starting to notice all of the different versions of words for men vs. women and are wondering why that is, stay tuned for the next chapter!

Tú and usted

First, it's important to note two subject pronouns that are not straightforward for English speakers to learn. They are *tú*, the informal word for "you," and *usted*, the formal word for "you."

The major difference between these pronouns and their English equivalent is that Spanish has two words that mean *you*, used depending on the level of formality. The idea of using "tú" informally and "usted" in more formal situations might seem confusing at first. But when you think about it, every language has formal and informal uses. For example, there are people you might greet with "Hey, what's up?" and there are other people you'd greet with "Good morning. How are you?" The first greeting would be used in casual conversation with someone you know well. The second would be preferable in a more professional environment, where you'd want to convey respect more than familiarity.

Tú and *usted* work very much the same way. There are no rules that make it one hundred percent clear as to when you must use one or the other, but generally, you can use *tú* with people you are very close to, like a sibling, a best friend, or a classmate. An adult speaking to a child might also refer to them as *tú*. *Usted* would normally be used in the opposite situation: when a younger person is talking to an older person. *Usted* is a simple way of conveying respect. That's also why you'd use it in professional settings, such as when talking to a boss.

Still, there are plenty of gray areas that can appear with *tú* and *usted*. For example, *usted* is more appropriate for a boss, but how should you address a coworker? How should you address your parents, or your partner's parents? Is it okay to be more informal with them as an expression of familiarity or closeness, or will using *tú* seem too casual? These kinds of situations really come down to the individuals you are interacting with. Some families are more informal and will use *tú* to refer to one another, while others require younger family members to use *usted*.

When you're in doubt about which form to use, a good rule of thumb is to use *usted*. Better to be too formal than too casual; if you are referring to someone as *usted* and they prefer *tú*, that is something they can explicitly tell you. For example, I once had a professor who told the class to please refer to him informally, as he did not expect us to address him as *usted*. I would not, however, assume that this would be the case for every professor. See what I mean when I say it depends on the person? So when in doubt, it's probably best to use *usted*.

Variations and Abbreviations

Going back to the subject pronoun chart, you will see that there is a *vosotros/vosotras* box. As with *tú* versus *usted*, *vosotros* would be the informal version of a pluralized "you" in some areas, and *ustedes* would be the formal version. However, when we start conjugating verbs, we will not be focusing on this form, as it is mostly used in Spain, which is one of twenty-one official Spanish-speaking countries. When you become conversational in Spanish, you will be able to understand the *vosotros* form, just like Spanish speakers from countries that don't use *vosotros*. If you do plan to go to Spain, then you can add the *vosotros* form to your language study. In this book, however, we will be focusing all of the examples on using the word *ustedes* whenever we need to communicate the plural "you." (And in terms of rule-of-thumb usage in Spain, it's similar to *tú* versus *usted*: using the more formal *ustedes* version won't offend anyone!)

Where you live, do you say "you all," "y'all," or "you guys"? Notice how all those terms are essentially a plural of "you," but which one you tend to use varies depending on where you live. For example, if you say "y'all" to someone from the Northern United States, they might look at you funny for a second. But even if they assume you're from another area of the country, they will still be able to understand and communicate with you. That is an example of a linguistic variation in English. Since Spanish is spoken in so many countries, there are tons of linguistic variations! I will be pointing out many throughout this book.

| 1 | The Essentials

There are a few common subject pronoun abbreviations that you will see in Spanish. Abbreviate *usted* as *Ud.* and *ustedes* as *Uds.* Just like the days and months in Spanish, the subject pronouns are not capitalized. However, when you write the abbreviated forms, they are capitalized.

There is one other variation of Spanish subject pronouns, referred to as "el voseo," that is used in some areas of Latin America. In some cases, you might hear the subject pronoun *vos* being used. Generally, this is similar to the word *tú*. Some countries tend to use *vos* instead of *tú*, and some areas use a mixture of both forms. *Vos* has its own conjugations that we will not focus on in this book, but do be aware that you may hear this form, as it is used in some varieties of Spanish.

For those who do not identify as masculine or feminine, users of the Spanish language have started a movement toward more gender-inclusive language. For example, the pronoun *elle* was created as a combination of the pronouns *él* and *ella* with a gender-neutral *e* at the end. Many individuals have started using *e* or *x* at the end of adjectives instead of *o* or *a*; we will cover this in chapter 2. Some Spanish dictionaries have been hesitant to recognize these as official parts of the language. However, if you do identify as nonbinary, know that you are a Google search away from communities of Spanish speakers who are working to find ways to more accurately express their identities through their use of the Spanish language.

Applying Subject Pronouns

Now that we have covered the basics of subject pronouns, we can talk about how to apply them. For example, if I am telling you a story about someone named Laura, instead of having to say "Laura" in every single sentence, I can use the subject pronoun "she" once I have established that I am talking about Laura. That same concept is going to apply to Spanish and will be very important when we start conjugating verbs in part II.

Let's go over a few more examples of how subject pronouns can be used in place of the people we are talking to or about.

Mi familia y yo (My family and I)	Instead of saying "my family and I" repeatedly in each sentence that I talk about them, I could just say *we*, which in Spanish would be *nosotros*.

Ana y Andrea (Ana and Andrea)	If I am talking about these two girls, I would use *ellas* for "they," since they are both girls. If I am talking directly to these two girls, I would use *ustedes* to address them, which is *you* plural.
Andrea y José (Andrea and José)	In this case, I am talking about a boy and a girl, so I would use the masculine version of "they," which is *ellos*. If I were talking directly to these two, I would use *ustedes*, just like we did for Ana and Andrea.
José y tú (José and you)	Here, because we have the word *tú*, it is clear that I am talking directly to José and another person, so I would use *ustedes* to refer to the two of them directly.
Las chicas (the girls)	In this situation, I am talking about a group of girls, so I would use *ellas*, the feminine version of "they."
Mis estudiantes (my students)	Since I am talking about my students, I would use *ellos*, the masculine version of "they."

Now you have a basic understanding of the subject pronouns and how they can be used to replace people we are talking to or about, while also accounting for the gender of those people. This is crucial to know, as we will be revisiting this concept repeatedly throughout the text.

Question Words

When we're traveling in a Spanish-speaking country or simply communicating with a Spanish-speaking person, there are some basic question words that are key in helping us ask for important information. Let's go over some of these terms, along with examples of some very common questions in Spanish.

¿Cuál?	Which one? Which? (singular)
¿Cuáles?	Which ones? Which? (plural)
¿Cuándo?	When?
¿Cuánto?	How much? (masculine)
¿Cuánta?	How much? (feminine)
¿Cuántos?	How many? (masculine)
¿Cuántas?	How many? (feminine)
¿Cómo?	How? What?
¿Dónde?	Where?
¿Por qué?	Why?

¿Qué?	What?
¿Quién?	Who? (singular)
¿Quiénes?	Who? (plural)

It is important to mention that not all question words are going to translate to exactly how we would use them in English. One such word is the question word *¿Cuál?*—it can take on the meaning of "what" in addition to "which." For example, the English question "What is your name?" would translate to *¿Cuál es tu nombre?*

To English speakers, that is like asking someone, "Which is your name?" In other words, it assumes that the person you're asking has an answer to that question. When I ask someone their name, I already know they have a name, I just don't know which name it is out of all the names in the world. That's an assumption we make in English, too, but it's not reflected in the phrasing; we use "what" rather than "which" in that situation. Rather than the Spanish equivalent of "what" (*¿Qué?*), the language uses *¿Cuál?* for a number of similar questions:

¿Cuál es tu número de teléfono?	What is your phone number?
¿Cuál es tu dirección?	What is your address?
¿Cuál es tu postre favorito?	What is your favorite dessert?

As you can see, these are all questions that you know the person has an answer to.

There are other instances, however, where the question word *¿Qué?* works in Spanish just as it does in English. For example:

¿Qué hora es?	What time is it?
¿Qué es esto?	What is this?

Here are a few other common questions in Spanish using the question words we have covered:

¿Dónde está (el baño)?	Where is (the bathroom)?
¿Cuándo es (la fiesta)?	When is (the party)?
¿Cuánto cuesta?	How much does it cost?
¿Quién es (ella)?	Who is (she)?
¿Quiénes son (ellos)?	Who are (they)?

Do you see how all the questions have an upside-down question mark before the first word? In Spanish, questions are always written with an upside-down question mark at the beginning of the sentence and a regular question mark at the end. When you think about it, this is pretty helpful. In English, many times we don't know we are reading a question until we get to the end of the sentence, but in Spanish, we know it right away!

Formal versus Informal Questions

In this section, we will revisit the concept of *tú* versus *usted* by looking at how those words play a role in asking questions. This will help you navigate asking questions in a way that is appropriate for either casual or formal contexts.

¿Cómo estás (tú)?	How are you? (informal)
¿Cómo está (usted)?	How are you? (formal)

You can see that there are two ways to ask someone how they are; one is formal, and the other is informal. This will be covered in greater detail when we get into conjugating verbs. But for now, think back to the discussion of the formal and informal uses of "you." Similarly, there are formal and informal ways to ask someone a question directly.

Here are a few more examples using different ways to ask someone's name:

¿Cómo te llamas (tú)?	Literally translates to the **informal** way to ask "What do you call yourself?"
¿Cómo se llama (usted)?	Literally translates to the **formal** way to ask "What do you call yourself?"
¿Cuál es tu nombre?	Literally translates to the **informal** way to ask someone "Which is your name?" (In this case, *tu* is a possessive meaning "your," which is why it doesn't include the accent on the *u*.)
¿Cuál es su nombre?	Literally translates to the **formal** way to ask someone "Which is your name?"

In part II, we will be diving deeper into verb conjugations, including making sure you are asking or telling someone something in either a formal or informal way, depending on the situation.

Infinitives

As we approach the end of this chapter, it is important that we talk about another foundational part of the Spanish language: infinitives. ***Infinitives*** are verbs in their original state before we do anything with them. For example, English infinitives include to *walk*, to *eat*, to *read*, etc. We then conjugate a verb to tell who does that action. For example, we can take the infinitive verb to *walk* and put it into sentences:

I walk to school.   **She walks** to work.

Do you see how "I" and "She" are different people? Do you also notice how the verb changed slightly from "walk" to "walks" depending on who was performing the action? This is called conjugating a verb, and we will discuss it more in part II. But first we need to learn verbs in their original state (as infinitives) before we will be able to conjugate them.

Now look at some infinitive verbs in Spanish (table 1.7).

table 1.7

-AR VERBS	-ER VERBS	-IR VERBS
hablar to speak/talk	**comer** to eat	**vivir** to live
caminar to walk	**leer** to read	**escribir** to write
estudiar to study	**aprender** to learn	**decidir** to decide

The infinitive verbs are divided into three categories according to the last two letters of the word: -AR, -ER, and -IR. It is important to recognize the three different endings of infinitives, as this will be important when we cover verb conjugation.

To learn more infinitives, consider making flashcards of common infinitive verbs to study the verbs and their meanings.

Now that we have covered the fact that all infinitive verbs in Spanish end in -AR, -ER, or -IR, consider the following paragraph. Focus on the bolded infinitives. Can you decipher the main idea of the paragraph?

Yo necesito **aprender** español. Es difícil **estudiar** otro lenguaje, pero es posible con mucha dedicación. Es importante **hablar** español porque muchas personas son hispanohablantes. Es necesario **comunicar** con muchas personas. Me gusta **aprender** a **leer** y **hablar** español.

Did you find that you understood more of that paragraph than you expected to? That may be because I wrote it using a lot of cognates—words that look similar to English words. We'll talk more about cognates in the next chapter.

Chapter Recap

In this chapter, we covered material that I consider vital to forming a foundation of language for you to build on:

» The alphabet and pronunciation are necessary for communication in almost any language.

» Numbers can help with so many important topics: a bus route, a house number, a date, and so on.

» Question words also help us navigate a multitude of situations.

» Subject pronouns and infinitive verbs will constantly be referred to throughout the rest of the book.

In fact, everything we covered in this first chapter will continually be revisited, so you will get plenty of opportunities to reinforce this information as we apply it to a variety of contexts.

| 2 |
Spanish–English Comparisons

When I started learning Spanish, I found it helpful to find connections with my first language, English. So every time I teach a beginner Spanish course, I take time to show my students how much they already know about Spanish just by being speakers of English. The great thing about Spanish is that it has many similarities to English, and I've found that drawing attention to these similarities (and differences) in reference to your native language makes things easier to learn and understand. Not only can this make language-learning feel less overwhelming, but it can also help us better understand the functions of our own language.

In this chapter, we'll be taking a closer look at some similarities and differences between Spanish and English, including the history of the language, which reveals why we find many similarities between the two. We will also go over the concept of gender, one of the bigger differences between Spanish and English, and how it applies to Spanish nouns. Then we'll work on combining articles, such as the words *the*, *a/an*, *this*, *that*, and so on, to start building sentence fragments in Spanish. All this will help you continue to build your foundational knowledge of how the language functions in comparison to English while also increasing your language fluency.

Chapter Overview

By the end of this chapter, you will be able to do the following:
» Understand a brief history of the Spanish language.
» Identify cognates and be aware of false cognates.
» Categorize high-frequency Spanish nouns into gender categories.
» Apply the concept of gender to basic articles and adjectives.
» Apply the concept of gender agreement to demonstrative adjectives and pronouns.

Origins, Evolutions, and Connections

Despite their many differences, Spanish and English do share some common ground, in part because of the way their histories overlap. Briefly examining the history of the Spanish language helps us to better understand that common ground.

A Brief History of the Spanish Language

We won't cover this history in great detail, but it does inform how we learn the language, especially as English speakers. Let's begin with the Iberian Peninsula, which today is Portugal and Spain. Throughout time, many different tribes occupied those lands, and little by little their languages influenced each other. In 218 BC, the Romans invaded the Iberian Peninsula and slowly began what is referred to as the Romanization of Hispania. During the rule of the Romans, Latin was the official language. When the Roman Empire fell in the fifth century, different Latin dialects evolved into what are the five romance languages today, one of which is Spanish.

The Spanish spoken in the Iberian Peninsula slowly evolved and was subsequently influenced by various languages that were brought to the Peninsula; one was Arabic, due to the invasion of the Moors in the eighth century. Many Spanish words, such as *almohada* (pillow) and *azúcar* (sugar), originate from Arabic. Eventually, colonization took the Spanish language across the ocean to the Americas, which is how it became so widely spoken here. The arrival of the Spanish in the Americas brought a variety of problems, even atrocities, to the natives of these lands, as the colonizers imposed their language and culture on indigenous groups. The Spanish also adopted words from the various indigenous groups that they came in contact with. Many Spanish words we use today, such as *aguacate* (avocado) and *chocolate* (chocolate), among many others, originate from indigenous languages that are still spoken in the Americas today, such as Náhuatl and Quechua. Many of these borrowed words were for items completely new to the Spanish coming from Spain.

Did you know that more than 500 indigenous languages are spoken throughout Latin America today? Many Spanish-speaking countries still have large indigenous populations, and it's important to note that not everyone living in Latin America speaks Spanish. For many indigenous peoples, Spanish is their second language.

As all languages do, Spanish continues to evolve. Now that it is very commonly in contact with English, the two languages have borrowed words from one another. For example, food words like *taco*, *tortilla*, and *quesadilla* are commonly understood Spanish words that English speakers use. You may also hear some words that are referred to as "Spanglish," which means a mixture of Spanish and English. For example, *parkear* is the Spanglish word for the verb "to park." You may hear Spanish speakers using Spanglish especially if they live in or near a country where English is also widely spoken.

Cognates

Those origins and evolutions of the Spanish language are why you may have seen or heard some Spanish words that remind you of English words. Even if you haven't experienced this before, you likely will encounter it as you continue your language-learning journey. For example, the word *carro* looks a lot like the English word *car*, and the word *apartamento* looks like the English word *apartment*. This can be extremely helpful, as sometimes you can recognize words in Spanish that you haven't explicitly learned yet, based merely on how they look and/or sound. These words that appear to be similar to English words are called **cognates**. The many cognates between English and Spanish can make learning Spanish a lot easier for English speakers.

Look at this next paragraph, and think about what English words the bolded words resemble:

Mi ciudad es **enorme**. Tiene dos **aeropuertos**, y tenemos mucho **tráfico** porque hay muchos **carros** y **accidentes**. También, hay muchos **restaurantes excelentes**. Me gusta **explorar diferentes restaurantes** y **parques**. En los **restaurantes**, me gustan las **pastas**, los **sándwiches** y los **platos tradicionales** de **diferentes** países. En los **parques**, me gusta hacer **ejercicio**.

Some cognates between English and Spanish are due to their common Latin roots: English has borrowed many words from Latin.

False Cognates

Generally, the presence of cognates makes learning Spanish a little easier than it might otherwise be for English speakers. One potential downside, however, is the existence of *false cognates*; some Spanish words that seem familiar to you as an English speaker won't mean what you think they mean. For example, look at the following sentence below.

Ella está **embaraza**.

When you read that sentence and apply your knowledge of cognates, you might reasonably assume it means "She is embarrassed," right? But unfortunately, you've come across a false cognate; the word actually means "pregnant." Can you imagine trying to tell someone you're embarrassed, when instead you're telling them you're pregnant? That would likely cause even more embarrassment! This is why it is important to pay attention to context and be aware that not every word you think you recognize necessarily means what you think it does.

The following are a few examples of false cognates:

Éxito	Looks like the English word "exit," but it actually means *success*.
Fábrica	Looks like the English word "fabric," but it actually means *factory*.
Sopa	Looks like the English word "soap," but it actually means *soup*.

Many of the Spanish words you come across that look like an English word will be true cognates and mean what you think they mean. The sprinkling of false cognates makes learning the language a little more exciting and certainly isn't worth worrying about. Just be aware that you cannot assume the meaning of the word with one hundred percent accuracy even if it looks a lot like an English word. Cognates are a rough (and fun!) guide, not a rock-solid principle of language learning.

Word Order

An important difference between Spanish and English has to do with word order. Specifically, Spanish adjectives usually go *after* the **noun** (the person, place, or thing) in a sentence. For example, in English, I would say "the red car," but in Spanish it is said "*el carro rojo*," which translates to "the car red." Although this word order is very different from English, arguably it makes a lot of sense: the thing or person being described is established before you hear the adjectives describing it. So when I hear *el carro*, I know we are talking about a car, and any adjective afterward is modifying and enriching my mental picture of this car. In English, if I refer to "the big, red, beautiful car," you don't know what I am describing until I get to the very end. In Spanish, that same phrase would be "*el carro* *grande, rojo y hermoso,*" and I immediately know I am describing a car. Here are two more examples of this word order:

| The tall boy | El chico alto (literally "the boy tall") |
| The tall girl | La chica alta (literally "the girl tall") |

Besides the word order, you might notice something else about these examples: the same adjective—the one that means "tall"—changes depending on the gender of the noun. This is another major difference between English and Spanish.

Other aspects of word order in Spanish are quite similar to English. For example, Spanish generally follows a Subject-Verb-Object (S-V-O) pattern, just like English does. "I eat a salad" in English becomes "*Yo como una ensalada*" in Spanish. However, the Spanish language does have a bit more flexibility in the structuring of sentences. In the case of the salad example, it's permissible to form the sentence without the subject, too, and just say "*Como una ensalada.*" This is because many of the verb conjugations already imply who is doing the action in the sentence.

Another major difference is that questions tend to follow Verb-Subject-Object (V-S-O) format, especially for yes-or-no type questions. For example, ¿*Vives tú en una casa?* is literally asking "Do you live you in a house?" (Though, as with the previous example, it's possible to omit the "tú" in the question, because the verb conjugation already implies it.) There are also instances of Subject-Object-Verb (S-O-V) and Object-Subject-Verb (O-S-V) structures being used in Spanish. Although these forms aren't as commonly used, they do exist, typically for the purpose of placing emphasis on different parts of a sentence. Here is one sentence with the same meaning in three different structures—none of them incorrect:

Subject-Verb-Object (S-V-O)	Yo hago la tarea.	Literally translates to: *I do the homework.*
Subject-Object-Verb (S-O-V)	Yo la tarea hago.	Literally translates to: *I the homework I do.*
Object-Subject-Verb (O-S-V)	La tarea yo hago.	Literally translates to: *The homework I do.*

You can see with the three sentence examples above, different parts of the sentence are being emphasized. However, I would recommend that you stick to forming most sentences following the Subject-Verb-Object (S-V-O) format since it is the most commonly used. Throughout this book, you will become more familiar with sentence structure and also better understand when certain sentence structures do not follow the pattern that we are used to using in English.

The Concept of Gender

You've likely started to notice that many words in the previous chapters have ended with the letter *o* or *a*. This is because, unlike with English, words in Spanish have two gender categories: masculine and feminine. For example, in English, when someone uses a phrase like "a friend" without context clues, you can't tell if the friend in question is male, female, or nonbinary. Also, English words like "chair," "house," "car," and so on do not have a gender. In Spanish, however, almost all words are either feminine or masculine. And some words, like "friend," can have a masculine or feminine form to refer to the gender of the person you are talking about. The feminine form of "friend" is *amiga*, and the masculine form is *amigo*. The letter *a* on the end of a word is understood to indicate that the word is feminine, and the letter *o* at the end of a word indicates that it is masculine.

Most Spanish nouns do not have interchangeable masculine and feminine forms like *amigo/amiga* but rather are randomly assigned as masculine or feminine. For example, the word "dress" in Spanish, *vestido*, is a masculine word and ends with the letter *o*. Even though you might expect, based on stereotypes and tradition, that "dress" would be a feminine word, that does not determine the gender. A good practice when learning new words is to learn them with the Spanish word for "the" in front to help you remember their gender; *el* indicates masculine and *la* indicates feminine.

Here are a few words that can interchangeably be feminine or masculine:

el chico	the boy
la chica	the girl
el amigo	the friend (male)
la amiga	the friend (female)
el hermano	the brother
la hermana	the sister

You can see that the feminine versions of these words end in *a* and the masculine versions end in *o*. That one letter is enough to tell you what gender the person is. But with other words, ones that aren't generally meant to apply to people, the word itself has a gender that cannot change.

Here are some examples:

la casa	the house (feminine)
la silla	the chair (feminine)
el piso	the floor (masculine)
el cepillo	the brush (masculine)

Again, the gender of a word has nothing to do with what you might think of as a feminine or masculine object. Usually, you can tell the gender of a noun by looking at the last letter. If the word ends in *o*, it is likely a masculine word, and if it ends in *a*, it is likely a feminine word. However, as with most rules, there are some exceptions. We will cover that in the next section.

Definite Articles and Gender Agreement

As you've seen in previous sections, many of the word examples have the word *el* or *la* in front of them, with translations showing that those words both mean "the"—which is known as a ***definite article***. There are actually two more words meaning "the" in Spanish. All four versions are listed in table 2.1

table 2.1

DEFINITE ARTICLES		
	MASCULINE	**FEMININE**
SINGULAR	el	la
PLURAL	los	las

As you can see in table 2.1, there are masculine and feminine words for "the." The masculine *el* is paired with masculine singular nouns, and the feminine *la* is paired with feminine singular nouns. The words *los* and *las* also mean "the" and are used with plural words that are masculine or feminine. Table 2.2 shows some examples.

table 2.2

DEFINITE ARTICLES		
	MASCULINE	**FEMININE**
SINGULAR	el carro the car	la rosa the rose
PLURAL	los carros the cars	las rosas the roses

As you can see in table 2.2, *carro* is a masculine word, so in order to say "the car," you have to put the masculine singular *el* in front of *carro*. To say "the cars," you put the masculine plural *los* in front of *carros*. The same rules apply to the feminine word *rosa*.

Do you notice how most of the endings of the definite articles match the endings of the nouns? I have bolded them in the chart to draw your attention to this. Although not every word in Spanish ends in *o* or *a*, this is a helpful way to visualize it: make sure that the definite article and the noun match in gender (feminine or masculine) and number (singular or plural).

Making Words Plural

As you probably noticed in the definite article chart above, there are singular and plural versions of words in Spanish. So, how do you make a Spanish word plural? There are two major rules for making Spanish words plural. The first is that if the word ends in a vowel (*a, e, i, o, u*), then just add the letter *s*. For example:

carro → carros	car/cars
hombre → hombres	man/men
casa → casas	house/houses
mesa → mesas	table/tables

The second rule is that if the word ends in a consonant (any letter that is not a vowel mentioned above), you normally add *es*:

color → colores	color/colors
mes → meses	month/months
sándwich → sándwiches	sandwich/sandwiches
flor → flores	flower/flowers

There are a few other common patterns you should know about for making words plural. For most words ending with *s*, you don't have to add anything to make it plural. Just add the plural version of the definite article in front of it to indicate the plural meaning:

el lunes → los lunes	Monday/Mondays

For words that end in *z*, the *z* changes to a *c*, and you add *es* to the end:

el pez → los peces	the fish/the fishes
el juez → los jueces	the judge/the judges

Indefinite Articles and Gender Agreement

We've established that definite articles in Spanish are the equivalents of the word "the." But as you know from your own English usage, "the" isn't always appropriate; sometimes you use the words "a," "an," or "some," which are called ***indefinite articles***. To help students remember the difference between definite articles and indefinite articles, I use this trick: When I use the word "the" in English—let's say I say "the marker"—you know I am talking about a very specific marker. You *definitely* know what marker I am talking about because of my use of a *definite* article. If I say "a marker" or "some markers," you're *not* definitely sure what marker I'm talking about, because I'm using *indefinite* articles. Saying "a marker" or "some markers" is more indefinite than saying "the marker" or "the markers."

In English, our indefinite articles are *a*, *an*, and *some*. In Spanish, the words for a/an are *un* and *una*. Masculine singular nouns are paired with *un* and feminine singular nouns are paired with *una*. The same applies for *unos* and *unas*, which mean "some." Table 2.3 serves as a quick guide.

table 2.3

INDEFINITE ARTICLES	MASCULINE	FEMININE
SINGULAR	**un** a/an	**una** a/an
PLURAL	**unos** some	**unas** some

And here are some examples of the indefinite articles from table 2.3 paired with nouns:

un hombre (m)	a man (or one man)
un niño (m)	a boy (or one boy)
una mujer (f)	a woman (or one woman)
una niña (f)	a girl (or one girl)

NOTE: Since the Spanish word for the number "one" is *uno*, the words *un* and *una* can also carry the meaning of "one," depending on the context.

In English, when we want to make words plural, we use the terms "some" or "a few." In Spanish, however, the indefinite articles themselves are pluralized: *unos* and *unas*. Here are examples of how to put nouns with indefinite articles into a plural form.

unos hombres (m)	some/a few men
unos niños (m)	some/a few boys
unas mujeres (f)	some/a few women
unas niñas (f)	some/a few girls

More on Gender Agreement: Unknowns, Irregulars, and Adjectives

Making words plural is easy enough if you already know the definite article; *el* becomes *los* and *la* becomes *las*. But what if you don't have the definite article, and the word does not end with an easy signifier of its gender, like *o* or *a*? In those cases, it's not possible to know by simply looking at the word. You must learn the gender of these words when you first learn the words. For example, if I am learning the word for "flower" in Spanish, I can go to a dictionary, and it will tell me whether the word is *masculino (m)* or *feminino (f)*.

Look at figure 2.1; you can see that if I were to type the word "flower" into the search bar of an online bilingual dictionary, it would bring up the Spanish word *flor*. When I put my cursor over the letter *f* next to the word, a description pops up showing that the *f* means *feminino*, or feminine. You can also see that they put the definite article *la* in front of *flor*, another signal. This will not only help you learn the gender of the word, but it will be extremely helpful when you want to add adjectives to describe the word, because you'll be able to make the adjectives agree with the word's gender—which we will practice in the next section.

In figure 2.2, you can see that I searched for the word "man" in the online dictionary. The first Spanish word to come up was *el hombre*, which translates to "the man." Next to *el hombre* is the letter *m*, and when I put my cursor over it, it shows me that it means *masculino*, or masculine.

fig. 2.1 and fig. 2.2

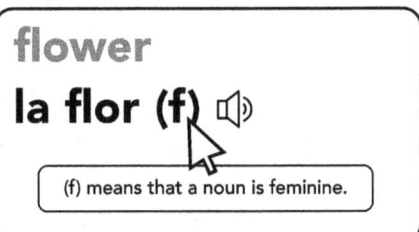

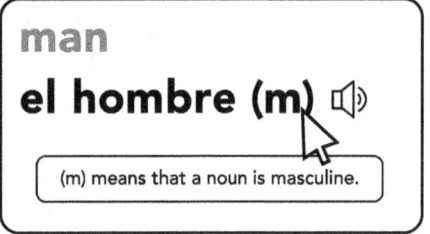

If you make a habit of writing down new vocabulary words or making flashcards with the definite article along with the word (as shown in figures 2.1 and 2.2), it will help you better learn the gender of the words.

As I mentioned earlier, there is almost always an exception to the rule. Here are a few examples of words that do not follow the rule we just discussed and are therefore considered irregular in gender:

el agua, las aguas	the water(s) (feminine)
el alma, las almas	the soul(s) (feminine)
la mano, las manos	the hand(s) (feminine)
el problema, los problemas	the problem(s) (masculine)
el clima, los climas	the climate(s) (masculine)
la foto, las fotos	the photo(s) (feminine)

As you can see, these words either combine the feminine definite article *la* with a word that appears to be masculine because it ends in *o*, or combine the masculine definite article *el* with a word that appears to be feminine because it ends in *a*. Even more confusing, there's not an easy rule for which indicator to follow; *el agua* is considered feminine (despite the "el"), and *el problema* is considered masculine (despite ending in *a*). You can also see that when the words are made plural, some of the definite articles change to a definite article of the other gender, while others don't.

The majority of words you come across in Spanish that end in *o* or *a* will follow the straightforward pattern we already talked about. Just be aware that there will be some words that appear to be a mixture of both genders but are assigned to one overall gender category. These are the most difficult for non-native speakers to learn, because it goes against the pattern that makes sense to our brains. The only way to learn these words is to add them to your flashcards or vocabulary notes and memorize and practice them.

Now, let me tell you: I used to sweat over these irregular-gender words, and I would get very nervous that I was going to mess them up when speaking Spanish—and I did many times. I still occasionally mess them up to this day. What's changed is that I no longer obsess over needing to be one hundred percent flawless when speaking my second language. In my first few years of practicing fluency, I missed out on many opportunities to practice because I was too afraid of saying something like *el mano* instead of *la mano*. Eventually, though, I realized my perfectionism was getting in my way and keeping me from progressing in the language. Most non-native speakers of Spanish are going to confuse these words from time to time. But guess what? Even if you say *el* instead of *la*, they both mean "the." Therefore, although you might not sound perfect, you're still achieving the general purpose of language: to communicate. So I recommend that you try to learn the tricky words when you can, and if you don't always get them right, just remember that it's okay not to be perfect. Honestly, my native English is far from perfect, so how is it realistic for me to expect my Spanish to always be perfect?

Adjective Agreement

Now that we have a handle on article–gender agreement, let's take a look at gender agreement with adjectives. This is the next step in your being able to form full sentences in Spanish.

Adjectives are words that we use to describe nouns: big, red, tall, beautiful, etc. Earlier in this chapter, we discussed the word order of these sentence fragments in Spanish and how it differs in English. Remember that an English sentence fragment such as "the red car" would, in Spanish, be arranged as *el carro rojo* (the car red).

Notice how *carro* is a masculine singular word, so it is paired with the masculine singular definite article *el*. Now consider the adjective at the end, *rojo*. A lot of adjectives in Spanish can change from masculine to feminine to fit the gender of what we are describing. Therefore, the word "red" can be *roja* or *rojo*. Here we would use the masculine *rojo* because it matches the gender of *carro*. And to make the example plural, we would say *los carros rojos*.

This is another English/Spanish difference. In English, we cannot make the word "red" plural; in Spanish, we can. And if we are describing more than one red thing, that adjective "red" also has to become plural. The same is true for adjectives like the Spanish word for "pretty," which can be *bonito*, *bonita*, *bonitos*, or *bonitas*; or the Spanish word for "tall," which can be *alto*, *alta*, *altos*, or *altas*, depending on what they're describing. For learners, these adjectives are usually written with the masculine ending *o*, with the option of the feminine ending *a* in parentheses. This implies that the adjective can switch genders depending on the gender of the noun it is describing. It looks like this:

rojo(a)	red
bonito(a)	pretty
alto(a)	tall

When studying adjectives, make flashcards or a list of the adjectives, following the format I used above. This will help you remember that the adjectives have the ability to be masculine or feminine.

If I wanted to describe a feminine noun, such as a chair, I would use the feminine definite article *la* and pair it with the feminine version of the adjective—in this case, *roja*:

la silla roj**a**	the red chair
la**s** silla**s** roj**as**	the red chairs

I bolded the endings of the words above so that you can see the singular and plural versions of this sentence fragment centered around the Spanish word for "chair." It's important to remember that endings won't always match perfectly like this, since not all nouns in Spanish end in *o* or *a*. For example, *mujer* is the Spanish word for "woman," and, as such, it's feminine—but it doesn't end with an *a*. Similarly, *hombre* is the Spanish word for "man," but it doesn't end with an *o*. In these cases, the definite articles can tell you how to use gender agreement:

la mujer bonita	the pretty woman
el hombre alto	the tall man

Even without the nouns ending in *o* or *a*, you can see that the gender, and whether it is singular or plural, is indicated by the definite articles in front of the nouns, as well as the adjectives. Keep in mind that this same concept applies to indefinite articles. So in that case the previous two examples would be as follows:

| una mujer bonita | a pretty woman |
| un hombre alto | a tall man |

Adjective Agreement with Gender-Neutral Adjectives

Some adjectives in Spanish do not have the ability to switch their endings from *o* to *a* to agree with the gender of the noun. Here are some examples:

azul	blue
gris	gray
grande	big
amable	kind
inteligente	intelligent
feliz	happy

Therefore, we will leave these adjectives as is when describing any masculine or feminine noun that is singular. For example:

la chica feliz	the happy girl
el hombre inteligente	the intelligent man
el carro azul	the blue car
la casa gris	the gray house

However, these adjectives can be pluralized, and if their accompanying nouns are made plural this still needs to happen, using the rules for plurals we've already established:

las chicas felic**es**	the happy girls
los hombres inteligent**es**	the intelligent men
los carros azul**es**	the blue cars
las casas gris**es**	the gray houses

You can see that I bolded the plural endings that were put on the definite articles, nouns, and adjectives so that every single word was made plural. You can also see that the definite articles and nouns are either both feminine or both masculine. Since the adjective cannot be made feminine or masculine, it simply has to be made plural.

Remember that the concept of gender agreement takes lots of practice to master, so be sure to continue to practice this concept throughout your studies of the language. To help, the Digital Asset library for this book includes a practice exercise on gender agreement. Visit go.quickstartguides.com/spanish.

Demonstrative Adjectives and Pronouns

So far we have learned how to put the articles "the," "a/an," and "some" in front of nouns, which in itself is already helpful in communicating basic needs and ideas in Spanish. The last concept we will cover in this chapter is demonstrative adjectives and pronouns, which also require application of the concept of gender agreement. Demonstrative adjectives and pronouns are words such as "this," "that," "these," and "those." These words help us clarify what object, person, or place we are referring to. Table 2.4 introduces this new set of words.

table 2.4

		THIS/THESE	THAT/THOSE	THAT/THOSE (further away)
MASCULINE	SINGULAR	este	ese	aquel
	PLURAL	estos	esos	aquellos
FEMININE	SINGULAR	esta	esa	aquella
	PLURAL	estas	esas	aquellas

DEMONSTRATIVE ADJECTIVES AND PRONOUNS

First, let's talk about the difference between demonstrative adjectives and demonstrative pronouns. You can see that table 2.4 is titled demonstrative adjectives *and* pronouns. What is the difference between the two? Demonstrative adjectives are used to describe the location of a noun (person, place, or thing). For example, if I say, "That girl is my friend," the word "that" is being used as a demonstrative adjective to describe which girl I am referring to. However, if I wanted to use a demonstrative pronoun instead, I would just say, "That is my friend." The word "that" in this case is being used as a pronoun to refer to the girl I am talking about, without my having to put the word "girl" with it. Therefore, you can see that demonstrative adjectives and pronouns are the same set of words. Whether you are using a demonstrative adjective or a demonstrative pronoun comes down to the grammatical technicality of how you are using those words.

Let's take a closer look at the first column of words in table 2.4, which starts with the word *este*. Those words are all ways to say "this" or "these," depending on whether the object we are referring to is singular or plural. Take a minute to think about when you would use the words "this" or "these" in English. Typically, they're used to communicate the distance of an object from the speaker; you are signaling that the objects are in close proximity to you. And in English, if we are speaking about something that is further away, we might use the words "that" or "those." The words in the second column starting with *ese* are equivalents of "that" and "those."

As you can see, there's also a third column of words, beginning with the word *aquel*—a set of Spanish words that also mean "that" or "those" but at an even greater distance. When you think about it, we also communicate this in English, but in a different way. For example, we might say "that house way over there." The words originating from *aquel* are basically equivalent to saying "that" or "those" *way* over there.

There will be some scenarios where you want to use a demonstrative word but don't know exactly what you are referring to—perhaps because you are seeing something new for the first time, or perhaps because you haven't learned the Spanish word for it yet (which makes it hard to refer to something using a demonstrative adjective that has a specific gender). This is when demonstrative pronouns come in handy. For example, in English, when we don't know what something is, we can ask, "What is that?" But English doesn't have the concept of gender agreement, so how can I ask a similar question in Spanish, when all the demonstrative pronouns in table 2.4 have a specific gender? That's where the set of bonus words listed in table 2.5 comes in handy.

table 2.5

GENDER NEUTRAL DEMONSTRATIVE PRONOUNS		
THIS/THESE	THAT/THOSE	THAT/THOSE (further away)
esto	eso	aquello

The three demonstrative pronouns in table 2.5 do not have a gender; they are among the few words in Spanish that are considered gender-neutral. You would use one of these words in situations where you don't know the gender of the object you are referring to (technically, this makes it a demonstrative pronoun). *Esto*, *eso*, and *aquello* enable you to refer to an unknown object while still being able to communicate the distance of the object. For example, you could ask something like this:

¿Qué es **esto**?	What is this?
¿Qué es **eso**?	What is that?
¿Qué es **aquello**?	What is that (way over there)?

If someone was to answer one of the above questions, they could start their answer with the gender-neutral word used in the question. For example, if you ask someone, *"¿Qué es esto?"* they might respond with *"Esto es una comida típica que se llama _____,"* or "This is a typical food that is called _____." Or they might respond with the correctly gendered demonstrative pronoun like, *"Esta es una silla,"* or "This is a chair."

When we do know the word for what we are referring to, we must use the correct gendered demonstrative adjective that agrees with the gender of the word and also clarifies its distance. Figure 2.3 shows a more concrete example.

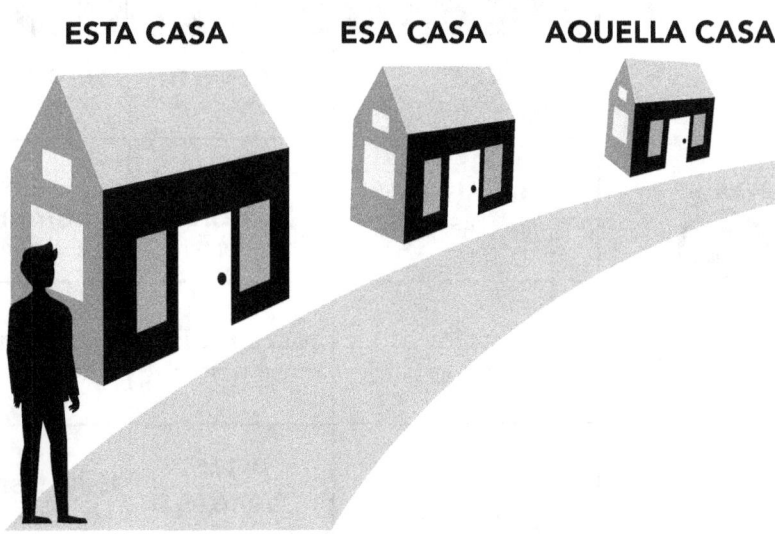

fig. 2.3

| 2 | Spanish-English Comparisons

Looking at figure 2.3, you can see how *esta*, *esa*, and *aquella* can all be combined with the word *casa*, because it is a feminine singular noun. You can see the location of the speaker and how the houses are referred to as they get further away in distance from the speaker. Therefore, to say "this house," you would say *esta casa*, for "that house" (a bit further away) you would say *esa casa*, and for "that house way over there" you would say *aquella casa*. Now, if we wanted to get technical with grammar, I could ask you which house you like the most, and you could respond with a demonstrative pronoun and say, *"Me gusta esa,"* basically meaning "I like that (one)." *Esa* still agrees with the subject of the conversation, *casa*, but you wouldn't have to explicitly say the word "casa" since the topic of the conversation had already been established.

Let's go through a few more examples of how to use these demonstrative adjectives with different Spanish nouns. We'll work with the following nouns:

carro (masculine singular)	car
hombres (masculine plural)	men
mujer (feminine singular)	women
tiendas (feminine plural)	stores

table 2.6

	CLOSEST TO SPEAKER	FURTHER AWAY FROM SPEAKER	VERY FAR FROM SPEAKER
carro (masculine, singular)	este carro (this car)	ese carro (that car)	aquel carro (that car *way over there*)
hombres (masculine, plural)	estos hombres (these men)	esos hombres (those men)	aquellos hombres (those men *way over there*)
mujer (feminine, singular)	este mujer (this woman)	esa mujer (that woman)	aquella mujer (that woman *way over there*)
tiendas (feminine, plural)	estas tiendas (these stores)	esas tiendas (those stores)	aquellas tiendas (those stores *way over there*)

Table 2.6 shows masculine and feminine words as well as singular and plural forms for a visual example of how these demonstrative adjectives pair up with nouns in Spanish.

I would say that the hardest demonstrative adjectives and pronouns to learn and remember are the words in the first two columns of table 2.6, those that start with *este* and *ese*. These forms are almost exactly alike except for one letter!

The way I remember the difference between them is that the words that have the letter *t* in them are for objects that are closest to me. Since "to me" starts with a *t*, I make that connection with the *t* in the forms of *este*. So, if it's helpful, think of how something close to you requires the word with the letter *t* in it, and something further away doesn't.

Again, the really important thing to remember is not to let yourself get overwhelmed by grammatical rules, especially when it comes to applying the concept of gender agreement. Because gender agreement doesn't exist in English, your brain will need a lot of practice and repetition before this concept will come more naturally to you. During the learning process, don't freeze up because you're overthinking about the trickier concepts. Something else that Spanish has in common with English—and with many other languages!—is that imperfect grammar doesn't have to stop you from achieving the overall goal of communication, and the more you put yourself out there, the faster you will master these concepts through practice.

Chapter Recap

The goal of this chapter was to highlight both similarities and differences between English and Spanish. My hope is to draw as many similarities to English as possible, to make the language-learning process feel easier to you. I am a big believer in the idea that learning a language shouldn't feel overwhelming to the learner. The following are two points of emphasis in these comparisons:

» Cognates, similar-sounding words that mean the same thing in English and Spanish. These are a useful concept to explore at this stage as you're just getting used to Spanish vocabulary.

» The concept of nouns being masculine (often but not always ending in *o*) or feminine (often but not always ending in *a*) and requiring gender agreement in their accompanying adjectives and articles. This is one of the biggest differences between the two languages, and a potentially overwhelming one.

I think it's important to explain the concept of gender agreement early so you have time to grow accustomed to it, but you should know that this concept isn't usually mastered until you're more in the intermediate to advanced proficiency levels of Spanish. For now, you should simply be aware of this language concept so you can notice it and practice it—while also being patient with yourself as you work to master it. It will come with time, but give yourself some grace if you don't feel you have it down yet. This is a normal part of your development as a Spanish-language learner. And although the gender concept is a major one, not everything you'll learn depends on it. In the next chapter, we will cover some basic phrases and conversation to get you more comfortable with the language. We'll revisit the concept of gender agreement in part II, where you'll see it in action through the use of full, complete sentences. For now, we'll move on to some basic conversation and phrases.

| 3 |

From Hello to Goodbye
Basic Spanish Conversation and Phrases

In the past two chapters, we covered a lot of bits and pieces of the language that are foundational in working toward a sentence-level ability. That information will come into play throughout the rest of the book—starting with this chapter, where we'll begin to work toward more sentence-level discourse. Through exploration of greetings, goodbyes, introductions, and basic conversational techniques, as well as some common expressions that can't be translated literally into English, you'll gain a greater understanding of how the culture and the language work together. Most exciting: you will be able to start participating in everyday uses of the language! There's something thrilling (and motivating) about conducting a conversation in another language when you're understanding others and being understood! This is what I consider to be the fun part of the language: the communication.

Chapter Overview

By the end of this chapter, you will be able to do the following:
» Understand the cultural importance of greetings and formal vs. informal forms of address.
» Learn common greetings and goodbyes in Spanish.
» Identify core phrases and words to communicate basic needs and emergencies.
» Practice common conversation questions and answers.
» Examine common expressions in the language, such as idioms.

Greetings/Goodbyes

Greetings and goodbyes may seem like the simplest possible expressions of a language; countless people who don't speak Spanish nonetheless understand that *hola* means "hello" and *adiós* means "goodbye." But these types of phrases have cultural importance beyond being simple pleasantries—and they illustrate some cultural differences between English and Spanish as well.

These differences extend to physical space. In the United States, people tend to prefer more personal space than in many other cultures. In Latin America, the personal space bubble tends to be smaller. Also, it is very common to kiss someone (usually on their right cheek) when greeting or meeting them. When I first started living in Mexico, I was very taken aback when I met new people and they would kiss me on the cheek. Generally, this is not done in professional settings such as work environments, but in most other casual situations, such as at parties or with family and friends, it is common. It felt very uncomfortable to me at first, especially with male strangers. Why would I kiss a man on the cheek that I don't even know? But in Latin America, this isn't as "forward" an action as it is in the States.

I also noticed a cultural importance placed on greetings. For example, any time I was at someone's house and any additional friends or family members arrived, they would go around and greet every single person, no matter how many people were there. And when it came time for people to leave, they would typically make the rounds to everyone present, to give them another kiss on the cheek and say goodbye. I also observed many families greeting each other in this way every time they left or returned home from work, school, and other places. This was surprising to me, coming from an American family where we would sometimes yell "I'm home!" or "I'm leaving! Bye!" without initiating a personal interaction with everyone in the house. Similarly, if my family had a party at our house, I would of course greet people, but it wasn't as big of a deal; I could walk into the kitchen and issue a blanket hello to everyone there. And when people left a gathering, they might say their goodbyes to those in their immediate vicinity, but they wouldn't necessarily reach out to every person in every room. My time in Mexico helped me to realize that relationships are highly valued in Latin America, and therefore proper greetings and goodbyes tend to be taken pretty seriously. Of course there are going to be differences depending on the country, the area you are in, and the individual people you come in contact with. However, I can say that the expectations for greetings and goodbyes are likely going to be a bit different from what you are used to in typical American culture.

Basic Greeting Phrases

Now that we have covered some of the main cultural differences with greetings and goodbyes, let's cover some basic words and phrases that you can use to greet people. We'll start with the three essentials.

Buenos días	Good morning
Buenas tardes	Good afternoon
Buenas noche	Good night (or good evening)

In Latin America, these three greetings are used constantly and according to the time of day. They work the same way they do in English, with a slight exception for *buenas noches*. In English, we tend to say "good night" almost as a way of saying goodbye, and often to communicate that we are going to sleep. In Spanish, *buenas noches* can have that meaning, but it is also used to greet people at nighttime, similar to the English phrase "good evening." Thus *buenas noches* can be used as a greeting or a goodbye depending on the situation. Another more casual way to use any of the above greetings is to simply say *buenas*; it can imply good morning, afternoon, or evening. When you think about it, we do something similar in English when we say "morning," "afternoon," or "night" as a more casual way to get the message across.

Here are some more common greetings:

Hola	Hello
Bienvenido(a)(s)	Welcome
¿Cómo estás (tú)?	How are you? (informal)
¿Cómo está (usted)?	How are you? (formal)
¿Qué tal? / ¿Qué pasa?	What's up?

Of course, most of us are probably already familiar with the greeting *hola*. It can be combined with any of the greetings we have covered so far. For example, I could say, *"Hola, ¡buenos días! ¿Como estás?"* to a friend.

When it comes to the word *bienvenido(a)(s)*, you can see that I wrote it with an *a* and an *s* in parentheses. This indicates that if I am welcoming a man, I can say *bienvenido*, as that version of the word has the masculine singular ending. If I was welcoming a woman, I would use *bienvenida*. If I was welcoming more than one man or a mixture of men and women, I would use the masculine plural form, which is *bienvenidos*. And if I was greeting a group with only women, I would use *bienvenidas*. This is the gender agreement concept we just learned about in chapter 2.

Next, let's examine differences between "*¿Cómo estás (tú)?*" and "*¿Cómo está (usted)?*" I put the pronouns *tú* and *usted* in parentheses because you don't have to say them as part of the question if you don't want to, because the verb itself communicates who is being spoken to. Using pronouns in a sentence is often optional (we will get into that more in part II when we cover verb conjugation). If your encounter is with someone like a close friend, you can use *¿Cómo estás?* If it's an encounter that requires more formality, you can use *¿Cómo está?* It can be easy to mix these two questions up at first, since there is only a one-letter difference, so it might be better to say *¿Cómo está usted?* if you want to clarify that you are trying to be formal.

Finally, we have *¿Qué tal?* and *¿Qué pasa?* These are very casual ways to greet someone. As an employee, I probably shouldn't ask my boss "what's up?" as a greeting, and the same applies with these questions in Spanish. You should only use more informal greetings with people you have a close relationship with, as we discussed in chapter 1 where we introduced *tú* and *usted*.

Of course, communication isn't a one-way street, so it's helpful to have answers to those questions we've just learned. Here are some common responses:

Estoy (muy) (bien/más o menos/mal), gracias	I am (very) (good/so-so/bad), thank you
¿Y tú?	And you? (informal)
¿Y usted?	And you? (formal)

Just like in English, asking someone how they are often functions as a greeting and is not so much about finding out how they are doing at a deeper level. Therefore, just like in English, we tend to answer "How are you?" with something along the lines of "I'm good, how are you?" In Spanish, a typical answer would be *"Estoy bien, gracias."* Then, for the part of your response where you want to ask someone how they are in return, instead of repeating the question, you can just say *"¿Y tú?"* if it's an informal situation or *"¿Y usted?"* if you are in a formal situation.

The phrases *¿Y tú?* and *¿Y usted?* can be used in any context where you essentially want to ask someone, "What about yourself?"

Of course, there are situations when we have conversations in which we want to be a bit more honest or detailed about how we are doing, and that's when it's useful to know other adjectives to describe how we're feeling. We will also go over more vocabulary regarding our feelings in part III.

Basic Goodbye Phrases

Now that we've covered some basic greetings, let's look at some common ways to say goodbye.

Adiós	Goodbye
Chau	A variation of goodbye commonly used in some parts of Latin America
Nos vemos	We'll see each other later
Hasta luego/pronto/mañana/ (el lunes, la próxima semana, etc.)	See you later/soon/tomorrow/ (on Monday, next week, etc.)
Cuídate	Take care (informal)
Cuídese	Take care (formal)

Regarding the list of goodbyes in Spanish, both *adiós* and *chau* are very straightforward. The next goodbye is *nos vemos*, which literally translates to "we see each other" but implies something along the lines of "we'll see each other later." The next goodbye starts with the word *hasta*, which can be combined with a variety of words. *Hasta* literally means "until," so when you say something like *"Hasta el lunes,"* you are literally saying "Until Monday," but in English we would normally say "See you Monday."

The last two greetings come from the same verb, *cuidarse*, which means to take care of oneself. *Cuídate* is the informal *tú* version of "take care," and *cuídese* is the formal *usted* version of "take care." *Cuídate* and *cuídese* are actually commands, which we will be learning more about in chapter 11.

Although we can say "take care" in many situations, we can also use it as a goodbye. I personally use this one a lot to say goodbye, as I think it is a nicer way to show you truly care about someone than simply saying a curt "Bye." You can even add more sentiment to it by saying, for example, *"Cuídate mucho."* The word mucho means "much" or "a lot," and in this case it's implying that I really want you to take care.

Of course, you also need words and phrases to fill in that conversation that happens between hello and goodbye. That's where we're heading next.

Introductions and Basic Conversation

Now that we've covered the basic greetings and goodbyes, let's get a little deeper into the middle of the conversation. I've found that it's motivating to get out into the world and participate in small conversations. Hopefully it will leave you wanting to learn more!

First, let's take a look at some vocabulary and common phrases that are used when introducing yourself and meeting others.

¿Cómo se llama? / ¿Cuál es su nombre? (formal usted)	What is your name?
¿Cómo te llamas? / ¿Cuál es tu nombre? (informal tú)	What is your name?
Me llamo _____. / Mi nombre es ____.	My name is _____.
Mucho gusto / Encantado(a)	Nice to meet you / Delighted
Igualmente	Likewise
Un placer	A pleasure

Looking at the words above, you can see there are two different ways to ask someone their name. (We briefly covered this in chapter 1.) The first question, *¿Cómo se llama?*, would literally translate to "What do you call yourself?" The second question, *¿Cuál es su nombre?*, literally translates to "Which is your name?" Either of these is a perfectly appropriate way to ask someone their name, so I suggest you start by learning one and sticking with it for now. Note that I've listed both the formal *usted* form of the questions and the informal *tú* versions, and I will continue to do that throughout the remainder of part I. In part II, we will introduce verb conjugations, and you won't need as much support with formal and informal conjugations.

Once you ask someone their name, you usually say something along the lines of "Nice to meet you." In Spanish, you can communicate that by saying either *mucho gusto*, which literally translates to "much pleasure," or *encantado(a)*, which translates to "delighted." Both mean essentially the same thing.

If you use *encantado(a)*, recognize that this word will be masculine or feminine depending on your gender, as it is an adjective indicating that you are delighted. And if you want to answer something like "It's nice to meet you too," you can say *mucho gusto* or *ecantado(a)*

60   SPANISH QUICKSTART GUIDE

or you can simply say *igualmente*, which translates to "likewise," or *un placer*, which translates to "a pleasure."

Here are a few more questions you might typically ask or be asked when meeting someone:

¿De dónde es (usted)? (formal usted)	Where are you from?
¿De dónde eres (tú)? (informal tú)	Where are you from?
Soy de _____.	I am from _____.
¿Cuántos años tiene (usted)? (formal usted)	How old are you?
¿Cuántos años tienes (tú)? (informal tú)	How old are you?
Tengo _____ años.	I am _____ years old.

You can see that I have again listed the formal and informal ways to ask someone a question. Note that the question "How old are you?" in Spanish would literally translate to "How many years do you have?" and you would answer with something like "I have twenty-nine years" (*"Yo tengo veintinueve años"*). We will cover the verb *tener* in more depth in part II. (Also, if you need a refresher on numbers so that you can express your age, look back at chapter 1).

fig. 3.1

Figure 3.1 brings everything we have been working on so far in this chapter together in two conversation examples.

More Basic Questions and Phrases

In addition to exchanging pleasantries, there are some other fundamental questions, words, and phrases that can be used to enrich your basic conversation and communicate your needs in a clear and respectful way. As with any language, manners are important—and I would say that, culturally speaking, manners are considered to be of particularly high importance in the Spanish language. As you might have noticed in the discussion of greetings and goodbyes, some aspects of Spanish and its cultures are a bit more formal than those of English. This means that you have the opportunity to get far with Spanish speakers by being sure to use your manners. We'll also go over some questions and phrases that can help you get around—and in emergencies, should they arise.

Mind Your Manners

Here's a set of words that you might recognize:

Sí	Yes
No	No
Por favor	Please
Gracias	Thank you
De nada	You're welcome

Simply knowing these words can add a lot to your conversational fluency in Spanish and help you to add some extra politeness. There's a reason they're some of the Spanish words non-speakers seem most likely to be familiar with! Here are some additional phrases to communicate politeness that aren't quite as well-known:

Con permiso	Excuse me
Perdón	Excuse me
Disculpe (formal) / Disculpa (informal)	Excuse me
Lo siento	I'm sorry

As you can see, *con permiso*, *perdón*, and *disculpe/disculpa* can all mean "excuse me" in certain contexts, so I will explain each a little further to give you a clearer idea of when to use which term. First, *con permiso* is a way to say "Excuse me" mostly in situations such as when you are physically trying to get around someone. *Perdón* would commonly be used in situations such as when you accidentally bump into someone, burp, or engage in some other minor social slip-up. *Disculpe/disculpa* are commands and are used more for apologizing (the infinitive verb *disculpar* literally means "to forgive"), so you are literally telling someone to forgive you. However, you can also use *disculpe/disculpa* as a way to get someone's attention. For example, in English, we often ask a store employee or a waiter for assistance by saying "Excuse me." Finally, *lo siento* doesn't mean "excuse me," but it can also be a useful phrase in some of the scenarios I just described.

Communicating Languages and Understanding

Let's look at some additional questions that commonly come up in simple conversation and can aid in basic understanding. First, here are some ways to ask someone if they speak a certain language, and how to let them know what you speak. This can be helpful when traveling.

¿Habla (usted) _____?	Do you (formal) speak _____?
¿Hablas (tú) _____?	Do you (informal) speak _____?
(Yo) hablo (un poco de) _____.	I speak (a little bit of) _____.
inglés	English
español	Spanish
chino	Chinese
hindi	Hindi
francés	French

(Notice that languages are not capitalized in Spanish.)

Though these questions are useful for travelers, they're certainly not exclusive to that situation. I've been in places such as at a store checkout where I heard someone ask a cashier, *"¿Habla español?"* and when I saw the panicked look on the cashier's face, I jumped in to say, *"¡Yo sí hablo español!"* I have been able to help people communicate in many situations, and for me, that is one of the most satisfying things about knowing another language. Other people will doubtless help you out from time to time on your language-learning journey, so you'll likely savor the day when you will be able to do it for someone else!

Now, we might not always be in a picture-perfect situation as described above, so let's go over some ways to get clarification in those times when you don't quite understand someone.

No entiendo	I don't understand
Más lento/despacio, por favor	Slower, please
Repita, por favor (formal) / Repite, por favor (informal)	Repeat, please

If I had a dollar for every time I've had to use *no entiendo*, I would have *mucho dinero* (a lot of money). It's definitely a phrase new learners will use often—and one I still use from time to time. As we have discussed, there are twenty-one official Spanish-speaking countries. Even if you are an advanced speaker of the language, when you talk to people from different countries there will be moments when communication is challenging, because they are likely to use certain colloquial words and phrases you are not familiar with. So keep these phrases handy.

Also, at first it's going to sound like Spanish speakers are talking very quickly. Any language is going to sound fast to you if you're a beginner, so sometimes you need to ask someone to speak *más lento* and/or to *repita por favor*, and then you will be able to understand them. The more you advance in your language skills, the less fast Spanish will seem to you. (However, in any language there are some people who just naturally talk really fast.) This might also make you more aware of the experiences of others who are just starting to learn English!

Getting Around Town

Plenty of people attempt to pick up the language in preparation for a trip to a Spanish-speaking country, but there are many other great reasons to learn Spanish. The questions and accompanying nouns that you might use in a travel situation are helpful for finding your way through basic conversation. Let's go over some common questions that will help you in situations such as traveling, shopping, or eating out.

¿Dónde está _____?	Where is _____?
el baño	the bathroom
el restaurante	the restaurant
la tienda / el mercado	the store / the market
el hotel	the hotel
el aeropuerto	the airport
¿Cuánto cuesta?	How much does it cost?
¿Qué recomienda? / ¿Qué recomiendas?	What do you recommend? (formal/informal)

One of the common phrases I often hear people say they know in Spanish is *¿Dónde está el baño?* That's definitely a good one to know, and the *el baño* part of the question can be replaced with any place or person you want to find. And if you're out and about, you will also likely need to purchase something at some point. This is where the numbers we learned in chapter 1 are going to be helpful yet again, as you'll be able to ask how much something costs and communicate the price of an item or product.

I think asking someone what they recommend is a good thing to be able to do, while traveling or otherwise. Although that might seem a bit advanced for this part of the book, I love being able to ask a local for a recommendation when I am traveling, such as a good dish to try or a place to visit. Gleaning information from locals, whether you're in a Spanish-speaking country or a predominantly Spanish-speaking neighborhood, can definitely enrich your experience.

When you're out and about, other needs may come up; here are some major ones you might need to address:

Tengo hambre	I'm hungry
Tengo sed	I'm thirsty
el agua	the water
la comida	the food
el taxi / el autobús	the taxi / the bus

Even knowing just the words and phrases above can get you a long way in a Spanish-speaking country. Being able to communicate your basic needs, such as for food and water, is definitely of high importance. And if you're traveling, you'll likely need to use some form of public transportation at some point, and being able to simply communicate *autobús* and have someone point you in the right direction to catch the bus can be enough to help you get where you need to go.

Emergency Essentials

Of course, a best practice is to be prepared for emergencies. Hopefully, you won't have to use these words, but I definitely don't want to let you get through part I without covering our bases.

¡Cuidado!	Careful!
¡Ayuda!/¡Auxilio!	Help!

la emergencia	the emergency
las alergias	the allergies
el hospital	the hospital
la ambulancia	the ambulance
el/la policía	the police (masculine/feminine)
el fuego / el incendio	the fire (fuego is for fire in general, and incendio refers to when something is on fire)
el terremoto	the earthquake
el tornado	the tornado
la inundación	the flood
el huracán	the hurricane

These words should be enough to help you communicate in case of an emergency. I think *las alergias* is a particularly important word to have in this section, as serious allergies are arguably more common than bigger, flashier disasters. If you have a specific allergy (or any medical condition, for that matter), I highly recommend looking it up in your Spanish dictionary and committing it to memory. It is also important to know which kinds of natural disasters are more common in areas where you're traveling and to inform yourself of the best safety procedures. I apparently slept through an earthquake when I was living in Mexico, and luckily it was a minor one. But after that happened, I realized I had no idea what to do in a more intense one. I really hope you will learn from my mistakes!

Dynamic Dialogue

You have already started to learn that not everything in one language translates perfectly to another language, which means that it's helpful to have certain phrases and expressions on hand that can help you gain clarity in basic conversation, as both a communicator and a listener.

Clarifying, Well-Wishing, and Filler

Let's start with some phrases that you can use to express yourself in simple and understandable terms.

Yo también	Me too
No sé	I don't know
Está bien	It's okay
Todo bien	Everything's good

No hay problema	Not a problem
Por supuesto	Of course
¡Qué bueno/excelente/triste/difícil/sorpresa!	How good/excellent/sad/difficult/surprising!

These phrases can help you add a little more detail to your basic conversation. You might notice that Spanish has a lot of phrases about everything being "good" or "not a problem" and so on. My personal sense has been that many Spanish speakers I've encountered tend to frame things pretty positively. I did some research on this idea and found some studies that had gathered corpuses (bodies of text pulled to use as a database) of different languages, and, indeed, they found Spanish to be one of the most positive languages. I think this helps explain the concept of how language shapes our worldviews, and I definitely think this is part of the reason why Spanish-speaking countries are often noted for having such happy people. Speaking of positivity, let's go through some more positive phrases and expressions below.

¡Salud!	Cheers! / Bless you!
(Buen) provecho	Bon appétit
Felicidades	Congratulations
Buena suerte	Good luck

If you ever share a meal with Spanish speakers, you might find yourself clinking glasses with everyone and saying *"¡Salud!"* This literally translates to *"Health!"* In English, we would say "Cheers!" The word *salud* is also used to tell someone "Bless you" after they sneeze. In both situations you are technically wishing someone good health.

Another word you will often hear during meals is *buen provecho*, which is a way to tell someone to enjoy their meal. When I lived in Mexico, sometimes even random people walking by my table as they left a restaurant would say *provecho* out of politeness. Going back to the point of manners being important, generally anytime you come in contact with a person who is eating, it would be polite of you to say *provecho* to recognize the fact that they are enjoying a meal.

Continuing with more positive words, *felicidades* is a way to congratulate someone, and *buena suerte* is used to wish someone good luck. I personally prefer to tell someone *éxito*, which means "success" rather than "good luck," but either is appreciated!

Because I'm mentioning a lot of words and phrases in this chapter that have some form of *bien/bueno*, I also want to note the words *pues* and *este*.

| Bueno/Pues/Este | Well.../So.../Umm... (as filler words) |

While *bueno* would normally translate as "good," and we previously learned that *este* is a demonstrative adjective and pronoun meaning "this," they are also often used as filler words, as well as the word *pues*. In English, some common filler words we use are "um," "like," "well," and "so," and we aren't really using them to communicate anything specific but rather to fill in the silence between our other words. There are many filler words in Spanish, but *bueno*, *este*, and *pues* are the ones I've come across most frequently—and the ones that confused me as a beginner learning Spanish. People kept saying "good" and "this" when it made no sense in the context (when I translated them literally). But once I understood they were filler words, I was able to pay attention to context and better understand when a word was being used as a filler word rather than a literal word in a sentence.

Beyond the Dictionary: Linguistic Variations, Slang, and Idioms

Some expressions in Spanish vary greatly depending on location. As I've mentioned, linguistic variations are extremely common in Spanish. One phrase that varies a lot depending on where you are is the expression for "cool."

fig. 3.2

You can see in figure 3.2 how many different words can be used to express the Spanish equivalent of "cool," and what Spanish-speaking country you're in greatly impacts which one you might hear. For example, when I lived in Mexico, I would hear ¡*Qué padre!* and ¡*Qué chido!* a lot. However, if I went to Spain or Argentina, people would probably look at me funny if I used one of those terms. These linguistic variations make Spanish such a diverse language; you'll never run out of words and phrases to learn.

Linguistic variations like this can be daunting too, because you can't very well instantly memorize every local variation of various words and phrases and have all of them correctly correlated to the given country or region. When I meet a Spanish speaker from a country where I haven't spent much time (or haven't encountered other speakers from there), it can be harder to understand them. However, I've also found that the more advanced I have gotten with the language, the easier it has been for me to pick up on the context of a situation and more or less figure out what they are saying despite not knowing the exact word or phrase they're using.

On the other hand, there are times when I have been completely lost and have had to ask people to explain what they were saying. For example, one of my past coworkers is from Venezuela, so she uses some words that I did not learn when I studied Spanish in Mexico. We had many laughs as I had to ask her, "What in the world are you talking about?!" She would explain to me that, for example, to her, a T-shirt is a *franela*, whereas I learned that a T-shirt is a *camiseta* or a *playera*. Those words sound nothing alike! The linguistic variations are unpredictable. However, you will definitely learn something new and probably even develop relationships with people where you can make fun of each other's vocabulary differences in good spirit.

I should also mention that some words that are used in one Spanish-speaking country can actually be inappropriate or offensive in other countries! For example, in Spain the verb *coger* can be used to communicate a variety of things, such as "to take" (a bus), "to grab" (something off the floor), etc. However, I can tell you that in Mexico, this verb was used to refer to sexual intercourse. You can imagine that this word alone has caused some pretty awkward situations between speakers of different regions. The important thing to remember is that these differences are not worth stressing over. There are many words that can have different meanings depending on the country, and it's something that Spanish speakers are used to facing.

If you are interested in looking at more examples of linguistic variations, do an online search for Spanish words that vary by region. If you know you'll be traveling to a specific country, you could also search for common words and phrases used in that country or region to do a little preparing beforehand.

Every language has formal and informal uses, and with informal language use comes slang. I do not consider myself to be well-versed in any kind of Spanish slang, and it can be pretty difficult for a non-native speaker to learn it. That's true of any language; I even struggled to learn (and stay up to date with) some of the English-language slang my students used when I taught high school. So don't be surprised if you hear people engaged in casual conversation in Spanish and you feel as if you're hearing another language. Anyone learning a language is going to feel that way when they come in contact with slang.

Just like slang, idioms can be very difficult to learn as a non-native speaker. Think about it: in English, if we said something like "It's raining cats and dogs!" can you imagine how confused someone learning English would likely be? Those types of phrases cannot be translated literally; they are meant to imply something completely different. Table 3.1 shows some examples I've come across.

table 3.1

IDIOM	LITERAL TRANSLATION	IMPLIED MEANING	ENGLISH EQUIVALENT
Ser pan comido	To be eaten bread	To be easy	A piece of cake
Encontrar a mi media naranja	To find my half of an orange	To find the love of your life	To find your soulmate/ other half

You can see that if you were to translate these idioms literally, you would not get the implied meaning, and the way we say them in English is completely different (though sometimes there's basic common ground, such as using food like bread or cake to indicate ease). Which idioms are used can also vary by region. Basically, what I'm getting at is that none of us can know everything in a language, and idioms can really keep us on our toes!

 **QUICK TIP** If you are interested in learning more idioms, do an internet search and you will find tons. There are even some pretty entertaining YouTube videos about the challenges that you can encounter with Spanish: idioms, variations of Spanish, the different accents, etc.

So how do we navigate linguistic differences without committing a whole lot of them to memory? I find two particular questions to be helpful in this regard.

¿Cómo se dice _____?	How do you say _____?
¿Qué significa _____?	What does _____ mean?

For example, if you are with someone who knows English, you could ask them "¿Cómo se dice *car*?" and they would answer you with "Se dice *carro*" to tell you how to say the word in Spanish. You can also use *¿Cómo se dice?* by simply holding an item or pointing to it, and then someone can tell you the word. This is a great way to keep yourself speaking Spanish while you learn, instead of resorting to asking your entire question in English or looking it up online.

If someone says something you don't understand, try asking them *¿Qué significa?* or *¿Qué significa _____?* (inserting a word in the blank). Once you get to a more conversational level in the language, you'll be able to experience asking someone what something means in Spanish and comprehending their explanation in Spanish. It's such a neat feeling when you can keep learning more in a language while you're speaking that language! But regardless of what stage you're at, these two questions are likely to come in handy, especially if you are encountering speakers from many different regions. You'll be able to navigate those linguistic differences and learn a lot of ways to communicate the same idea.

Chapter Recap

In this chapter, we covered basic phrases, words, and expressions to enrich your conversational skills in Spanish and to help you communicate basic needs and be prepared for emergency situations. These types of words and phrases include the following:

» Greetings and goodbyes
» Introductions and basic conversational tools
» Common questions and phrases for clarifications and conversation

Hopefully you are leaving this last chapter of part I feeling as if you have a basic understanding of the major functions of the language and feeling confident that you could find your way through a number of day-to-day interactions and situations.

The rest of the book is going to be topic-based and will give you a context for how everything in part I fits together in the language. Although it is important to cover certain grammatical points, my passion is studying language through the lens of everyday circumstances rather than purely by grammar and memorization drills. This means looking at the language as a whole, focusing on comprehension and communication and what role grammar plays in real-life settings. So buckle up, because we are about to go on an amazing journey together, where we will explore the language through different lenses and meet lots of Spanish speakers from all over the world as we go!

PART II

THIS IS ME

Now that we have covered many of the bare essentials of the language, we will start building on that foundation. This involves expanding on the basic concepts we covered in part I, with the goal of getting you to a place where you can participate in more complex uses of the language. This part will mostly center around you, focusing on your ability to share information about yourself, such as who you are, what you like to do, and what your typical daily activities are. Toward the end of this part, we will start expanding outward and work on sharing information about those around us, such as our family.

| 4 |
Defining Yourself

Through our work in part I, you learned how to say your name, how old you are, and so on. But to really master language concepts, we need to constantly recycle and revisit topics and see how they work in different contexts. Revisiting these basic phrases while adding some new concepts will help you expand your language proficiency. We start with talking about ourselves because it's an intuitive starting place for language acquisition: as children, for example, we often master self-description before branching out to describe others. Therefore, this chapter will prioritize looking at things from a "me, myself, and I" point of view.

Chapter Overview

By the end of this chapter, you will be able to do the following:
» Know the uses of the verb *ser*.
» Conjugate the irregular verbs *ser* and *tener* in the present tense.
» Use *tener* and *ser* to describe yourself and others.
» Conjugate regular -AR, -ER, and -IR verbs in the present tense.

For an overview of the concepts we will be working with in this chapter, listen to the following QuickClip. As you listen, follow along with the script below. You will hear the native speakers describe aspects of themselves such as their profession, personality, and activities they enjoy. These are all concepts you will learn in this chapter so that you will be able to provide similar descriptions of yourself.

In this clip, María from Venezuela and Sunciree from Guatemala hold a conversation. Follow along with the script below as you listen.

To watch the QuickClip, use the camera on your mobile phone to scan the QR code or visit the link below.

or www.quickclips.io/spanish-4

María:	Hola, yo soy María. ¿Cómo te llamas?
Sunciree:	Mucho gusto, María. Mi nombre es Sunciree. ¿De dónde eres?
María:	Yo soy de Venezuela, pero ahora vivo en los Estados Unidos. ¿Y tú?
Sunciree:	Soy de Guatemala, pero ahora vivo en el estado de Texas. ¿Y en qué trabajas?
María:	Yo trabajo en una universidad como tutora de matemáticas. Me encanta enseñar. ¿Dónde trabajas tú?
Sunciree:	Yo trabajo como maestra de español en una escuela de secundaria. ¿Y qué te gusta hacer en tu tiempo libre?
María:	En mi tiempo libre, me encanta trabajar en el jardín. Me gusta que mi casa se vea bonita. Y a ti, ¿qué te gusta hacer?
Sunciree:	A mí me gusta mucho cocinar y me encanta viajar.
María:	¡Qué bien! ¿Cómo eres?
Sunciree:	Yo soy muy extrovertida. Me gusta tener muchos amigos. ¿Cómo eres tú?
María:	Yo soy muy activa y como a ti, me encanta viajar.
Sunciree:	Pues mucho gusto, María. Es un placer conocerte.
María:	Igualmente, mucho gusto. ¡Adiós!

To Be or Not to Be? An Introduction to the Verb *Ser*

To start off, let's look at our first conjugation chart, for the Spanish verb *ser*, which means "to be." (There is another verb, *estar*, that can also mean "to be," and we will cover that in chapter 7 to avoid learning both verbs simultaneously.) Conjugation, as we've touched on before, is the process of modifying a verb to match how it's being used. In other words, making the general verb "to be" agree with "I" ("I am"), "you" ("you are"), "we" ("we are"), and so on.

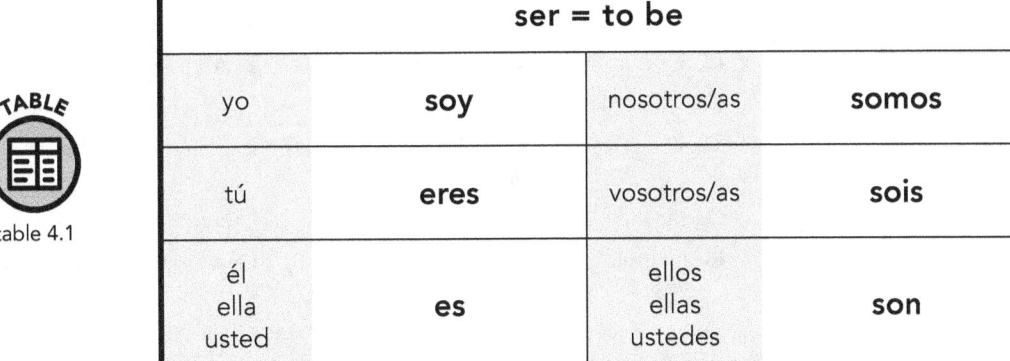

table 4.1

ser = to be			
yo	**soy**	nosotros/as	**somos**
tú	**eres**	vosotros/as	**sois**
él ella usted	**es**	ellos ellas ustedes	**son**

As mentioned in chapter 1, the order of the pronouns in the chart is intentional and important, and that's why I recommended memorizing them in this exact format and order: *yo*, *tú*, *él*, *ella*, and *usted*, and then *nosotros(as)*, *vosotros(as)*, *ellos*, *ellas*, and *ustedes*. As you can see in table 4.1, each box of the conjugation chart contains a variation of the verb *ser*. These variations are referred to as *conjugations*—forms of a verb that change depending on who is doing the action (the one doing the action is known as the *subject*).

Our verbs in English work similarly. In English, the conjugations of the verb "to be" are as follows: I *am*, you *are*, he/she *is*, we *are*, and they/you all *are*. The verb changes depending on the pronoun that is in front of it. You will be seeing many verb charts like the one pictured above, using the same pronouns but with different verbs, so you can learn verb conjugations in a consistent pattern.

The verb *ser* is a major building block of the language, but it's also an irregular verb, which means its conjugations don't follow a pattern like some of the verbs we will cover later in this chapter. This makes it more important to memorize the pronoun organization above with the corresponding conjugations: soy, eres, es, somos, sois (if you want to learn the vosotros conjugations), and son. This is how I learned to conjugate verbs, drilling them in my head over and over. Picturing this box in my head helps me to quickly pull out the correct conjugation of a verb when I'm speaking the language.

| 4 | Defining Yourself

Uses of the Verb *Ser*

Since you know the English equivalent "to be," you might have guessed that there are a number of contexts in which we use *ser*. Many people use the acronym DOCTOR to remember these contexts. I will give you an example sentence for each letter in DOCTOR, and we will work more extensively with all these uses throughout the next few chapters.

Date	Hoy es lunes.	Today is Monday.
Occupation	Soy una maestra.	I am a teacher.
Characteristics	Soy rubia y atlética.	I am blonde and athletic.
Time	Son las diez y media de la mañana.	It is ten thirty in the morning.
Origin	Soy de South Dakota.	I am from South Dakota.
Relationship	Soy la hija de mis padres.	I am the daughter of my parents.

As you can see, each example sentence contains a conjugation of the verb *ser* that is provided on the verb conjugation chart.

Describing Yourself with *Ser*

Using the verb *ser* to describe yourself—the *C* in DOCTOR—involves revisiting the concept of gender agreement. When describing yourself, you will use the verb conjugation *soy*, and any adjectives you use to describe yourself will have to match the gender that you identify with.

For example, if you identify as male, you could say something like this:

Yo soy alto, rubio y amable.	I am tall, blond, and kind.

That same sentence for a female describing herself would be as follows:

Yo soy alta, rubia y amable.	I am tall, blond, and kind.

You can see that the adjectives that were able to change gender did indeed change depending on the gender of the person doing the describing. The gender-neutral adjective *amable* stayed the same because it was describing a single person in each scenario.

Here are some basic adjectives that might be helpful for describing yourself:

alto(a)	tall
bajo(a)	short
atlético(a)	athletic
guapo(a)	good-looking
simpático(a)	kind
extrovertido(a)	extroverted
introvertido(a)	introverted
tranquilo(a)	calm
fuerte	strong
inteligente	intelligent

Let's look at an example sentence of me describing myself:

Soy Maria. Soy simpática, tranquila e inteligente.

Any adjectives that can end in *o* or *a* will in this case end in *a*, because I identify as a woman and use feminine adjectives to describe myself. As we discussed before, inteligente ends in *e*, so I didn't have to do anything with that ending. Also notice that instead of writing *y* for "and," I wrote *e*. The reason is that when you say *y* out loud, it makes the same sound as the beginning of the word *inteligente*, so if I were to say/write *"y inteligente,"* the two words would run together and you wouldn't hear a distinction between them. So whenever the word that follows the word "and" in Spanish starts with the same sound as *y*, it is changed to *e* (pronounced like the English "eh") to communicate the word "and."

You can also use *ser* to describe yourself without adjectives. For example, instead of saying something like "Me llamo Maria," I could say "Soy Maria," which translates to "I am Maria." You can also use *ser* to tell someone where you are from, or your nationality. To say where you are from, say "Soy de _____." In my case, I would say "Soy de los Estados Unidos," meaning the United States (abbreviated as EE.UU. in Spanish). To describe your nationality, use "Soy _____." In my case, I would say "Soy estadounidense," meaning American (from the United States—see how it looks similar to the words for United States in Spanish?).

Do you see how my sentence examples above start with "Soy" instead of "Yo soy"? This is because the conjugation *soy* is only used with the pronoun *yo*, which means I don't have to include *yo* because *soy* on its own can communicate "I am." (You can include *yo*, but it's not necessary to convey the meaning clearly.) Other conjugations of *ser*, such as *es*, are used with the pronouns *él*, *ella*, and *usted*. In these cases, you might want to include the pronoun with the verb conjugation to clarify who you are talking about. But once you have established the subject of the sentence, you don't have to put the pronoun in front of the verb each time. We will revisit this concept repeatedly throughout the book as we continue to practice conjugating verbs.

You might also like to share your profession—the O from the acronym DOCTOR—when describing yourself to others. Here are some examples:

el/la maestro(a)	teacher
el/la doctor(a)	doctor
el/la abogado(a)	lawyer
el/la estudiante	student
el/la carpintero(a)	carpenter
el/la cocinero(a)	cook
el/la policía	police
el/la secretario(a)	secretary

Let's look at an example sentence:

Yo soy una maestra.	I am a teacher.

You can see that I put the indefinite article meaning *a* in front of the word for teacher, and I used the feminine ending for teacher. Some professions, such as *policía* and *estudiante*, don't have gender-specific endings; for those you can indicate gender by putting either *un* or *una* in front of the word. For example, "Soy una estudiante" communicates that I am a female student.

Describing Yourself with the Verb *Tener*

Another way of describing yourself is to use the verb *tener*, which means "to have." The conjugation chart is shown in table 4.2.

table 4.2

tener = to have			
yo	**tengo**	nosotros/as	**tenemos**
tú	**tienes**	vosotros/as	**tenéis**
él ella usted	**tiene**	ellos ellas ustedes	**tienen**

Like the verb *ser*, *tener* is also an irregular verb (we will dive into many more irregular verbs throughout the book), so I recommend memorizing *tengo*, *tienes*, *tiene*, *tenemos*, *tenéis* (if you're learning the *vosotros* conjugations), and *tienen*. For this section, we will stick to talking about ourselves using the *yo* conjugation: "tengo."

We can use the verb *tener* to describe many aspects of our appearance. To do that, we need some new vocabulary terms that can be combined with *tener*.

el pelo/el cabello	hair
largo	long
corto	short
rizado	curly
liso	straight
rubio	blonde
pelirrojo	redheaded
café/castaño/marrón	brunette or brown
negro	black
la piel	skin
clara	white/light complexion
morena	brown/dark complexion
negra	black
los ojos	eyes
azules	blue
verdes	green
cafés/castaños/marrónes	brown
negros	black

| 4 | Defining Yourself   81

NOTE: Keep in mind that if you are describing your hair, you would have to use the masculine singular form of the adjectives in the list because *pelo* and *cabello* are masculine singular words. When describing your skin, the adjectives must take the feminine singular form to agree with *piel*. And when describing your eyes, you must use the masculine plural form to agree with the word *ojos*.

Here are a few more vocabulary words that can be helpful when describing physical features:

las pecas	the freckles
el lunar	the mole
la cicatriz	the scar
el tatuaje	the tattoo
la barba	the beard
el bigote	the moustache

Here's how I would put some of our new vocabulary words into practice to describe myself:

» Tengo el cabello muy largo y rubio. Tengo la piel clara y tengo ojos verdes. También tengo pecas y lunares.

I used the verb *tener* in each sentence to describe many aspects of my appearance using the vocabulary we covered above. Now, because there is usually more than one way to communicate an idea in a language, I am going to write the same idea in a slightly different way:

» Mi cabello es muy largo y rubio. Mi piel es muy clara y mis ojos son verdes. Mi piel tiene pecas y lunares.

In the paragraph above, I used the verb *ser* in some of the sentences instead of *tener*. However, in my last sentence, I still use *tener* to communicate that I have moles and freckles. You can see that *ser* and *tener* can be used in similar situations depending on what you are trying to say. Now that we have covered the basics of *ser* and *tener* and seen a little of how they can work together when describing appearance, let's look at a few more ways to use them.

Birthdates and Ages Using *Ser* and *Tener*

One frequent use of both *ser* and *tener* is to communicate about age. We briefly touched on this earlier in the book, but let's take a more detailed look at this form of communication and a few different ways to go about it. First, when using the verb *ser*, we can describe our age by using words like *old* or *young*.

joven	young
menor	younger
mayor	older
viejo(a)	old

You can see that *joven* is used to say that someone is young. However, there are two words to communicate that someone is old—and you should be careful which one you use. *Mayor* means "older" in a polite and human-focused way. The other word, *viejo(a)*, means simply "old" and is more appropriately used to describe objects rather than people.

Calling someone "viejo" or "vieja" would sound blunt and impolite to many people. Think of it as the difference between saying "she's older than I am" and just flatly stating, "she's old." Some couples do call one another "mi viejo" or "mi vieja" as a term of endearment to communicate the idea of "my old guy" or "my old lady," but notice that the closeness of the relationship determines whether that's an appropriate use. The word *mayor* can also be used to express that someone is older than you, like an older brother, for example, and *menor* would be used to express that someone is younger than you. We will learn more about comparing ourselves to others with age and other characterisitcs in chapter 6.

In part I, we learned how to say how old we are using the verb *tener*. We will now revisit that along with a few other ways to discuss birth dates.

Tengo veintinueve años.	I am 29 years old.

To express my age, I used the verb *tener*. In English we don't say "I have 29 years," but that's the construction used in Spanish. We have also touched on the concept of dates, and I want to review and expand on that while we are talking about ages and birth dates.

Mi cumpleaños **es** el 18 de febrero.	My birthday is February 18th.

| 4 | Defining Yourself

Notice that I used the verb *ser* to communicate my birth date. Also, remember that when dates are written out numerically, they are styled with the day first, then the month, and then the year, as shown below.

- » 4/5/2022 would represent May 4, 2022
- » 3/10/2019 would represent October 3, 2019

The date examples that I used above are the birth dates of my dogs. Next you will read a paragraph about each of my dogs, and I will apply many of the concepts we have covered in this chapter using *ser* and *tener* to describe them. But this time I will be talking about someone else (pets in this case) instead of myself.

- » Mi perro menor **es** Anakin. El cumpleaños de Anakin **es** el 4 de mayo. Anakin tiene un año. Él **es** negro y **tiene** ojos cafés. **Es** muy extrovertido e inteligente.

- » Carlita **es** mi perra mayor. El cumpleaños de Carlita **es** el 3 de octubre. Ella **tiene** tres años. Ella **es** blanca y gris y **tiene** ojos negros. **Es** simpática y atlética.

Notice that the verb conjugations in bold font come from the verbs *ser* and *tener*. Also, do you notice how I varied the phrasing to communicate similar ideas about my dogs? And because Anakin is a male and Carlita is a female, I used different adjective endings in each description as well.

You have now learned several ways to describe different ideas about yourself (and about others, which we will focus more on later in part II). Next, let's take a look at present-tense conjugation for regular verbs, so we can describe things we do.

Activities Using Regular Present-Tense Verbs

Verbs are referred to as *regular* when they have a very clear conjugation pattern (unlike *ser* and *tener*). Most of us are probably familiar with the present tense and what it's used for—obviously, it's to talk about the present! The present tense in Spanish is indeed used to talk about things you do regularly or on an ongoing basis, just like in English, but it can also be used to talk about things you are doing right now.

For example, in English, we would use the present tense to communicate something like "I work in an office." The same goes for Spanish: you would say "Yo trabajo en una oficina." In that case, the present tense is used to communicate something that's done presently and/or regularly.

However, in Spanish, I could also say something like "Yo como un sandwich," which means "I eat a sandwich," but it could also mean "I am eating a sandwich." In English, we use the present progressive (adding -ing to a verb to indicate that we are performing that action right now), but in Spanish we can use either the present progressive (which will be covered in chapter 7) or the regular present tense. So if someone says something like "Como un sándwich," it could mean they eat a sandwich on a regular basis or that they are eating one right now.

Before we look at our new conjugation charts, I want you to read the paragraph below and pay close attention to the bolded words.

Yo **hablo** inglés. **Estudio** español, pero no **hablo** mucho español. Mi amigo **habla** inglés y francés. Nosotros **estudiamos** español en la escuela. Yo **trabajo** en un restaurante italiano, y mi amigo **trabaja** en una oficina. Nosotros **pasamos** tiempo en el parque y practicamos fútbol. Mis otros amigos **practican** béisbol en el parque. Ellos no **practican** fútbol con nosotros.

The paragraph uses conjugations of the verbs *hablar* (to speak/talk), *estudiar* (to study), *trabajar* (to work), *pasar* (to pass), and *practicar* (to practice). All Spanish verbs in their infinitive state (that we talked about in part I) end with -AR, -ER, or -IR. For this paragraph, we will focus on -AR infinitive verbs only. However, you can see that those verbs don't end in -AR anymore. This is because I conjugated them to match the different people I was writing about. With that in mind, I suggest that you take another look at the paragraph and pay attention to the subjects (people) being referred to. For example, do you see *yo*, *mi amigo*, *nosotros*, etc.? You might be starting to notice how the verb endings change depending on who is doing the action. To explain this further, we will focus exclusively on the verb *estudiar* shown in the conjugation chart in table 4.3.

Each box of pronouns seen in table 4.3 is correlated with a different variation of the verb *estudiar*. I have bolded the verb endings to draw your attention to the differences. You can see that all the conjugations of the verb *estudiar* look very similar to one another, which was not the case with the two irregular verbs *ser* and *tener* that we covered earlier. We will learn more irregular verbs in later chapters, but the rest of this section is dedicated to regular present-tense verbs, which have consistent endings.

table 4.3

estudiar = to study			
yo	estudi**o**	nosotros/as	estudi**amos**
tú	estudi**as**	vosotros/as	estudi**áis**
él ella usted	estudi**a**	ellos ellas ustedes	estudi**an**

Conjugating an -AR Verb

Let's go over the three steps for conjugating a regular -AR verb in the present tense:

Example using the verb *estudiar* (to study)

1. Take the infinitive form of the verb and drop the ending (-AR in this case).
   - estudiar

2. Write down what is left (*estudi* in this case).
   - estudi

3. Add the appropriate ending (*o*, *as*, *a*, *amos*, *áis*, or *an*) depending on who is doing the action.
   - estudio, estudias, estudia, estudiamos, estudiáis, estudian

This conjugation pattern applies to any regular -AR verb that you want to conjugate in the present tense. Therefore, I recommend memorizing the endings, drilling them into your mind—"*o*, *as*, *a*, *amos*, *áis*, *an*"—so that when you need to conjugate an -AR verb, the endings and conjugation chart are readily available in your head.

Do an online search for regular present-tense -AR verbs in Spanish (as well as -ER and -IR verbs, which we will cover next), and make them into flashcards. Practice writing or reciting all the conjugations. An example flashcard you could make is shown in graphic 4.1.

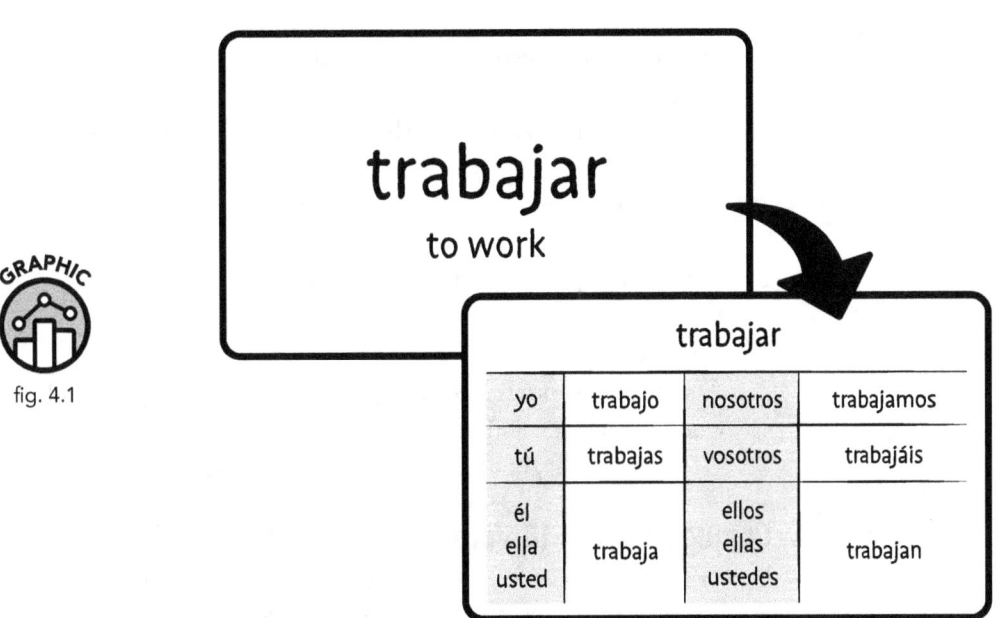

fig. 4.1

Next, let's consider regular present-tense -ER verbs. Look at the verb chart (table 4.4) and pay close attention to the endings in bold.

table 4.4

comer = to eat			
yo	com**o**	nosotros/as	com**emos**
tú	com**es**	vosotros/as	com**éis**
él ella usted	com**e**	ellos ellas ustedes	com**en**

As you probably noticed, the endings for -ER verbs are very similar to those of -AR verbs, except the letter *a* is replaced with the letter *e*. So to learn -ER verbs, memorize the endings *o*, *es*, *e*, *emos*, *éis*, and *en*, and practice conjugating regular -ER verbs in the present tense. Let's look at one more example of conjugating an -ER verb.

Example using the verb *beber* (to drink)

1. Take the infinitive form of the verb and drop the ending (-ER in this case).
   - beb**er**

2. Write down what is left (*beb* in this case).
   - beb

3. Add the appropriate ending (*o*, *es*, *e*, *emos*, *éis*, or *en*) depending on who is doing the action.
   - beb**o**, beb**es**, beb**e**, beb**emos**, beb**éis**, beb**en**

Conjugating an -IR Verb

Now that we have seen a few examples of how -AR and -ER verbs are conjugated in the present tense, we will look at our last category of present-tense verbs, -IR verbs:

table 4.5

vivir = to live			
yo	viv**o**	nosotros/as	viv**imos**
tú	viv**es**	vosotros/as	viv**ís**
él ella usted	viv**e**	ellos ellas ustedes	viv**en**

In the verb chart (table 4.5), you can see that the regular present-tense -IR endings are *o*, *es*, *e*, *imos*, *ís*, and *en*. These are almost identical to the -ER verb endings, except for two pronoun categories: *nosotros* and *vosotros*. The *nosotros* ending replaces the *e* with an *i* and the *vosotros* ending drops the *e* and uses only *ís* as the ending. An easy way to remember this is that these two letters, *ei* change to a letter *i* for the -IR verbs.

Here's one more example of how to conjugate an -IR verb.

Example using the verb *escribir* (to write)

1. Take the infinitive form of the verb and drop the ending (-IR in this case).
   - escribir

2. Write down what is left (*escrib* in this case).
   - escrib

3. Add the appropriate ending (*o*, *es*, *e*, *imos*, *ís*, or *en*) depending on who is doing the action.
   - escrib**o**, escrib**es**, escrib**e**, escrib**imos**, escrib**ís**, escrib**en**

Getting used to conjugating regular verbs takes some practice. Although this book is not intended to be a workbook, I want to show you some workbook-style exercises that can help you truly master these verb conjugation patterns.

Present-Tense Conjugation Exercise Examples

For your reference, all the regular present-tense verb endings we just covered are in table 4.6. This is what I highly recommend you memorize so that conjugating regular present-tense verbs can become quick and easy for you.

table 4.6

REGULAR PRESENT-TENSE VERBS			
-AR VERBS			
yo	**o**	nosotros/as	**amos**
tú	**as**	vosotros/as	**áis**
él ella usted	**a**	ellos ellas ustedes	**an**

| 4 | Defining Yourself

REGULAR PRESENT-TENSE VERBS

-ER VERBS

yo	o	nosotros/as	**emos**
tú	**es**	vosotros/as	**éis**
él ella usted	**e**	ellos ellas ustedes	**en**

-IR VERBS

yo	o	nosotros/as	**imos**
tú	**es**	vosotros/as	**ís**
él ella usted	**e**	ellos ellas ustedes	**en**

1. Yo __hablo__ (habl**ar**) inglés.
   (I speak English).

2. Ella __escribe__ (escrib**ir**) mi nombre.
   (She writes my name).

3. Usted __aprende__ (aprend**er**) español.
   (You (formal) learn Spanish).

The first three examples are very straightforward conjugations. As you can see, the subjects, *yo*, *ella*, and *usted*, are listed in our conjugation chart. So all I had to do was identify whether the verb in parentheses was an -AR, -ER, or -IR verb, drop the ending, then locate the appropriate verb chart and find the ending that correlates with the pronoun. Now that we've covered the basics, let's crank up the difficulty level one notch.

4. Mi padre __viaja__ (via**j**ar) mucho.
   (My dad travels a lot).

5. Mi amiga no __come__ (com**er**) queso.
   (My friend doesn't eat cheese).

In exercises 4 and 5, the subjects *mi padre* and *mi amiga* are not pronouns on the verb conjugation chart. Therefore, I have to apply what we talked about in part I regarding pronouns. For number 4, *mi padre* means "my dad," so the pronoun that could replace it is "he." Therefore, I drop the ending of the verb, go to the -AR conjugation chart, and locate the ending for *él*, giving me the conjugation *viaja*.

I got my answer for number 5 using the same process. *Mi amiga* means "my friend," and *amiga* ends in *a*, so I know it is a female friend. Therefore, I could replace my friend with the pronoun "her." So I drop the verb ending, go to the -ER verb chart, and locate the ending for *ella*, giving me the conjugation *come*.

Now let's look at two more examples with a similar difficulty level.

6. Él y yo __vivimos__ (viv**ir**) en esta casa.
   (He and I live in this house).

7. Tú y ella __caminan__ (camin**ar**) al parque.
   (You and she walk to the park).

For numbers 6 and 7, you'll note that the subjects of the sentences, *él y yo* and *tú y ella*, are all listed as individual pronouns on the conjugation chart, but these sentences each have more than one pronoun. Therefore, *él y yo*, which means "he and I," could be replaced with *we*. I drop the ending of the verb, go to the -IR verb chart, and find the verb ending for *nosotros*, giving me the conjugation *vivimos*.

For number 7, *tú y ella* means "you (informal) and she" and could be replaced with "you all/you plural," which is *ustedes*. I dropped the ending, went to the -AR verb chart, and located the ending for *ustedes*, resulting in the conjugation *caminan*. Now that you are getting the hang of conjugating, I am going to crank up the difficulty one more notch, and then you'll have a very solid understanding of how to conjugate verbs in the present tense!

8. El carro __usa__ (us**ar**) gasolina.
   (The car uses gasoline).

9. Los empleados __comen__ (com**er**) el almuerzo.
   (The employees eat lunch).

10. Mis perros __corren__ (corr**er**) afuera.
    (My dogs run outside).

When you look at examples 8, 9, and 10, you'll see that none of these pronouns can be found on our verb conjugation chart. In number 8, we are actually talking about a thing rather than a person. So let's look closely at number 8. *El carro* means "the car," and we know it's a singular noun since there is just one car. The only category in our verb conjugation chart that could work in this situation is the category that can describe singular people who are not ourselves: *he* or *she*. Although a car isn't really a *he* or a *she*, we can pretend *the car* is a *he* because it is a masculine noun. All singular objects that perform an action are going to use the conjugation ending in the *él, ella, usted* box. Therefore, I will drop the ending of the infinitive form of the verb *usar*, then add the appropriate ending from the *él, ella, usted* box to get the conjugation *usa*.

What if we are talking about plural things or groups of people? Numbers 9 and 10 are examples of how to do that. The appropriate pronoun to replace "the employees" or "the dogs" (or even "the cars") would be "they," which is *ellos*. So for 9 and 10, drop the ending, find the correct verb chart, and locate the ending for *ellos*. You will use the *ellos, ellas, ustedes* conjugation box for anything that is plural, such as objects or groups of people you are talking about.

Conjugating verbs is a huge part of learning Spanish and becoming fluent. This concept takes lots of practice and, honestly, a lot of memorization and drilling. I can't stress enough how helpful flashcards can be in this situation. I used to give myself an infinitive, such as *hablar*, and then I would conjugate out loud: "*hablo, hablas, habla, hablamos, habláis, hablan,*" and then continue with more verbs. Another thing you can do is use Conjuguemos (conjuguemos.com) to help with practice and drilling of present-tense -AR, -ER, and -IR verb conjugations. However you practice, these patterns need to be ingrained if you want to speak fluidly. And I highly recommend mastering the regular present-tense verbs before you move on to mastering any other verb tenses, such as irregular present-tense verbs, past tense, future tense, and so on. It's totally fine to move on to the following chapters and expose yourself to more types of verb conjugations before you've completely conquered the present tense, but keep in mind that knowing regular present-tense verb conjugation is the foundation for being able to conjugate other tenses.

It never hurts to get more practice in conjugating verbs. For a set of practice exercises reinforcing subject pronouns and conjugating present-tense -AR, -ER, and -IR verbs, visit this book's Digital Assets at go.quickstartguides.com/spanish

Chapter Recap

In this chapter, we started learning about one of the most important grammar points in Spanish: verb conjugation, changing the form of verbs to match how they're used. We focused on the following:

» The verbs *ser* and *tener*, because although they are irregular, they are high-frequency verbs and necessary for communicating lots of basic ideas, especially when describing ourselves and others.

» Regular present-tense conjugation, because the regular present-tense verbs will help you start to describe activities that you commonly perform.

» Basic vocabulary that is helpful when describing ourselves and others.

Mastering regular present-tense verb conjugation will also enable you to more effectively learn the other conjugations we cover throughout this book. In conjunction with the verbs we covered in this chapter, we also learned some basic vocabulary that is helpful when describing ourselves and others. Now that you are familiar with these concepts, if you go back to the audio recording at the beginning of this chapter, you will hear it in a new way. Take a moment to pat yourself on the back, because conjugating verbs is a huge part of becoming fluent in the language!

| 5 |
A Day in the Life

In the previous chapter, we focused on verbs and vocabulary needed to provide simple descriptions of yourself. In this chapter, we will expand from that point by learning how to describe your day, in terms of both specific events and the typical activities of your daily routine. The present tense works perfectly for describing daily activities, so we will continue to focus on that tense while covering some new verb conjugation patterns that will make it possible for you to talk about your everyday life in Spanish.

Chapter Overview

By the end of this chapter, you will know how to do the following:
- Apply the verb *ser* to telling time.
- Review regular present-tense conjugation and apply it to describing your daily routine and frequency of activities.
- Learn how to conjugate regular reflexive verbs in the present tense.
- Become familiar with a few irregular present-tense verb conjugation patterns.
- Understand phrases used to express obligation.

For an overview of the concepts that we will be working with in this chapter, listen to the following QuickClip of a native speaker and follow along with the script below. You will hear the native speaker describe their typical day, which will include many activities using the present tense in Spanish.

Valentín: Hola, ¿qué tal? Soy Valentín y soy de Argentina. Voy a describir mi día típico. Normalmente me levanto a las 6 de la mañana. Me preparo café, desayuno y luego me visto. Después, tomo el tren para llegar al trabajo. Soy cajero en un banco y tengo que llegar al trabajo a las ocho de la mañana. Paso el día ayudando a clientes. Como mi almuerzo alrededor de las doce, y luego salgo del trabajo a las cinco. Después de regresar del trabajo, voy a jugar un partido de fútbol con unos amigos. Jugamos una hora y después cenamos. Al final del día, regreso a mi casa y veo una serie en la televisión. Después, me preparo para dormir. Y así es un día típico en mi vida.

What Time Is It?

When talking about daily activities, you'll likely need to communicate specific times. So before we get into explaining our daily activities in great detail, let's start with the concept of telling time.

Talking about Time Using *Ser*

When we learned the present-tense conjugations for the verb *ser*, we used the acronym DOCTOR, in which the *T* represented time. However, when talking about time, we need only the singular *él*, *ella*, *usted* conjugation *es* and the plural *ellos*, *ellas*, *ustedes* conjugation *son*. We don't need the other conjugations because we would never say something like "I am five o'clock," or "We are 8 a.m."

There are two expressions you can use to ask what time it is:

- » ¿Qué hora es?
- » ¿Qué hora son?

The following are some examples of how we could reply to "What time is it?" in Spanish:

1:20	**Es** la una y veinte.
2:45 p.m.	**Son** las dos y cuarenta y cinco de la tarde.
5:00	**Son** las cinco (en punto).
8:15	**Son** las ocho y quince. / **Son** las ocho y cuarto.
9:00 a.m.	**Son** las nueve de la mañana.

The conjugations of the verb *ser* are bolded, and you can see that in each sentence, I use either the *es* or the *son* conjugation. Notice that I use *es* in only one sentence, and the rest of them use *son*; this is intentional. Look at the formula below for specifying the time.

For 1:00	Es la _____. **For example:** Es la una. (It is one o'clock.)
For all other hours (2:00 – 12:00)	Son las _____. **For example:** Son las tres. (It's three o'clock.)

The chart focuses on communicating simply the top of the hour. For 1:00, we have to say, "Es la una." Notice that *una* is not the same as *uno*, which was discussed in part I when we covered numbers. Since we are talking about the *hora*, or hour of time, which is feminine, the number for *one* becomes *una* to be feminine as well.

Now let's focus on all other hours. To denote any hour besides one o'clock, we start with "Son las _____." We use the plural conjugation for the verb *ser* since the hours are plural (more than one). We then finish the sentence stem with whatever number the hour is, and we do not change the ending of any of those numbers like we did for one o'clock.

Next, let's go over how to add minutes if the time in question is not exactly the top of the hour. You have a few options for forming a sentence to express the number of minutes past the hour.

1:10	Es la una [y] diez.
3:21	Son las tres [y] veintiuno.
5:50	Son la cinco [y] cincuenta.
1:46	Es la una con cuarenta y seis.
2:05	Son las dos con cinco.

Notice that between the hour and the minute you can insert the word *y*, or leave it out. For example, "*Son las tres y veinte*" is literally saying "It's three and twenty," and "*Son las tres veinte*" is literally saying, "It's three twenty." That format might make more sense to you because it's closer to how we tell time in English. But another option is to put the word *con* between the hour and the minutes. For example, "*Son las tres con veinte*" would be like saying, "It's three with twenty." I personally tend to favor the option of putting *y* between the hour and the minute, but you are welcome to stick to whatever option is easiest for you. Just know that you may hear any one of the three from a Spanish speaker.

While we are on the topic of time, I want to mention the fact that some Spanish-speaking countries use what we refer to as "military time," or the 24-hour clock. So don't be surprised if you hear people say something like "Son las dieciocho y cuarenta." In military time, 18:40 would be equivalent to saying it's 6:40 p.m.

There's one last thing I'd like to mention about time. If you've taken a Spanish course before, you've likely learned to tell time a bit differently than what's presented here. Many traditional textbooks teach that if it is thirty minutes or more past the hour, you must round up to the next hour and use the word *menos* (meaning "minus") between the hour and the minutes to communicate that it is that many more minutes until the next hour.

Take, for example, "Son las cinco menos diez." This literally says it is five minus ten, meaning that in ten minutes it will be five o'clock.

MY TAKE

Personally, I've never liked this way of telling time (or using military time) because it involves a lot of extra math, which I don't tend to be very good at. And I have yet to actually hear anyone express the time using *menos*. So be aware that this way of telling time does exist, and I am sure there are people out there who use it, but don't let the Spanish textbooks convince you that this is the *only* way to communicate that it is thirty or more minutes past the hour.

Now that you know the basic formula for telling time, I want to cover a few other useful time-related vocabulary terms.

y cuarto	a quarter after (note that *cuarto* is not the same as number four, *cuatro*)
y media	half past the hour
en punto	on the dot
de la mañana/tarde/noche	(morning) a.m. / (afternoon and evening) p.m.

Here are a few examples using some of this vocabulary:

Es la una y quince. / Es la una y cuarto.	Both communicate the time 1:15
Son las tres y treinta. / Son las tres y media.	Both communicate the time 3:30
Son las cinco en punto.	It's 5 o'clock on the dot.
Es la una y seis de la tarde.	It's 1:06 in the afternoon.

Of course, our communication about time is not limited to asking and/or answering what time it is. We're also likely to be asked something like "What time is your doctor's appointment?" and we want to be able to answer with "It's at _____ o'clock." Let's look at how to ask what time a certain event is scheduled for.

¿A qué hora es/son _____?	At what time is _____?

As you can see, when asking for the time of a specific event, we have a choice between two conjugations of the verb *ser*: *es* and *son*. Because these conjugations will refer to an event at a particular time, we have to decide if it's something that is singular, requiring *es*, or plural, requiring *son*. So if I'm asking about the time of a single appointment, I would say, "¿A qué hora es la cita?" But if I'm asking about a series of appointments, I would say, "¿A qué hora son las citas?"

Here is the construction for answering these types of questions:

A la/las _____.	It's at _____.

You can see that instead of saying something like "It's 2:00," we are now saying "It's at 2:00." When we are being asked what time something is scheduled for, we basically follow the same formula we already covered, but instead of starting with "Es la _____" or "Son las _____," we replace the verb *ser* with the word *a* in Spanish, which in this case means "at." All the other parts of the formula stay the same; 1:00 remains *una* instead of *uno*, and so on.

Below are some example questions and answers.

Question:	Answer option 1:
¿A qué hora **es** tu cita con el doctor?	A las dos. (At two o'clock).
(At what time is your doctor's appointment?)	Answer option 2: Mi cita con el doctor **es** a las dos. (My doctor's appointment is at two o'clock).

Notice how the original question and answer option 2 both use the verb *ser* with the *es* conjugation. It is *es* because we are referring to the appointment, which is singular. Look for the bolded conjugations of *son* in the next example to see the difference with an event that is plural.

Question:	Answer option 1:
¿A qué hora **son** los partidos?	A las cinco y media. (At 5:30).
(At what time are the [sports] games?)	Answer option 2: Los partidos **son** a las cinco y media. (The games are at 5:30).

You can apply this knowledge of communicating about time when you practice speaking in the present tense, to add more details about when you do certain things. This will also come into play as we continue to learn different ways to talk about our daily lives, as time will be integrated with many of the upcoming concepts.

When talking about the concept of time, cultures tend to view time differently. Generally, the United States follows a culture of monochronic time, meaning that we highly value punctuality and see time as being very structured. However, in Latin America, there tends to be more of a polychronic culture of time. The concept of time is seen as more fluid, and because of that it is common for guests to show up to your party thirty minutes to a few hours late. In fact, this is extremely common and almost even expected.

As someone who grew up in a family that struggled to be punctual, I easily adjusted to that cultural aspect when living in Mexico. I felt less rushed and more able to go with the flow. I'm not saying that if you were to get a job in Latin America it would be totally acceptable for you to be two hours late to work every day; it depends on the situation. And I've met many Spanish speakers who are extremely punctual, so this concept doesn't apply across all people or all Spanish-speaking cultures. But it's important to be aware that if you find yourself in a situation where a Spanish speaker is not as punctual as you are, know that there could be some cultural factors in play.

From Sunrise to Sunset: A Typical Day

With the basics of time taken care of, let's examine how to communicate about our daily activities, adding time to those descriptions as needed.

One way that we can apply time to daily activities is by using adverbs of frequency, as well as some other useful words/phrases that help us clarify how often and in what order things are performed. Here's a quick list of some of the more common adverbs, words, and phrases:

primero	first
después	after
entonces	then
siempre	always
normalmente	normally
frecuentemente	frequently
a veces/muchas veces/pocas veces	sometimes/many times/few times
nunca	never
en/por (la mañana/la tarde/la noche)	in the morning/afternoon/evening
durante (la mañana, etc.)	during (the morning, etc.)

QUICK TIP

You can make the words *la mañana, la tarde,* and *la noche* plural to communicate that you do something more than once. For example, "Yo me baño por las noches" means "I bathe myself in the evenings," communicating that I tend to always bathe at that time of day.

Now that we have some more vocabulary with which to talk about our daily activities, let's review the present tense and add some more verbs to our library of knowledge.

More Present-Tense Verbs

Present-tense conjugation can be combined with the words just listed, as well as some new verbs, to help us refer to common daily activities. Here is a list of some regular infinitive verbs that are helpful in this regard:

preparar	to prepare
tomar	to take
manejar	to drive
llegar	to arrive
regresar	to return
pasar	to pass/spend time
mirar	to look at/watch

The following paragraph combines all the concepts we just covered so you can see them working together:

Por la mañana, yo siempre **preparo** un café. También, **preparo** mi desayuno y mi almuerzo. **Manejo** mi carro a mi trabajo. **Llego** a mi trabajo a las siete y media. **Paso** ocho horas en el trabajo. También como mi almuerzo en el trabajo a las once y media. Después, **regreso** a mi casa. Normalmente **miro** la televisión y **paso** tiempo con mis perros.

In this paragraph I bolded the regular present-tense conjugations that I used to describe some of my typical daily activities. I also integrated the concept of time and many of the vocabulary words from this chapter to give a clearer idea of when I do those activities during my day.

Try writing your own paragraph describing things you typically do, using some of the verbs and vocabulary words we just covered.

Let's look at a few workbook-style exercises to review regular present-tense conjugation. I will provide you with a subject pronoun, an adverb of frequency, a verb to conjugate, and a time. I will then show you how to write everything in a complete sentence.

1. Yo / siempre / trabajar / 8:00 a.m.

   <u>Yo siempre trabajo a las ocho de la mañana.</u>

2. Yo / a veces / preparar un café / 6:00 a.m.

   <u>Yo a veces preparo un café a las seis de la mañana.</u>

3. Yo / siempre / regresar a casa / 4:00 p.m.

   <u>Yo siempre regreso a casa a las cuatro de la tarde.</u>

In each example above, I conjugated the -AR verb the way we practiced in chapter 4 so that I could communicate that I am the one doing those activities at those times. Remember, we talked about how the *yo* could be left out of the sentence, since the verb itself already indicates that I am the one doing that action.

Reflexive Verbs

Another important type of verb we use when talking about our daily activities is the reflexive verb. *Reflexive* verbs describe actions that you do to *yourself*. For example, when you take a shower, you are bathing *yourself*. When you get out of a chair, you are getting *yourself* up.

Let me show you some examples of reflexive verbs at work in Spanish:

En las mañanas, **me levanto** a las seis. Mis papás **se levantan** a las seis y media. Mi hermano **se levanta** después de las nueve. Cuando estamos de vacaciones, nosotros **nos levantamos** tarde.

The paragraph above centers around the reflexive verb *levantarse*, which means "to get up." I bolded the various conjugations of that verb to draw your attention to them. What you probably noticed is that each verb has a word such as *me*, *se*, or *nos* in front of it. These are called reflexive pronouns, and we will discuss them in a moment. After each of the reflexive pronouns is a present-tense conjugation using the verb endings we have already learned for present-tense verbs.

Before we talk about the conjugation process, let's look at how we write reflexive verbs as infinitives before we conjugate them:

bañar**se**	to bathe oneself
lavar**se**	to wash oneself
despertar**se**	to wake up
levantar**se**	to get up (physically)
cepillar**se**	to brush one's hair/teeth/etc.

I bolded the *se* part of the verbs above. That *se* is what tells us that they are reflexive verbs. Pretend for a moment that the *se* isn't there, and you will see that all those verbs look like the -AR verbs we worked with when we were conjugating verbs in the present tense. Once we remove the *se* from the ends of the verbs above, we are left with *regular* present-tense -AR verbs. So we will conjugate these just like we did the regular -AR verbs, but we will add one more step to the process: we will have to do something with the reflexive pronoun *se*.

Table 5.1 shows the reflexive pronouns and how the *se* at the end of the verb can change depending on who is doing the action.

The reflexive pronoun *me* when used in conjunction with a reflexive verb means "myself." For example, *me baño* means "I bathe myself." Since the *me* comes first, it's like saying in English, "Myself I bathe." This kind of sounds like Yoda speaking—but remember, word order isn't always the same in Spanish.

table 5.1

Reflexive Pronouns			
yo	**me**	nosotros/as	**nos**
tú	**te**	vosotros/as	**os**
él ella usted	**se**	ellos ellas ustedes	**se**

I recommend that you memorize the reflexive pronouns. The *se* at the end of a reflexive verb will change into any of the pronouns in table 5.1 depending on the subject of the sentence, so it's important to know them.

table 5.2

bañarse = to bathe oneself			
yo	**me baño**	nosotros/as	**nos bañamos**
tú	**te bañas**	vosotros/as	**os bañáis**
él ella usted	**se baña**	ellos ellas ustedes	**se bañan**

Table 5.2 gives us a visual example of how a reflexive verb is conjugated in all forms. Before we get into the specifics of conjugating, take a look at the explanations below that show what the conjugations communicate. You'll see that the reflexive pronoun helps communicate who is doing the action to themself.

me baño	I bathe myself
te bañas	You bathe yourself
se baña	He bathes himself/She bathes herself/You (formal) bathe yourself
nos bañamos	We bathe ourselves
os bañáis	You (plural/informal) bathe yourselves
se bañan	They (masculine/feminine) bathe themselves/You (plural/formal) bathe yourselves

Now, let's talk about how I got these conjugations. When you look at the conjugation chart, you can see how I took the *se* off the end of the verb and moved it to the front of the verb, and it became *me*, *te*, *se*, *nos*, *os*, and *se*. Then I followed the regular present-tense conjugation steps (in this case for an -AR verb) that we learned in chapter 4. Note that each verb conjugation contains the -AR verb endings that we already learned: *o*, *as*, *a*, *amos*, *áis*, and *an*. This is essentially the same process that we used with regular present-tense conjugation, except here we're adding one more piece: placing the reflexive pronoun *se* in its correct form in front of the regular present-tense conjugation.

| 5 | A Day in the Life

QUICK TIP If you decide to practice conjugating reflexive verbs, or want to look up more reflexive verbs on the internet, just make sure they are *regular* present-tense reflexive verbs for now, as we have not yet covered irregular verb patterns! Below are some common reflexive verbs that follow a regular present-tense conjugation pattern.

apurarse	to hurry
calmarse	to calm down
cepillarse	to brush (hair, teeth)
ducharse	to take a shower
enfermarse	to become ill
enojarse	to get upset/angry
lavarse	to wash (body part)
maquillarse	to put makeup on
levantarse	to get up
peinarse	to comb (hair)
quitarse	to take off (clothing)
secarse	to dry (body part, hair)
llamarse	to call oneself

Let's look at a few workbook-style exercises to further practice conjugating regular present-tense reflexive verbs:

1. Ella / bañarse / por las mañanas

   Ella se baña por las mañanas.

2. Yo / cepillarse / el cabello frecuentemente

   Yo me cepillo el cabello frecuentemente.

3. Mi hermano y yo / despertarse / a las seis de la mañana

   Mi hermano y yo nos despertamos a las seis de la mañana.

Now that we've covered regular present-tense reflexive verbs, I recommend that you integrate them into your studying and practicing of the language. In the next section we will start to see some irregular verbs, and later on we will come across irregular reflexive verbs.

Passing the Time

It's likely that we all have some hobbies we enjoy doing to pass time. Basic discussion of hobbies (*los pasatiempos*) in Spanish will give us a chance to go over more verbs and start learning some irregular verb patterns as well.

The chart below shows some common regular present-tense verbs that can relate to hobbies:

correr	to run
leer	to read
escuchar [a] (música)	to listen to (music)
tocar (un instrumento)	to touch / to play (an instrument)
descansar	to rest
comprar	to buy

The chart below shows some common irregular verbs that can relate to hobbies:

salir (go verb)	to leave / go out
hacer (go verb)	to do/make
jugar (u-ue)	to play
ir	to go

The regular verbs all follow the regular present-tense conjugation pattern that we learned in the previous chapter. However, I want to briefly explain that the verb *escuchar* (and some others) will sometimes need to be followed by the word *a*. That's because Spanish has something called the "*a* personal," which means that the word *a* must be used between a verb and its direct object (the person receiving the action of the verb). For example, if we are using the verb to *listen*, and we are listening to a person, then we would say something like "Escucho a mi amigo," or "I listen to my friend." If we are not listening to a person, then we would leave the *a* out and say something like "Escucho música," meaning "I listen to music." The other verb I want to point out is *tocar*, which can mean to touch something, but if I pair it with a word like *un instrumento*, then it means "to play an instrument."

Irregular "Go" Verbs

Let's take a closer look at the irregular verbs listed on the hobby chart. The words *salir* and *hacer* are referred to as "go verbs." The conjugations of *salir*, meaning "to leave" or "to go out," are listed in table 5.3.

table 5.3

salir = to leave / to go out			GO
yo	salgo	nosotros/as	salimos
tú	sales	vosotros/as	salís
él ella usted	sale	ellos ellas ustedes	salen

You can see that the verb *salir* is an -IR verb, and the chart has most of our usual regular present-tense -IR verb endings, except for one conjugation. The *yo* conjugation still ends in *o*, but where did the letter *g* come from? Well, that's the irregular part of this type of verb, and that's why we call them "go verbs." For the present-tense *yo* conjugation, we drop the -IR from the verb, and instead of adding the regular *o*, we add *go*. The rest of the words retain the regular present-tense -IR verb endings, so this verb is irregular only in the *yo* form.

With the verb *salir*, you can say something like "Salgo con mis amigos," or "I go out with my friends." However, if you are going to order someone to leave, then you will need to use the command form (we'll see this later on). The last go verb we'll cover in this section is *hacer*. See if you can predict what the conjugation chart will look like (table 5.4).

table 5.4

hacer = to do / to make			GO
yo	hago	nosotros/as	hacemos
tú	haces	vosotros/as	hacéis
él ella usted	hace	ellos ellas ustedes	hacen

Like the verbs *salir* and *decir*, the verb *hacer* also ends with "go" in the *yo* form, but since *hacer* is an -ER verb, all the other conjugations follow our regular present-tense conjugation pattern for -ER verbs. With the verb *hacer*, you can say something like "Yo hago ejercicio," or "I do exercise."

Go verbs are just one of the many irregular verb conjugation patterns that we will cover in this book. I am going to introduce them in small bites, because the concept of irregular verbs can seem very overwhelming at first. But although there are many irregular verb patterns, you can learn them! You just have to take it one verb at a time—actually, we've already covered a few irregular verbs in previous chapters. I've tried to sneak them in in a non-overwhelming way, and that will continue throughout the text.

The Verbs *Ir* and *Dar*

In this chapter, we've covered two irregular verbs, *salir* and *hacer*, with the same pattern. There are two more irregular verbs related to hobbies and activities that you should be aware of, and then we can take a break from irregular verbs for a bit!

Let's start with the verb *ir*, which means to go. This is a verb you will use often, as we are always going places in our daily lives. The strange thing is that the verb *ir* looks like the ending that we find on -IR verbs. If we follow our regular conjugation steps and drop the ending, which in this case is -IR, we are left with nothing! So of course it doesn't make sense to drop an ending here. Look at table 5.5 to see how this irregular verb is conjugated.

table 5.5

ir = to go			
yo	**voy**	nosotros/as	**vamos**
tú	**vas**	vosotros/as	**vais**
él ella usted	**va**	ellos ellas ustedes	**van**

You'll notice that the *yo* conjugation *voy* is circled and that the other endings, *as*, *a*, *amos*, *ais* (the lack of an accent mark is not a typo), and *an*, are in bold. The voy conjugation is completely irregular and has no logical explanation. As for the other conjugations, *ir* has somehow turned into the letter *v* and taken on our regular present-tense -AR verb endings. Trust me, if you're not liking this verb conjugation, you're not alone. That's why I recommend memorizing these conjugations. You're probably already familiar with the word "vamos," so hopefully that will help you remember that when you conjugate *ir* in the present tense, it starts with the letter *v* like in "vamos." So, vamos al próximo verbo—let's go to the next verb!

This is a good time for us to learn another verb that has an irregular conjugation pattern similar to that of *ir*. The verb *dar*, meaning to give, is conjugated in table 5.6.

table 5.6

dar = to give			
yo	doy	nosotros/as	**damos**
tú	**das**	vosotros/as	**dais**
él ella usted	**da**	ellos ellas ustedes	**dan**

You can see that *dar* and *ir* have a similar ending conjugation in the *yo* form. However, with *dar*, the rest of the conjugations after *doy* follow the regular -AR verb conjugation endings, except that the ending on the vosotros form does not have an accent mark. With the verb *dar*, you can say something like "Doy clases de español," which means "I give Spanish classes." You can also say something like "Doy un paseo," or "I go on a walk." (Note that this verb doesn't translate literally from English to Spanish, because *dar* usually means "to give.") But if you are going to give something to someone, then you will need to combine this conjugation with an indirect object pronoun, which we will learn about and practice in later chapters.

Introducing Stem-Changing Verbs with *jugar*

The last irregular verb we will cover in this section is *jugar*, which means "to play." The reason I wrote it as "jugar (u-ue)" in the vocabulary chart is to indicate that the verb *jugar* has what we call a "stem change" of *u* to *ue*. A stem change is a spelling change occurring inside a verb (in the stem rather than the ending) in some of the conjugations. Table 5.7 shows the conjugations for *jugar*.

table 5.7

When you look carefully at the chart, you will see our regular present-tense -AR verb endings: *o*, *as*, *a*, *amos*, *áis*, and *an*. However, you'll see that some of the conjugations contain the letters *ue*. This is the stem change. In this verb, the letter *u* in *jugar* changes to *ue*, but notice that's not the case in the *nosotros* and *vosotros* forms. This is what is often called a "boot verb," because if you draw a line around the forms that do take the stem change, it looks like a boot. So, for the verb *jugar*, the *u* to *ue* stem change takes place "in the boot," so to speak. The verb chart in table 5.8 visualizes how the irregular conjugations of *jugar* fit into a boot shape.

table 5.8

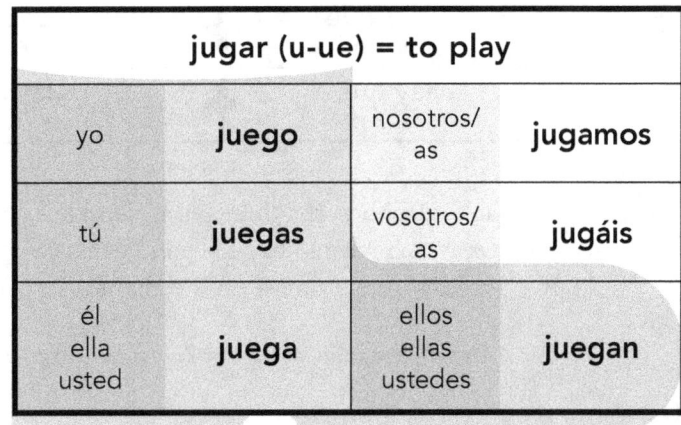

| 5 | A Day in the Life

As you've seen, there are many boot verbs, go verbs, and irregular verbs that have no logical pattern. However, there's no need to go down the rabbit hole of discovering all the irregular verbs at once. I'm going to keep introducing them in digestible pieces so that your brain can process the information and master it. Rest assured that we will have many opportunities to practice these types of verbs throughout the book.

Must Dos: Ways to Express Obligation

When learning Spanish, we have to learn irregular verb conjugations, even if they're not easy—and it's the same with our daily routines, where there are certain things we need to do whether we want to or not. This is another aspect of life that you should learn how to talk about. The good news is that you won't have a lot to conjugate on this topic!

Just like in English, when we combine two Spanish verbs, we conjugate only the first verb. For example, in English I would say "I have to clean my house." The verb phrase "I have" is conjugated (with "I") and combined with the non-conjugated infinitive "to clean." We follow that same pattern in Spanish. Let's look at three ways to express things we have to do.

table 5.9

PHRASE EXPRESSING OBLIGATION	INFINITIVES + DETAILS
Necesitar to need (to do something)	**limpiar la casa** to clean the house **ir a la tienda** to go to the store
Tener que to have to	**cocinar la cena** to cook dinner
Hay que one must	**lavar los platos** to wash the dishes

Table 5.9 shows the three phrases used to express obligation. The first is *necesitar*, which means "to need" or, in this case, "to need to do something." It is a regular present-tense -AR verb; here's a simple example of it in action:

| Nosotros necesitamos limpiar la casa. | We need to clean the house. |

I conjugated *necesitar* in the *nosotros* form, combined it with the infinitive, *limpiar*, and added the words *la casa* to give further detail about what we need to clean.

The next phrase uses *tener que*, meaning to *have to*. This has a slightly stronger sense than *necesitar*, as needing and having to do something are technically two different things. Here's an example:

| Yo tengo que ir a la tienda. | I have to go to the store. |

I conjugated the irregular verb *tener* that we covered in chapter 4. Then I combined it with the infinitive *ir a*, which means "to go to," and added *la tienda*, which is "the store." I'm telling you that I have to go to the store, meaning that I am obligated to. I may or may not want to, but that's what's going to happen.

Finally, we have the phrase *hay que*, which is a wonderful option because we don't really have to conjugate anything! The verb hay is technically a conjugation, and it comes from the verb *haber*, which is an auxiliary verb that can give the meaning "to have," but with a slightly different sense than the verb *tener*. The only conjugation for haber in the present tense is *hay*, which, standing alone, means "there is" or "there are." However, when we combine *hay* with the word *que* followed by an infinitive, it carries a very general message meaning "this needs to be done" or "someone must do this" without saying exactly who needs to do the action. The English equivalent would be to say something like "The clothes need to be washed." That could be a hint to someone else to wash the clothes, or it could be the speaker processing his or her to-do list out loud. Consider a few examples:

| Hay que hacer algo. | Someone needs to do something. / Something needs to be done. |
| Hay que preguntar. | Someone needs to ask. / It must be asked about. |

The sentences above convey that something needs to be done, but they don't directly state who needs to do it. This construction can be handy in situations where we don't want to overstep and take charge, but rather simply express our opinion about something that needs to be done.

When I was living in Mexico, I noticed a lot of indirect speech. For example, when I learned how to say I dropped something, the translation was basically "The cup fell," rather than "I dropped the cup." Phrases like "hay que" are also indirect ways to speak. I realized that it was common for people to do what I, as an American, would consider "beating around the bush." Culturally, I was more used to direct speech. That said, some Spanish-speaking cultures tend to be less direct than others. For example,

Spaniards are generally known for being quite direct. The first time I experienced this was when I had a professor from Spain. The feedback I got from her on an essay I wrote made me feel as if I had written the worst essay she'd ever seen, but once I finished reading through the feedback, I saw that my grade at the end was an A. I realized she was simply much more direct than I was used to. Be aware that some Spanish-speaking cultures tend to rely more on indirect speech to convey messages, whereas others are much more direct and straightforward.

Chapter Recap

In this chapter, we expanded on the ability to talk about ourselves by focusing on the topic of daily life and learning many ways to communicate about what our typical day looks like. This included the following:

» Learning how to tell time in Spanish so that we can speak about our daily schedules with clarity.

» Reviewing present-tense conjugation by learning some new verbs related to daily activities.

» Learning some regular present-tense reflexive verbs, most commonly used when describing daily activities: brushing your hair or teeth, bathing yourself, and so on.

» Learning a few irregular present-tense conjugation patterns through a series of irregular verbs that can be of use when discussing daily activities.

I will continue to weave in irregular verbs when they are relevant to the topic we are working with, so that your brain doesn't get overloaded with a full chapter on irregular verbs. Finally, we covered ways to express obligation, because that can be such a major part of our daily routine as adults—although if you're reading this book, you have obviously made some time in your day to do something you want to do! I truly hope that as you practice describing your daily life in Spanish, it will include activities that you find enjoyable and that bring a sense of balance to your life.

| 6 |
Life with Loved Ones

So far, we have spent part II developing the language skills needed to talk about ourselves and the many things that make us who we are. With that solid foundation, we are now going to start expanding beyond ourselves. In whatever form they take, our families impact who we are and how we interact with the world. Accordingly, this chapter expands on what we've learned in previous chapters to include aspects of family in the examples. This includes similarities but also differences between family members, which will give us a chance to practice comparisons in addition to likes and dislikes.

Chapter Overview

By the end of this chapter, you will be able to do the following:
» Practice communicating possession.
» Combine family vocabulary with the verb *ser* to describe others and make comparisons.
» Describe common family activities using the present tense.
» Know how to conjugate the verb *gustar* and similar verbs.
» Use conjunctions and transitions to connect words to build more complex sentences.

For an overview of the concepts that we will be working with in this chapter, listen to the QuickClip of two native speakers having a conversation; follow along with the script below. You will hear the native speakers talk about their families, including descriptions of various family members and activities that the family participates in.

Listen to Arantza and Daniel from México share about their families with one another. You will hear each of them share about siblings and pets, as well as make plans to get together.

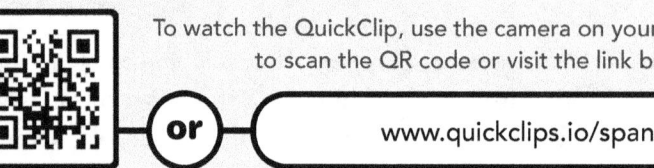

To watch the QuickClip, use the camera on your mobile phone to scan the QR code or visit the link below.

www.quickclips.io/spanish-6

Arantza:	Hola, Daniel. ¿Cómo estás?
Daniel:	Hola Arantza. Estoy muy bien, gracias. Y tú, ¿cómo estás?
Arantza:	Muy bien. Me siento muy feliz porque voy a pasar tiempo con mis hermanas hoy.
Daniel:	Ah, ¡qué emoción! ¿Cuántas hermanas tienes?
Arantza:	Tengo tres hermanas. Mis hermanas menores son gemelas. Se llaman Ana y Amely. También tengo una hermana mayor que se llama Alin.
Daniel:	Tres hermanas, ¡wow! ¿Y cómo son tus hermanas?
Arantza:	Ana es muy amigable y Amely es tímida. Yo soy más extrovertida que ellas. Y tú, ¿tienes hermanos?
Daniel:	No, yo no tengo hermanos. Soy hijo único. Pero tengo un perro que se llama Firulais y un gata que se llama Cometa.
Arantza:	¡Ay que bonito, me encantan las mascotas! Son una parte importante de la familia. Yo tengo una perra que se llama Mantecada y un gato que se llama Milaneso.
Daniel:	Sí, nuestras mascotas son miembros de nuestra familia. ¿Quieres ir un día al parque con nuestros perros?
Arantza:	¡Claro! ¿Quieres ir este viernes a las dos?
Daniel:	Sí, está bien. ¡Nos vemos pronto entonces!
Arantza:	Sí, ¡hasta pronto!

My Family, Our Home: Possessive Adjectives

When addressing the topic of family, it becomes necessary to describe various relationships—siblings, spouses, children. This involves some vocabulary words, of course, but it also means using possessive adjectives that help to clarify who someone is to you, or who you are to someone else. For example: Are you *her* daughter? Is that *your* dad? In this section, we'll start with the vocabulary and then move on to the adjectives that help further clarify them.

Here are a few basic family vocabulary words:

el/la esposo(a)	the husband/wife
la pareja	the couple
la madre/mamá	the mother/mom
el padre/papá	the father/dad
los padres/papás	the fathers or the parents
el/la hermano(a)	the brother/sister
los hermanos	the brothers or the siblings
el/la hijo(a)	the son/daughter
los hijos	the sons or the children
el/la abuelo(a)	the grandpa/grandma
los abuelos	the grandpas or the grandparents

This list includes the most essential and basic family-member words. One possible source of confusion with these words is some of the plural forms, such as *los padres* and *los papás*. Context is important here, because *los padres* is masculine plural and technically could mean either fathers or parents. The same thing applies to *los hermanos*, *los hijos*, and *los abuelos*. Those words refer to masculine plural forms that mean "brothers," "sons," and "grandfathers," but they can also include a feminine person(s) and mean "siblings," "children," and "grandparents."

Another important concept I want to explain is how to refer to stepfamily members. Take a look at the words below.

el padrastro	the stepfather
la madrastra	the stepmother
el hermanastro	the stepbrother
la hermanastra	the stepsister
el medio hermano	the half-brother
la media hermana	the half-sister

You probably noticed that the words above look a lot like the words we already learned for *mom*, *dad*, *brother*, *sister*, etc. However, stepfamily members have *astro* or *astra* added to the end of the word. You can also see the words *medio* and *media*, which refer to the *half* in half-brother or half-sister. Just like with our first set of family vocabulary words, these terms, when in the masculine plural form such as *los hermanastros*, can mean either "the stepbrothers" or "the stepsiblings."

Now that we've covered some basic family vocabulary, let's take a look at some examples of these words combined with possessive adjectives.

mi hermano	my brother
mis padres	my fathers/parents
tu hermana	your sister (informal)
nuestro abuelo	our grandpa
sus hermanastras	his/her/their/your (plural) stepsisters

Each of the terms above starts with a possessive adjective (in bold), which is the word that tells me whose family member it is. You probably noticed that the possessive adjective's ending tends to match the ending of the word that follows it. For example, both words in the term *mis padres* end in *s*, and neither word in *mi hermano* ends in *s*. In *nuestro abuelo*, both words end in *o*, and so on. This is because the possessive adjective can become singular or plural, and some possessive adjectives can also become masculine or feminine. The chart in table 6.1 contains handy information to help us go deeper into possessive adjectives.

table 6.1

yo	**mi(s)**	nosotros/as	**nuestro(a)(s)**
tú	**tu(s)**	vosotros/as	**vuestro(a)(s)**
él ella usted	**su(s)**	ellos ellas ustedes	**su(s)**

Let's talk about the possessive adjectives in table 6.1; however, I will skip the *vosotros* form.

mi(s)	my
	For example: *mi madre* means "my mom," and *mis hermanas* means "my sisters."
tu(s)	your (informal)
	For example: *tu madre* means "your mom," and *tus hermanas* means "your sisters."
su(s)	his, her, or your (formal) depending on the context
	For example: *su madre* can mean "his mom," "her mom," or "your (formal) mom," and *sus hermanas* can mean "his sisters," "her sisters," or "your (formal) sisters."
nuestro(a)(s)	our, and the ending depends on the number as well as the gender of the word that follows it
	For example: *nuestra madre* means "our mom," *nuestro padre* means "our dad," *nuestras hermanas* means "our sisters," and *nuestros hermanos* means "our brothers" (or siblings).
su(s)	this possessive adjective is the same as the one we see in the él, ella, usted box of table 6.1, which means that context will be important, because the su(s) from the ellos, ellas, ustedes box could mean "their" or "your" (plural)
	For example: *su madre* can mean "their mother" or "your (plural) mother," and *sus hermanas* can mean "their sister" or "your (plural) sister."

Possessive adjectives aren't used only to specify family relationships; they can also indicate who an object belongs to. So now that we have established how possessive adjectives work, let's do a few workbook-style translation exercises with objects instead of family members.

1. Your (informal) car

    _____Tu carro_____

2. Our house

    _____Nuestra casa_____

3. Her dog

   _____Su perro_____

4. Their dishes

   _____Sus platos_____

5. My family

   _____Mi familia_____

Remember when we learned the subject pronoun *tú* for the informal "you" in Spanish? See how it has a *tilde* (accent mark) over the letter *u*? Now look at our possessive adjectives chart and see how the word for "your" is written as *tu* without that accent mark. *Tu* and *tú*, although they look almost the same, (and sound exactly the same) are actually completely different words. In the same way that the word *el* means "the" and the word *él* means "he," that little accent mark technically does matter!

No Apostrophes, No Problem

Since we're on the topic of expressing ownership/possession, now is the perfect opportunity to go over another way to express a concept in Spanish that differs from English. In English, to communicate that an object belongs to someone, we take the name of the owner, add an apostrophe and the letter *s*, and then add the object. To explain that a house belongs to Jon, we say "Jon's house." But in Spanish I cannot say "Jon's casa," because Spanish doesn't have the concept of apostrophe *s* to show ownership or possession. Therefore, in Spanish, I have to say "the house of Jon" or "la casa de Jon." In other words, to express ownership or possession, we must use the following formula:

item of ownership + de + name of person who owns it

Here are a couple examples:

El carro de Claire	"The car of Claire," or in English, Claire's car
La casa de mi familia	"The house of my family," or in English, my family's house

In addition to expressing ownership or possession, we can use this formula to express our relationships to others. Let's look at a couple more examples:

| El amigo de mi padre | "The friend of my dad," or my dad's friend |
| La hermana de mi abuela | "The sister of my grandmother," or my grandmother's sister |

Below are some workbook-style questions that use this formula to describe a family member.

1. El padre de mi padre es ____mi abuelo____.

2. La hija de mis padres es mi ____hermana____.

3. El hermano de mi madre es mi ____tío____.

These exercises require a lot of thinking, but they're a great way to practice your family vocabulary! Now that we have covered some basic family vocabulary along with ways to express ownership, possession, and relationship, we will apply all this information to the practice of describing our family.

Relatives and Relationships: Describing Loved Ones

Describing family members involves reviewing some concepts you should find familiar, such as using the verb *ser* to describe others, and the concept of gender agreement. We will also add a few additional family vocabulary words to our repertoire:

el tío	the uncle
la tía	the aunt
los tíos	the uncles / the aunt(s) and uncle(s)
el primo	the cousin (male)
la prima	the cousin (female)
los primos	the cousins (all male or male and female)
la madrina	the godmother
el padrino	the godfather
los padrinos	the godfathers/godparents

I made sure to include the word *padrinos*, or "godparents," because in Spanish-speaking cultures it is common to find people practicing Catholicism. Godparents are not exclusive to Catholicism, but they have great significance in many Catholic families. Not only is it important for godparents to be present on the day of their child's baptism, but they are seen almost as secondary parent figures for the child. Many parents refer to their child's godparents as their *comadre* and *compadre*, which would be similar to "co-mother" and "co-father." This shows the deep connection and trust the parents have with the godparents. Although you may hear words like *compadre* or *compa* in other contexts to refer to a close friend, it is a great honor to be chosen to be the *madrina* or *padrino* of a child.

As we've discussed, family-member terms written in the masculine plural form can refer to either all males or a mixture of males and females. For example, if you say *los primos* you could be talking about several male cousins or male and female cousins. However, if someone says *los tíos*, they're more likely talking about their aunt and uncle, or both sets of aunts and uncles, although it could technically mean "uncles" as well. Context is important in these scenarios, and I know I've said that a lot, but I think this is a concept that can take a while for second-language learners to get used to.

Look up additional family vocabulary terms you want to learn using an online Spanish dictionary.

Now that we have a solid base of family vocabulary to work with, we are going to use that vocabulary as an opportunity to review the verb *ser*, the concept of gender agreement, and possessive adjectives, which are all used when describing others. There will also be some comparative words that we will be covering next. Listen to the audio from the following QuickClip and follow along with the paragraph below.

Pepe: Mi madre es muy bonita. Ella es alta, tiene ojos cafés, y su pelo es largo. Es paciente e inteligente. Mi padre es muy cómico. Tiene mucha energía. Sus ojos son azules y no tiene mucho pelo. Es simpático y trabajador. Mi hermano es el más alto de mi familia. Tiene ojos marrones y el pelo oscuro como yo. Él es inteligente y cómico. Yo soy menos alto que mis padres. Tengo el pelo corto, igual que mi hermano.

Listen to Pepe from Perú talk about his family. You will hear about different family members' personalities and physical traits; you will also hear Pepe compare his own characteristics with those of his family.

To watch the QuickClip, use the camera on your mobile phone to scan the QR code or visit the link below.

www.quickclips.io/spanish-7

You can see that Pepe used possessive adjectives, such as *mi*, to describe his family members' relationship to himself. In several sentences, he used the verbs *ser* and *tener* conjugated into present tense to describe his family members' appearances and personalities. The adjectives he used for each family member are either masculine or feminine to fit their gender, and any words describing other aspects of their appearance, such as their hair, match the gender of the word for that particular aspect. You can also see that he used some new comparative phrases, such as *el más alto*.

Many times when we describe people, we compare certain aspects of them to ourselves or to others. You probably have some physical characteristics and personality traits that are similar to those of certain family members. You likely have some differences as well. Consider the following phrases:

el más alto	the tallest (masculine)
la más alta	the tallest (feminine)

You can replace *alto* or *alta* with other adjectives to say that someone is the funniest, shortest, kindest, etc. Since *el* is the masculine word for "the," it would be used for a male, and *la* would be used for a female.

Let's look at a few more examples in complete sentences.

» Yo soy la más baja, y mi hermano es el más alto.

» Mi mamá es la más paciente, y mi papá es el más cómico.

Notice that when I describe myself as being the shortest, I use the feminine *la* as well as the feminine ending on the Spanish word for "short." My brother, on the other hand, is described with the masculine Spanish words for *the* and *tall*. The same idea applies to the sentence about my parents.

Along with designating yourself (or someone else) as having the most of a particular quality, you can also designate yourself (or someone else) as having the least of a particular quality:

el menos alto	the least tall (masculine)
la menos alta	the least tall (feminine)

Instead of saying I'm the shortest, like I did in the previous example, I could say I am the least tall, or that my dad is the least serious person in my family:

» Yo soy la menos alta. Mi papá es el menos serio.

I used the word *menos* to communicate the idea of someone being least. *Menos* looks a lot like the English word for "minus," which in math implies the idea of *less*. That connection helps me remember the meaning of menos.

We can also compare two people to each other in the same sentence. There are three options for this kind of comparison. First, we can say we have more of a certain attribute than someone else. Second, we can say we have less of a certain attribute than someone else. And third, we can say we are equal in a particular attribute or characteristic.

1. A comparison using "more" is formulated this way:
   (person) + (conjugation of ser) + más + (adjective) + que + (person)

Mi hermano es más alto que yo.	My brother is taller than me.
Yo soy más atlética que mis padres.	I am more athletic than my parents.

2. A comparison using "less" is formulated this way:
   (person) + (conjugation of ser) + menos + (adjective) + que + (person)

Yo soy menos alta que mi hermano.	I am less tall than my brother.
Mi padre es menos paciente que mi mamá.	My dad is less patient than my mom.

3. A comparison using the concept of equal amounts is formulated this way:

   (person) + (conjugation of ser) + tan + (adjective) + como + (person)

Yo soy tan paciente como mi mamá.	I am as patient as my mom.
Mi padre es tan cómico como mi hermano.	My dad is as funny as my brother.

Using these kinds of comparisons can help others better understand us and the people in our life. But this concept can be applied to objects as well, not just people. For example, you might want to say that your car is older than someone else's car, or that the shirt at this store isn't as pretty as the shirt you are wearing. We aren't done with comparisons yet—we'll review them when get to the topic of shopping later in the book—so be sure to practice them and be ready to apply them in other ways!

Family Fun

Another common topic of conversation when describing our family relationships and dynamics is the activities we do with our families. We'll start by introducing some new present-tense verbs.

celebrar	to celebrate
compartir	to share
discutir	to argue
pasar (tiempo juntos)	to pass/spend (time together)

These are all regular verbs, meaning that they can be conjugated using the endings you learned for regular present-tense verb conjugation. Since we've already reviewed this type of conjugation a few times, let's look at a workbook-style exercise using these new verbs alongside some regular verbs we've already learned.

Mi familia y yo __vivimos__ (vivir) en una casa muy grande. Yo __vivo__ (vivir) con mi mamá, mi papá, y mi hermano. Nuestra abuela también __vive__ (vivir) con nosotros. Mi hermano y yo __compartimos__ (compartir) un carro. A veces __discutimos__ (discutir), pero no mucho. En las noches, a las siete, todos __compartimos__ (compartir) una comida como familia. Cada año, nosotros __celebramos__ (celebrar) la Navidad con nuestra familia extendida. La familia es muy importante, y por eso nosotros siempre __pasamos__ (pasar) mucho tiempo juntos.

This paragraph is a great example of how to apply regular present-tense conjugation to the description of common family activities. I want to draw attention to a couple of verb conjugations. The circled verb *discutir* is conjugated in the *nosotros* form. Although the previous sentence doesn't contain the word *nosotros*, it was talking about "my brother and I." Thus, based on context, it is fair to assume that the topic is still "my brother and I," and therefore the *nosotros* form will be used.

The other verb I circled is *compartir*. It is also conjugated in the *nosotros* form. The subject of that sentence is *todos*, which is similar to "everyone." However, this is being written from a family member's point of view, so in this case the word *todos* is akin to saying "we all." This is why it is conjugated in the *nosotros* form. If you were talking about everyone else and not including yourself, *todos* would be conjugated with the *ellos/ellas/ustedes* form *comparten*.

Next, we are going to add a few more reflexive verbs to our library of knowledge. This will allow us to revisit the concept of reflexives while introducing some more verbs that might relate to family and family activities.

| reunirse (con/en) | to get together (with/at) |
| sentirse (e-ie) | to feel |

The first verb, *reunirse*, follows the overall conjugation pattern of a regular present-tense reflexive verb, but it does require some tildes, or accent marks, when conjugated into present tense. This small change technically makes it an irregular verb. I gave you the prepositions *con* and *en* because they are commonly used with *reunirse*. Take a look at the verb conjugation chart in table 6.2.

table 6.2

reunirse = to get together			
yo	**me reúno**	nosotros/as	**nos reunimos**
tú	**te reúnes**	vosotros/as	**os reunís**
él / ella / usted	**se reúne**	ellos / ellas / ustedes	**se reúnen**

For *reunirse*, we follow the normal steps of dropping the *se* off the end of the verb and putting it in front of the verb with the proper reflexive pronoun.

We then drop the -IR ending from the verb and add our regular present-tense ending for -IR verbs. However, in four of the conjugations the letter *u* has a tilde. (The accent mark on the *i* in the *vosotros* form is the normal present-tense ending and always has that accent.)

Some verbs are conjugated similarly to a regular verb but have some slight difference in accents. I feel as if this barely qualifies them as irregular verbs, because the change is so minimal, but it's still helpful to be aware of what I call "slightly irregular verbs."

Now let's look at a couple examples using this reflexive verb in complete sentences.

Mi familia y yo **nos reunimos** cada fin de semana.	My family and I get together every weekend.
Mis hermanos siempre **se reúnen** en un café.	My siblings always get together at a coffee shop.

Another reflexive verb has a much more irregular pattern: *sentirse*.

table 6.3

sentirse (e-ie) = to feel			
yo	**me siento**	nosotros/as	**nos sentimos**
tú	**te sientes**	vosotros/as	**os sentís**
él ella usted	**se siente**	ellos ellas ustedes	**se sienten**

Notice in the chart in table 6.3 that the verb *sentirse* is accompanied by a stem-change pattern in parentheses next to it: e-ie. That means that the *e* in *sentir* is going to change to an *ie* in all the forms within the "boot" (circled words). Outside the boot, we do not apply the stem change. This verb is a stem-changing boot verb like those we discussed earlier, but it is also a reflexive verb, which adds an extra step to the process. We have to drop the *se* off the end of *sentirse* and then put it in front of the conjugated verb as the correct reflexive pronoun for each subject.

Look at a couple examples of complete sentences using the verb *sentirse*.

Cuando paso tiempo con mi familia, **me siento** feliz.	When I spend time with my family, I feel happy.
Mi familia y yo estamos de vacaciones y por eso **nos sentimos** muy contentos.	My family and I are on vacation and for that reason we feel very content.

Once you get the the hang of reflexive verbs as well as irregular present-tense verb conjugation patterns, you'll have a solid foundation of Spanish knowledge and will be better-equipped to participate in more self-study of the language—so if you think of any verbs that are important to your life that aren't covered here, look them up! You should be able to apply what you're learning from this book to other Spanish verbs. Now let's continue on with another verb that can be helpful in a variety of situations.

Likes and Dislikes: The Verb *Gustar*

When talking about our daily life and the things that make us who we are, the need to express likes and dislikes will inevitably come up. In this section, we will focus on expressing our likes using the verb *gustar*, which literally translates to "to be pleasing to" but is more commonly understood to mean "to like."

Here are some example sentences expressing some of my personal likes:

» Me gusta practicar yoga. Voy a clases de yoga cada semana.

» Me gusta el café. Siempre tomo café por las mañanas.

» Tengo dos perros. Me gustan mucho los perros. Juego con mis perros todos los días.

In the sentences above, you can see I used either *me gusta* or *me gustan*. But all the sentences were about myself and what I like. So why do some have the conjugation *gusta* while others have *gustan*?

The answer is because most verbs are conjugated for the person in the sentence who is doing the action, but the verb *gustar* works differently. The reason for this difference goes back to that more precise definition. Because *me gusta* literally means "it is pleasing to me," the thing or the action is what is doing the pleasing, not the person who is being pleased. For example, technically you're not saying "I like coffee." You're actually saying "coffee is pleasing to me." (Sometimes I even think of it as "coffee likes me," because that's sort of what you're saying when you say something is pleasing to you: it gets along with you.)

This is the one confusing aspect of an otherwise relatively easy verb to learn (and why I didn't introduce this verb earlier, even though it's one that many beginning Spanish learners already know). Although *gusta* is technically the present-tense *él/ella/usted* conjugation, it's better to describe *gusta* as a third person singular conjugation. *Gustan* is the *ellos/ellas/ustedes* conjugation but is better described as the third person plural conjugation.

table 6.4

GUSTA VERSUS GUSTAN		
INFINITIVES	SINGULAR NOUNS	PLURAL NOUNS
Me **gusta** practicar yoga.	Me **gusta** el café.	Me **gustan** los perros.
Me **gusta** caminar.	Me **gusta** la pizza y la fruta.	Me **gustan** las montañas.
Me **gusta** estudiar y leer.	Me **gusta** el carro.	Me **gustan** las bicicletas.

So the first step in expressing your likes is knowing when to use *gusta* and when to use *gustan*. Table 6.4 provides some examples. According to the first column of the chart, *gusta* can be combined with infinitives, which are verbs that haven't been conjugated (in this case, *practicar*, *caminar*, and *estudiar*). The reason we don't need to conjugate the infinitives is because *gusta* is already conjugated from the verb *gustar*, and when we have two verbs together, we conjugate only the first verb, just like we do in English.

For example, the first sentence in the chart says "Me gusta practicar yoga," which means "I like to practice yoga." I wouldn't say "Me gusta practico yoga" because that would be the same as saying "I like to I practice yoga." I leave *practicar* in its infinitive form so it means "to practice," and when I combine it with *gusta*, it is correctly expressing that I like to practice yoga. I also use *gusta* if I am listing more than one activity that I like, by simply using infinitives for all those activities. For example, "Me gusta estudiar y leer" contains two infinitives back-to-back, communicating that I like to study and to read.

The second column of the chart also uses *gusta*, but with singular nouns instead of infinitives. Anything you like that is singular will also use *gusta*. And you can list multiple singular items that you like, such as "la pizza y la fruta."

The third column of the chart uses *gustan* with plural nouns. Anytime you are expressing something you like that is plural, you will use *gustan*. This also applies to listing multiple plural nouns. For example, I could combine all three sentences in the third column to say, "Me gustan los perros, las montañas y las bicicletas."

QUICK TIP

The way I have remembered *gusta* versus *gustan* is that when I talk about something plural, which is more than one, I need to add an extra letter, which is the letter *n* at the end of *gusta*. This makes sense to me since my noun also has an extra letter (s) to make it plural. Then I remember that if I'm not talking about something plural, I will rely on using *gusta*.

We will now look at a few conversational questions and answers using *gustar* to review *gusta* versus *gustan*, as well as to preview some of our indirect object pronouns that help us communicate who likes or doesn't like something.

Persona 1:	¿Te **gusta** el café?
Persona 2:	Sí, me **gusta** el café.
Persona 1:	Te **gustan** los dulces?
Persona 2:	No, no me **gustan** los dulces.
Persona 1:	¿Te **gusta** bailar?
Persona 2:	Sí, me **gusta** bailar.

In these examples, the rules for when to use *gusta* versus *gustan* are applied correctly. Also, you might have noticed a new phrase: *te gusta*. This brings us to our next topic: indirect object pronouns that help us communicate who likes what we are talking about.

table 6.5

Indirect Object Pronouns			
yo	**me**	nosotros/as	**nos**
tú	**te**	vosotros/as	**os**
él ella usted	**le**	ellos ellas ustedes	**les**

In the earlier sentence examples expressing my likes, you might have noticed that I used the pronoun *me* instead of *yo*. When we use the verb *gustar*, we don't use the subject pronouns that we use for regular present-tense verbs. Instead, we use what are called indirect object pronouns (shown in table 6.5): *me, te, le, nos, os,* and *les*. Here's how they work when combined with the verb *gustar*.

Me gusta el café.	I like coffee.
Te gusta el café.	You (informal) like coffee.
Le gusta el café.	He/she/you (formal) like(s) coffee.
Nos gusta el café.	We like coffee.
Os gusta el café.	You all (informal) like coffee.
Les gusta el café.	(They/you all) like coffee.

These sentences show how the indirect object pronouns indicate who likes coffee. The *gusta el café* part stays the same, because we follow the rules just covered concerning *gusta/gustan*, and the word "coffee" is singular. What does change is the first word in each sentence. We are already familiar with *me gusta* expressing "I like," and it's easy to understand that *te gusta* expresses "you like" in the informal form of address. The other very clear example is *nos gusta*, as it means "we like" and actually looks a lot like the word *nosotros*, which is the subject pronoun for "we."

The slightly less clear examples are the sentences "Le gusta el café" and "Les gusta el café." Because the indirect object pronoun *le* can refer to "he," "she," or "you" (formal), saying "Le gusta el café" with no other context would probably be confusing to most people, as it isn't one hundred percent clear who likes coffee. Someone likes coffee, and we know it's one person, but who exactly? The same applies to "Les gusta el café" because the pronoun *les* can refer to "they" or "you" (plural). We know a group of people likes coffee, but it's still not exactly clear who that group is. This is where context is important. Let's say I'm talking to someone about my friend Claire, and I have already established that I'm talking about her. If I say, "Le gusta el café," it will be inferred that I'm still referring to Claire. If I was telling a story about my parents and I said, "Les gusta el café," it would make sense that the *les* was referring to my parents. However, in scenarios where I haven't already clearly established the subject, there are some words I can put in front of my sentence to add clarification of who I'm talking about.

(**A mí**) me gustan los deportes.	I like sports.
(**A ti**) te gustan los deportes.	You (informal) like sports.
A él/ella/usted le gustan los deportes.	He/she/you formal like(s) sports.
(**A nosotros**) nos gustan los deportes	We like sports.
A ellos/ellas/ustedes les gustan los deportes.	They(m)/they(f)/you all like sports.

The sentences above show how to use a prepositional pronoun (the bolded part of the sentences) at the beginning of your sentence to provide more clarification about who likes something. I put parentheses around *a mí, a ti,* and *a nosotros* to indicate that in those sentences, the subject is still one hundred percent clear even if you don't add the parenthetical part.

Just as the *yo* pronoun in present tense is optional, the *a mí* phrase is optional when using *me gusta(n)*. The indirect object pronoun *me* already communicates that I like it, and it can't be used for anyone else. When I say something like "a mí me gustan las películas," I am saying "To me I like movies." The *a mí* part really just adds more emphasis to the fact that you are the one who likes something.

For a *él/ella/usted*, there are three subject pronouns you could mean when you say "le gusta(n) _____." So unless you've already clearly established who you are talking about, I strongly recommend including the prepositional pronoun phrase to provide clarification. The same goes for the *a ellos/ellas/ustedes* phrase: "les gusta(n) _____."

Now that we've covered *gusta* versus *gustan*, the indirect object pronouns, and the *a* phrases that can provide clarification, let's look at a chart putting all those steps together (table 6.6).

table 6.6

A mí		me		singular nouns/infinitives
A ti		te	gusta	
A él/ella/usted	no	le		
A nosotros/as		nos		
A vosotros/as		os	gustan	plural nouns
A ellos/ellas/ustedes		les		

This chart illustrates how the *a* phrases go at the beginning. If you (or someone else) didn't like something, you would use the word *no* followed by the appropriate indirect object pronoun, followed by either *gusta* and an infinitive or a singular noun, or *gustan* and a plural noun.

Keeping that formula in mind, let's look at a few workbook-style examples. I will provide you with a subject, the infinitive *gustar*, and either an infinitive, a singular noun, or a plural noun, and then I'll show you how that information would be compiled into a complete sentence.

1. ella / no gustar / las verduras

   _____(A ella) no le gustan las verduras._____

2. yo / gustar / jugar fútbol

   _____(A mí) me gusta jugar fútbol._____

3. ustedes / gustar / tomar fotos

   _____(A ustedes) les gusta tomar fotos._____

You can see that the sentence examples above follow the order shown in table 6.6. This pattern is also seen in some other Spanish verbs, which we will look at shortly.

There is one other word I want to introduce to you along with the word *gustar*, and that is the word *ni*. In Spanish, *ni* is equivalent to the English words *neither/nor*. See the example below.

No me gustan ni los dulces ni los postres.	I don't like neither candy nor desserts.
Su hijo ni estudia ni trabaja. No le gusta hacer nada.	Their son neither works nor studies. He doesn't like to do nothing.

You can see that the double use of *ni* is like our English equivalent of *neither/nor*, although the literal translations in English of the examples above sound a bit funny. For the first sentence, we would probably say, "I don't like candy or desserts," or "I like neither candy nor desserts." As you can see, the second sentence literally translates to "He doesn't like to do nothing." In English we would say, "He doesn't like to do anything." The reason we use *nada*, or "nothing," is because Spanish allows what are called *double negatives*. In English, we wouldn't use two negative words in the same sentence, such as "don't" and "neither" in the example above. But in Spanish, double negatives are freely used to express such ideas.

Verbs Similar to *Gustar*

Like the verb *gustar*, there are other verbs in Spanish that follow the same pattern we just learned. Let's look at an example of the verb *encantar*, which means "to love" (an item or activity). You can tell someone "Me encantas," but that's more like telling them "I like you" or "You're lovely to me," whereas a true "I love you" is either *Te quiero* (more casual) or *Te amo* (more serious). For simplicity purposes, I recommend that you focus on using *encantar* for items and activities you like, and when you are more advanced you can get into more complicated phrases like *me encantas*. So for now, let's focus on using only *encanta* and *encantan*.

I've left a blank where you could fill in the object of your love.

(A mí) me encanta(n) _____.

(A ti) te encanta(n) _____.

A él/ella/usted le encanta(n) _____.

(A nosotros) nos encanta(n) _____.

A ellos/ellas/ustedes les encanta(n) _____.

Here are a few other verbs that follow this pattern:

interesar	to be interesting (to)
fascinar	to be fascinating (to)
importar	to be important (to), to matter

Below are a few examples of the above verbs being used in a sentence, just to reinforce this concept.

A mi amiga le encanta ir a la playa.	My friend loves going to the beach.
A mí me interesa practicar yoga.	Practicing yoga interests me.
A mi hermano le fascinan los carros.	My brother is fascinated with cars.
Nos importan mucho los animales.	Animals are very important to us.

Do an online search for "verbs like gustar" (also called *verbos afectivos*) to learn more verbs that follow this pattern.

In these examples, the first and third sentences use "mi" (without an accent on the i)—the possessive adjective meaning "my," rather than mí (with the accent), meaning "myself."

134 SPANISH QUICKSTART GUIDE

To review the verb *gustar* as well as similar verbs, we will look at a paragraph using what we have just learned. However, before doing so, I want to introduce a few transition words that will help you connect your words to create more complex sentence structures.

de hecho	in fact
además	moreover, additionally
también	also
pero	but
todavía	still
por eso	that's why

With those connecting words in mind, look at the paragraph below.

Listen to hear Luisa from Colombia share all about coffee. You will hear about her and her family's preferences around coffee, and she will also share her favorite Colombian coffee drink with you!

To watch the QuickClip, use the camera on your mobile phone to scan the QR code or visit the link below.

www.quickclips.io/spanish-8

Luisa: Hola, soy Luisa y soy del hermoso país de Colombia. En mi país, el café es muy popular. A mis padres les encanta tomar café todos los días. A mí también me gusta mucho el café, pero a mi hermana no le gusta el café porque dice que no le gusta su sabor. A mí, me interesan todas las bebidas de café que hay en Colombia. De hecho, lo tomo dos veces al día. Una muy popular y de mis favoritas es el "tinto campesino," que es un café negro endulzado con panela. Y en mi opinión, ¡el café colombiano es el mejor del mundo!

Take some time with the paragraph above to notice the present-tense conjugations, as well as the conjugations of the verb *gustar* and similar verbs. Pay attention to the gender agreement of words and the two-verb constructions where the first verb is conjugated and the second verb is in the infinitive state. Finally, notice the connecting words used to make the sentences flow better.

 Try writing your own paragraph about some of your likes and interests, as well as interests of your family or friends who are close to you, and include comparisons when possible.

Chapter Recap

In this chapter we used the topic of family to help us expand on our ability to describe ourselves and our experiences in more nuanced ways—by describing those close to us. This included the following:

» Practicing descriptions of both possession and comparisons between people.

» Reviewing some present-tense verbs related to family activities.

» Learning some more irregular verb patterns, including the important verb *gustar*, which is crucial to expressing our likes and dislikes as well as the interests of those around us.

» Adding more connecting words to our vocabulary in order to create transitions between sentences and build more complex sentence structures.

Put together, these topics will help you improve your descriptions of yourself and the things that are happening in the world around you. We will go further out into that world in part III.

PART III

EVERYDAY LIFE

After studying aspects of the language related to communicating about yourself, you should be ready to widen the scope a bit. Part III will focus on developing the vocabulary and grammar needed to communicate about your surroundings. We will cover topics related to life at home and things you do in your environment, as well as describing your community and how it relates to who you are as a person. Being able to navigate your surroundings in another language is an exciting accomplishment, so get ready to take this next step in your journey!

| 7 |
Where I Live

Now that we have mastered how to talk about ourselves and those around us, it's important that we also build communication skills related to the environments we spend time in throughout our daily lives. For many people, that environment starts with the home—and occupying almost any living space can come with a never-ending to-do list. Beyond the home, there are probably places you frequent in the area where you live and people you encounter regularly in your daily life, such as neighbors, friends, and coworkers.

To best communicate about your daily life, you'll need Spanish-language tools related to your living space, your environment, and what you are doing in the present moment. This chapter will introduce a new verb tense—the present progressive—that enables us to discuss what we're doing *right now*, and another—the near future tense—that enables us to describe things that we *will* be doing. For example, if you run into a friend while doing errands, you might ask them what they're up to, and they'll use the present progressive to say something like "I'm buying a few things for dinner tonight." You also might want to express things you are about to do, such as "After this I'm going to grab a coffee," using the near future tense. In other words, this chapter will start at home and then take you out into your immediate environment, where you'll likely encounter some people you know.

Chapter Overview

By the end of this chapter, you will be able to do the following:
» Describe parts of the house and the location of items in your home.
» Learn how to conjugate the present progressive to express things you are doing currently.
» Describe the parts of a town and learn proper shopping etiquette.
» Learn to conjugate the near future tense to express things you will do.
» Learn the rules for the verbs *ser* and *estar*.

For an overview of the concepts we will be working with in this chapter, listen to the following QuickClip and follow along with the script below. You will hear the native speaker describe the city he lives in, his home, and typical activities that he takes part in with people from his city.

Listen to Isaac from Spain share about life in his hometown of Madrid, including where he lives, things he typically does around the house and around the city, and how he spends his weekends.

To watch the QuickClip, use the camera on your mobile phone to scan the QR code or visit the link below.

www.quickclips.io/spanish-9

Isaac: ¡Hola! Soy Isaac y soy de España. Vivo en la ciudad de Madrid con mis padres y mi hermano pequeño. Estoy haciendo este video desde mi apartamento. Aunque es pequeño, es muy bonito. Tiene dos habitaciones, un baño, y un patio con vistas de la ciudad. Me gusta mucho cocinar y siempre ayudo a mi mamá en la cocina y además lavo la ropa para ayudar a mi familia. También, durante los fines de semana, voy al supermercado para comprar comida para la semana. En las tiendas siempre veo a personas que conozco como compañeros de la universidad. También, a veces me encuentro con unos vecinos y amigos del colegio. Durante los fines de semana después de hacer los quehaceres, me gusta juntarme con mis amigos para tomar un café en una terraza del centro. A veces voy a una clase de baile para aprender a bailar fandango. Es divertido conocer a nuevas personas de mi ciudad y disfrutar de la vida de la ciudad.

Mi Casa es Tu Casa

You've likely heard the phrase "mi casa es tu casa" or the formal "mi casa es su casa." They both mean "my home is your home," and I've found the two versions of this phrase to be widely used by Spanish speakers, reflecting the cultural value of hospitality. Overall, the Spanish speakers I have come in contact with have been extremely welcoming to me, and when they've offered me their home, I could tell that they meant it beyond a polite formality. This is notable, because welcoming someone into your home is a big deal. Our homes are sacred places, with doors and walls drawing a line between us and the outside world. As you may already know from the popular phrase, the word *casa* means "house"—as opposed to *el apartamento*, which means apartment. *El hogar* is the Spanish word for "home." Technically, then, *el hogar* is a broader term than house, allowing for the fact that not everyone lives in a house. But to me, even the word *casa* means more than just a specific structure, and I think that word can give the meaning of a place that you live in, whether it's a house, an apartment, or something else entirely.

Before we get more into the cultural importance of homes, take a look at the essential vocabulary depicted in figure 7.1.

Be sure to take some time to familiarize yourself with the vocabulary words in the figure so you have a foundation to work with as you continue through this chapter. This topic brings up a lot of essential vocabulary, so it will take some time to master all the home-related words you want to learn.

You will see that the home layout in figure 7.1 is likely different from what you are used to. Needless to say, houses can vary a lot throughout Latin America. However, I will share some of the major home differences I noticed while living in Mexico. Driveways seemed to be less common. Carpet also tends to be not very common, as tile floors are preferred. Many people have a washing machine on a covered roof area and hang their clothes out to dry. It's not unheard of to have a dryer, but it's not considered a necessity.

While we are talking about homes, I want to bring up an important cultural point about living arrangements. In Spanish-speaking countries, it is not uncommon to live under one roof with your extended family—a different arrangement from that of mainstream American culture, where the expectation often involves some degree of independence when children turn eighteen. This individualistic value is less present in Spanish-speaking cultures, which place more emphasis on a collective approach to living. Though of course every cultural practice has its own unique set of strengths, the collective approach results in a strong sense of family and community. The raising of a child is usually taken on not only by the parents, but by grandparents, aunts, uncles, cousins, or whoever else occupies the household. In turn, when the grandparents grow old, there are family members around to help care for them. Although living with a few extra family members may seem simple, it has a profound effect on the upbringing of a child and extends into many other parts of the culture.

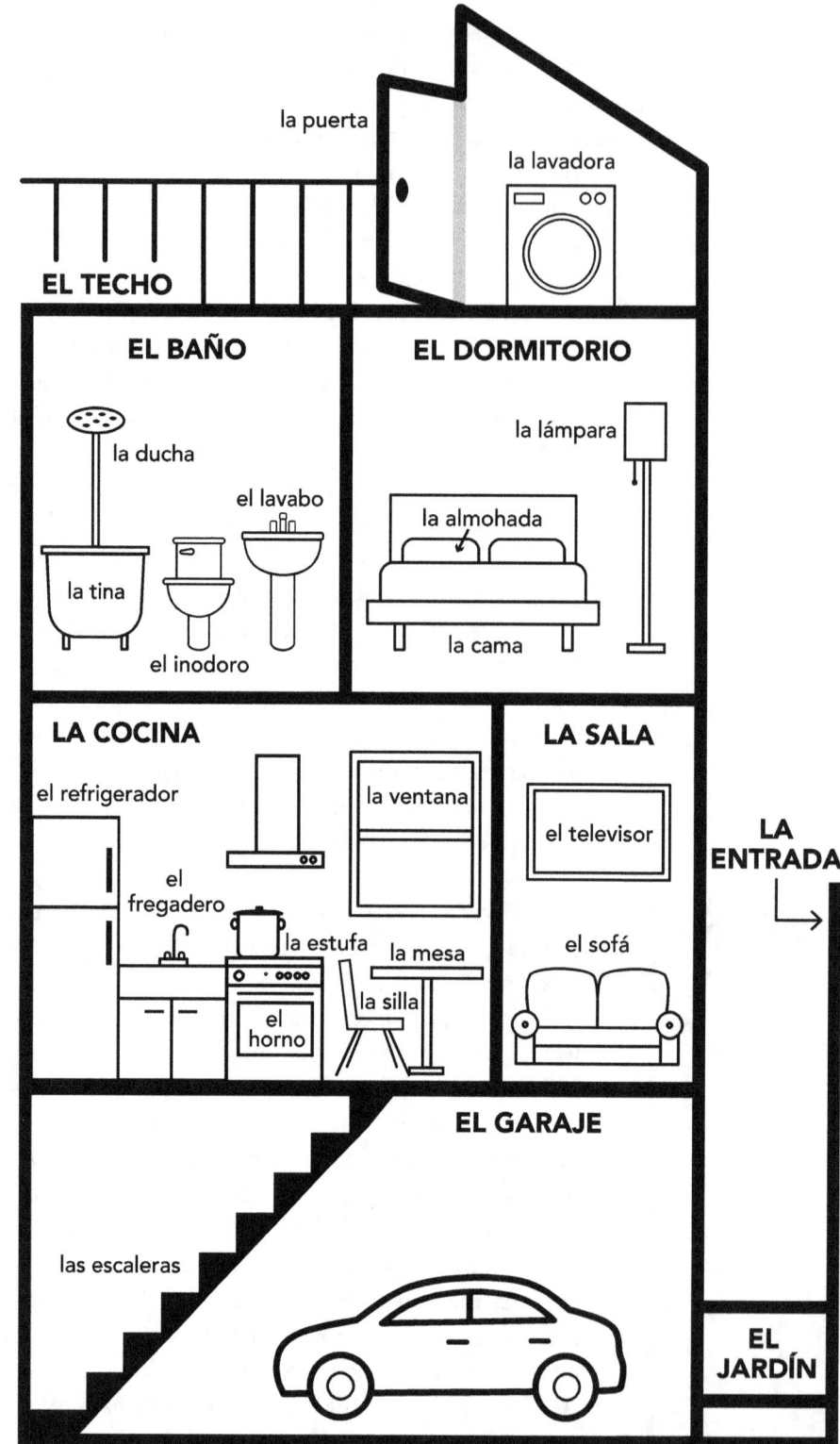

fig. 7.1

Prepositions

If you're like me, as organized as I try to keep my home, I always seem to be looking for something. If you live with someone, whether a partner, family member, friend, or just a roommate, you will more than likely be asked something like "Where is the remote?" or "Have you seen my phone?" To answer questions like that, you'll need some prepositions.

Prepositions are used to describe the location of something—words like *under*, *above*, *over*, and *across*—and can be extremely useful when explaining the layout of a house or when asking someone to go to another room to get something for us. To describe the location of something or someone, we use the verb *estar*, which means "to be." Although you have already seen some examples of this verb, be sure to examine the complete verb chart in table 7.1, as *estar* is considered an irregular verb.

table 7.1

estar = to be			
yo	**estoy**	nosotros/as	**estamos**
tú	**estás**	vosotros/as	**estáis**
él ella usted	**está**	ellos ellas ustedes	**están**

Now that you've reviewed the present-tense conjugations for the verb *estar*, look at the sentences below that describe where different rooms and items in a house are located; they give us an opportunity to learn some helpful prepositions to indicate location.

El garaje está debajo de la cocina.	The garage is under the kitchen.
La almohada está encima de la cama.	The pillow is on top of the bed.
El televisor está al lado del sofá.	The TV is next to the sofa.

In the examples above, we are working with four vocabulary terms:

debajo de	under
arriba de	above

encima de	on top of
al lado de	next to

These prepositions are very straightforward; however, if you look at the examples using them in complete sentences, you'll see that some say *de* and others say *del*. This is intentional, based on the word that follows the prepositional phrase; if the word following *de* is masculine, *de* becomes *del*, and if the word following *de* is feminine, we use *de la*.

de la	of the (feminine)
del	of the (masculine)

The reason for this is that if I said "encima de el carro" ("on top of the car"), placing the words *de* and *el* next to one another would blend together the pronunciation of the two *e*'s, eliminating the distinction between the words. Therefore, the *de* and *el* have to be combined into one word to become *del*. On the other hand, when I say "encima de la mesa" ("on top of the table"), the word "table" is feminine, so the *de* and *la* do not need to be combined, as there is a clear distinction between them. This is similar to how in English we can make contractions out of phrases such as "do not" to get "don't." Just think of *del* as a required contraction, where you don't have the option to use the wordier version.

Practice describing your home and the location of rooms and objects in relation to one another to work on your house vocabulary and prepositions.

Chores Around the House

Though some of your time at home is likely spent sleeping or relaxing, you probably attend to various household chores, often referred to as *los quehaceres*. Whether you live with others or by yourself, many responsibilities and duties come with occupying a living space. This creates the perfect opportunity to introduce some chore verbs:

lavar/doblar la ropa	to wash/fold the clothes
barrer el piso	to sweep the floor
aspirar	to vacuum
trapear	to mop
fregar	to scrub
sacar la basura	to take out the trash
regar (e-ie) las plantas	to water the plants

Do an internet search for Spanish chore vocabulary to learn more words you want to know. (Or don't, so that you can say you don't understand and get yourself out of doing said chore!)

All these chore verbs can be conjugated as regular present-tense verbs to say things like "Yo frego los platos," or "I scrub the dishes"—except for the verb *regar*, which is a stem-changing verb with an *e*-to-*ie* stem change in the boot of the verb chart. So "I water the plants" would be "Yo riego las plantas." (Revisit the previous sections covering stem-changing verbs in chapters 5 and 6 if you need a refresher.)

Present Progressive

Another tense that will likely come up a lot in conversation at home is the present progressive tense, which enables you to express things you are doing right now, in the current moment. For example, if your friend calls to ask what you're doing, you might need to say, "I'm cooking dinner and doing the laundry." I could use this tense to explain that right now you're reading this book: *Estás leyendo este libro*. We will be applying the present progressive tense to the chore verbs we covered in the previous section.

table 7.2

estar = to be				
yo	**estoy**	nosotros/as	**estamos**	
tú	**estás**	vosotros/as	**estáis**	
él ella usted	**está**	ellos ellas ustedes	**están**	

+

-ando
for -AR verbs

-iendo
for -ER and -IR verbs

Table 7.2 shows how to conjugate the present progressive. We first need to conjugate the verb *estar*, which means "to be," in the present tense. We have already learned this verb conjugation, but we will be adding what we call a *gerund*, (a verb with an -ing ending in English) so we can communicate that we are doing something currently.

Let's say I am folding the clothes right now. The first step is to conjugate the verb *estar* in the *yo* form, which is *estoy*. Next, I want the verb "to fold," which is *doblar*, to say folding. In English, I just add *ing* to the end of my verb. In Spanish, the first step is to drop the verb's ending, which in this case is *ar*. Then I will add *-ando* to the end, as shown in table 7.2. Finally, I get *Estoy doblando la ropa*, or "I am folding the clothes."

The chart shows two endings that are equivalent to the -ing ending in English: -ando is for -AR verbs, and -iendo is for -ER and -IR verbs.

Let's look at a few workbook-style exercises showing this process.

1. Yo (barrer) el piso.   __Yo estoy barriendo el piso.__
   (I am sweeping the floor).

2. Ella (regar) las plantas.   __Ella está regando las plantas.__
   (She is watering the plants).

3. Nosotros (limpiar) la casa.   __Nosotros estamos limpiando la casa.__
   (We are cleaning the house).

4. Él (preparar) la cena.   __Él está preparando la cena.__
   (He is preparing dinner).

As you can see, a form of the verb *estar* in the present tense is followed by a verb ending in either *-ando* or *-iendo*, depending on the ending of the verb in its infinitive form. I want to draw particular attention to the second example. This sentence uses the verb *regar*, which is an *e-ie* stem-changing verb. Because in this case I am not conjugating the verb *regar* into the present tense to say "I water," I do not make the stem change. To make the verb *regar* say "watering," I simply drop the *-ar* and add *-ando*. With -AR verbs, the stem change is not applied when forming a gerund. With certain -ER and -IR verbs, there are some special cases when you are creating a gerund in Spanish where a stem-changing rule will apply.

Irregular Gerunds in Spanish

As with most grammar concepts in Spanish, there are exceptions to the rules. For example, there are a few irregular gerunds in Spanish where the rule of dropping the -ER or -IR and adding *-iendo* does not apply.

One of the most important (and probably most common) irregular gerunds in Spanish is the verb *ir*, meaning "to go." To say "going," the verb *ir* becomes *yendo*.

Another common irregular gerund pattern is in verbs that have a vowel right before the -ER or -IR. Here are some examples:

leer → le**yendo**	to read/reading
creer → cre**yendo**	to believe/believing

Some -ER and -IR verbs that are also present tense stem-changing verbs will apply some form of a stem change when becoming a gerund. Here are some examples:

dormir (o-ue) → durm**iendo**	to sleep/sleeping

You can see that *dormir* is an *o-ue* stem-changing verb in the present tense, but when it is in the gerund form, the letter *o* only changes to *u*.

mentir (e-ie) → mint**iendo**	to lie/lying

Mentir is an *e-ie* stem-changing verb when conjugated in the present tense, but in the gerund form, the letter *e* only changes to *i*.

Luckily, the majority of verbs follow a regular pattern (ending with *-ando* or *-iendo*) when being formed into a gerund, but it's important to be aware that you will come across exceptions.

Stepping Out

When we step outside our home and venture into *la ciudad* (the city) or *el pueblo* (the town) to do errands or go out and about, it opens an opportunity for us to learn a lot more Spanish vocabulary! The list below provides some places we might visit in a town, city, or other type of community.

la tienda	the store
el supermercado	the supermarket
la estación de gas	the gas station
el centro comercial	the mall
la oficina de correos	the post office
el restaurante	the restaurant
la farmacia	the pharmacy
el banco	the bank
el parque	the park
el centro	downtown

el estacionamiento	the parking lot
el vecindario	the neighborhood
la lavandería	the laundromat
la estación de tren/autobús/metro	the train/bus/subway station
la calle	the street
la acera	the sidewalk
el semáforo	the traffic light
el mercado	the market

I want to go over a few vocabulary words from the list above. First is *el centro*, which looks a lot like the English word "center." *El centro* can indeed mean the center, but it can also mean downtown. The next word I want to focus on is *la lavandería* for "laundromat." You can see it looks similar to the verb *lavar*, which means "to wash," and *la lavandería* is where you wash your clothes. Making these associations when possible has made it easier for me to learn Spanish vocabulary.

If you travel to a Spanish-speaking country or even some southern states in the US, you will likely notice that many stores end with *ía*. For example, in Latin America, a common store is *la tortillería*, which is where you go to buy tortillas, and you can tell because the name has *tortilla* in it. The word *zapatos* means shoes, and you go to *la zapatería* to buy shoes. The Spanish word *pan* means bread; therefore, at *la panadería* you buy bread and other baked goods.

Finally, I want to highlight the term *el mercado*. In Latin America, markets can be outdoors in a series of tents (like a farmer's market in some areas of the US), or housed inside a permanent building or structure, and are very common; many families do most of their shopping there, while in the US "market" might refer to a farmer's market, grocery store, or small corner store. The way that shopping is set up in Spanish-speaking countries is often another significant cultural difference for Americans. We will dive into the topic of navigating markets in the appendix of this book.

The Near Future Tense

The topic of what we are going to do or where we are going to go comes up often in discussions, and the near future tense works perfectly for those situations. An example of this tense in English is "I am going to go to the supermarket." Table 7.3 shows how to form this tense in Spanish.

TABLE

table 7.3

To form the near future tense, you need the present-tense conjugation of the verb *ir*, meaning "to go," followed by the Spanish word *a*, meaning "to," followed by an infinitive verb. Here are a few examples:

Voy a estudiar para el examen.	I am going to study for the exam.
Ella **va a comprar** zapatos.	She is going to buy shoes.
Mis amigos **van a venir** a mi casa.	My friends are going to come to my house.
¿**Vas a ir** a la tienda para comprar jugo?	Are you going to go to the store to buy juice?

In these examples, I bolded the conjugation of *ir*, the word *a*, and the infinitive that follows it to draw your attention to the grammatical pattern. You can see that many of the sentences have more words after the bolded part to provide detail about what the people are going to do.

Now, instead of using the formula *ir + a + infinitive*, I can replace the infinitive with a specific place, in order to indicate what place I am going to. Look at the examples:

Voy al supermercado.	I'm going to the supermarket.
Voy a la tienda para comprar ropa.	I'm going to the store to buy clothing.
Voy al centro para comer con mis amigos.	I'm going downtown to eat with my friends.

Two of the sentences use the word *para*, which can have many meanings, but here it gives the meaning of "in order to." There are two words, *por* and *para*, that can be quite difficult for nonnative speakers of Spanish to learn, as they can both mean "for" in certain situations. They also have many other meanings, but there are rules as to when you can use which word. This is a more advanced grammar concept that I don't think should be covered in a beginner Spanish book. However, I want to mention it so you can start paying attention to when you see or hear *por* and *para* being used, because you can learn many of their uses just by paying attention to examples like the ones above.

Finally, I want to point out that examples 1 and 3 use the word *al*. We discussed the concept of *de el* having to become *del* (meaning "of the"). Here we have a similar situation with *a el* having to become *al* (meaning "to the"). This is, again, because we have two vowels side by side, so the words would not be clearly distinguishable from one another.

Now that you have built a foundation of being able to communicate about homes and cities, it's time to revisit the topic of people and how they relate to life in a city.

Talking To and Describing the People You Know

Being out on the town and running into people you know may or may not be something you look forward to, depending on whether you're an introvert or an extrovert. But it will happen, because living in a town, city, or other type of community usually involves some human interaction. So far, we have not covered many words for people who have some sort of relationship with you outside of being a family member, so let's learn some new words to help us communicate about non-familial relationships.

el/la compañero(a) de trabajo	the coworker
el/la compañero(a) de clase	the classmate
el/la compañero(a) de cuarto	the roommate
el/la vecino(a)	the neighbor
el/la (mejor) amigo(a)	the (best) friend
el/la conocido(a)	the acquaintance

To convey how we know these people, we can use one of two important verbs in Spanish that both mean "to know": *saber* and *conocer*. As you can see in table 7.4, they have nuanced differences in terms of what kind of knowing they describe. *Saber* involves having types of informational knowledge, and *conocer* is focused more on familiarity with people, places, or things.

table 7.4

saber = to know (information, facts, how to do something)			
yo	sé	nosotros/as	sabemos
tú	sabes	vosotros/as	sabéis
él ella usted	sabe	ellos ellas ustedes	saben

conocer = to be familiar with (people, places, things)			
yo	conozco	nosotros/as	conocemos
tú	conoces	vosotros/as	conocéis
él ella usted	conoce	ellos ellas ustedes	conocen

The verb *saber* has an irregular conjugation pattern, as the *yo* form, "sé," is irregular. The verb *saber* is used to communicate that you know information or facts, as well as how to do things. For example:

Yo sé que una semana tiene siete días.	I know that a week has seven days.
¿Sabes a qué hora sale el tren?	Do you know what time the train leaves?
Yo sé cocinar.	I know how to cook.

Conocer is also an irregular verb. The *yo* form, "conozco," looks very irregular with the letter *z* in it! The verb *conocer* is used to communicate that you know people and places and have knowledge about things. For example:

Yo conozco a tu hermana.	I know your sister.
Yo conozco esta ciudad.	I know (am familiar with) this city.
No conozco esta marca.	I don't know (am not familiar with) this brand.

It's initially confusing that there are two words that express "to know" in Spanish. However, real-life examples of *saber* and *conocer* will help you get used to the different uses, and soon it will become more intuitive.

Ser versus *Estar*

Now that we've covered talking about things in our home and around the town, it's a perfect time to revisit *ser* versus *estar*. Both these verbs mean "to be," and we have seen both used throughout the book thus far in isolated situations. In this chapter, for example, we used the verb *estar* to communicate where things are and what we are doing right at this moment.

After seeing many isolated examples of how to use *ser* and *estar*, you are ready to compare them side by side and learn the rules for when to use which. Start by looking at figure 7.2, with the acronyms representing the uses for *ser* and for *estar*.

fig. 7.2

WHEN TO USE "SER"

D ate
O ccupation
C haracteristics
T ime
O rigin
R elationships

WHEN TO USE "ESTAR"

P osition
L ocation
A ction
C ondition
E motions

Let's start by looking at the uses of *ser*. One acronym that is used to remember it is DOCTOR, which we learned about in chapter 4. To review this, I have written an example sentence for each letter of the acronym:

Date	Hoy es lunes.	Today is Monday.
Occupation	Soy una maestra.	I am a teacher.
Characteristics	Yo soy rubia e inteligente	I am blonde and intelligent.
Time	Son las siete cuarenta y seis de la noche.	It is seven forty-three in the evening.
Origin	Soy de South Dakota.	I am from South Dakota.
Relationship	Claire es mi mejor amiga.	Claire is my best friend.

For each of these sentences, I used a conjugation of the verb *ser*. We have already discussed all these uses, so hopefully this feels like a review for you. The uses of *ser* to communicate date and occupation are pretty straightforward. "Characteristics" refers to physical and/or personality traits. Time and origin are straightforward categorizations, and "relationships" simply refers to when we describe who someone is to us. All these uses require the verb *ser*.

Next, let's examine the uses of *estar*. PLACE is an acronym commonly used to remember them. This acronym has not been introduced, but you have seen many examples of the uses of *estar* throughout the book so far.

Below I have an example sentence for each letter.

Position	El libro está encima de la mesa.	The book is on top of the table.
Location	En este momento, estoy en mi casa.	At this moment, I am at my house.
Action	Estoy trabajando.	I am working.
Condition	No estoy enferma.	I am not sick.
Emotion	Estoy muy contenta hoy.	I am very content today.

Each of these examples contains a conjugation of the verb *estar*. Position and location are similar, as both refer to where things or places are, whether on a micro level (position) or a macro level (location). Earlier in this chapter we learned the present progressive tense, which is used to describe action. Condition and emotion are pretty clear-cut: Condition includes states such as sickness or something being broken; a store being open or closed could also fall under that category. And emotion, as you might guess, applies when you're feeling happy, sad, and so on.

Understanding the differences between *ser* and *estar* may seem overwhelming at first, but there is a more simplified way to comprehend them. If you consider the uses of *ser*, you will see that the situations are typically more permanent in nature, or at least longer-lasting. For example, your origin will never change. Your occupation might change, but it's likely not changing every day of the week. If you're tall, you'll likely have that trait for life.

Two possible exceptions are the uses of *ser* to describe date and time. However, even those have a type of permanence, in that it's always one of seven days of the week, and times of the day (despite there being many of them) are limited and recurring. With *estar*, you will see that most of the uses are more temporary in nature. For example, your location is constantly changing, as well as your action at a given moment. Your emotions probably change more often than your physical characteristics, and conditions like sickness or an open door are also likely to change.

Now that we've covered the uses of *ser* and *estar*, I want to give you a few examples of how these verbs can be used in the same sentence and/or paragraph:

> Claire **es** mi mejor amiga y **estamos** en el centro comercial. Las tiendas **son** muy bonitas. **Estamos** emocionadas porque el nuevo restaurante **está** abierto.
>
> Notice that these sentences contain a mixture of bolded conjugations of the verbs *ser* and *estar* to communicate various ideas.

Although it will take some time to master *ser* and *estar* (especially when you need to use them simultaneously as in the example above), the upside is that they both mean "to be." So if you use the wrong one, it will sound "off" to native speakers, but in most scenarios they'll understand the basic gist of what you're trying to communicate. These rules for *ser* and *estar* will also apply when you learn other tenses, such as past and future. For example, you'll eventually want to say something like "I was working" or "I was a teacher" or "I will be happy tomorrow." Keep these rules in mind when you learn *ser* and *estar* with new verb tenses, as the DOCTOR and PLACE rules will still apply.

Adjectives that Change Meaning with *Ser* and *Estar*

One more point of difference between *ser* and *estar*: there are some cases where *ser* and *estar* can be used with the same word, but the meaning of the word changes depending on which of the two verbs accompany it. Let me give you a few common examples of adjectives that have this ability to change meaning.

Estar listo(a)	to be ready (condition)
Ser listo(a)	to be smart (characteristic)
Estar nervioso(a)	to be nervous in the moment (emotion)
Ser nervioso(a)	to be a nervous person (characteristic)
Estar rico(a)	to be rich in taste / delicious (condition)
Ser rico(a)	to be a rich person / wealthy (characteristic)

For the three adjective examples above, I put one of the words from either the DOCTOR (*ser*) acronym or the PLACE (*estar*) acronym so that you can see the connection with the rules we just covered. Although it may seem confusing that the meaning of some words can change depending on whether they have *ser* or *estar* in front of them, the meanings do align with the rules. Thankfully there aren't a lot of these, but it is something to be aware of.

 Although *ser* and *estar* can seem overwhelming at first, the more you practice, the more you will start to see them as separate verbs. The Digital Asset library for this book includes a set of exercises to give you more practice on conjugating these two verbs, as well as knowing when to use which one. Visit go.quickstartguides.com/spanish

Chapter Recap

This chapter covered vocabulary and grammar concepts related to where we live, in terms of both home and the broader community. This included the following:

» Learning vocabulary words for parts of the house, and prepositions to communicate where various items in a house are located.

» Studying vocabulary words to express some chores to add to our to-do list, alongside the present progressive tense to describe actions that we are doing in the moment.

» Learning vocabulary related to places in a typical town, city, or other form of municipality, combined with the near-future tense to communicate places where we are going and things we are going to do.

» Learning the rules for *saber* and *conocer* to be able to correctly express "to know" in Spanish, distinguishing between knowing information and having familiarity with a person, place, or thing.

» Reviewing the many uses of *ser* and *estar* and looking at the overall rules for when to use *ser* and *estar* so that we can correctly express "to be" in Spanish.

All of this together has hopefully expanded your ability to communicate about your daily life in your home and other surroundings. Now that you've learned how to talk about your chores and errands, get ready to get out and have some fun in the next chapter!

| 8 |
Out and About

When we step out of the comfort of our home, we come in contact with the world that surrounds us, and being able to navigate that world is crucial to our survival. For example, we depend on being able to run errands to find the items we need. Knowing how to purchase goods and ask for assistance or recommendations helps us thrive. So now that we have a sense of our home and surroundings, let's broaden our scope to look at how we get around in our environment, focusing on communicating about places we go with friends as well as how to get to those places using direction words. This will include concepts related to shopping and eating out, which have a lot in common in terms of seeking specific information—and navigating the process of payment! This chapter will help you polish the necessary communication skills that will enable you to get around a Spanish-speaking city and problem-solve the many situations that can arise.

Chapter Overview

By the end of this chapter, you will be able to do the following:
» Use the names of places you go with friends, and know how to make plans.
» Make comparisons of items and prices when shopping.
» Learn vocabulary related to clothing and grocery shopping.
» Order food and customize food orders.

For an overview of the concepts we will be working with in this chapter, listen to the following QuickClip and follow along with the script below. You will hear the native speaker describe some plans he has with friends this coming weekend in the city.

Listen to Abdiel from Puerto Rico describe his upcoming activities, including plans to hit up his favorite beach and have dinner in Puerto Rico with some friends.

To watch the QuickClip, use the camera on your mobile phone to scan the QR code or visit the link below.

www.quickclips.io/spanish-10

Abdiel: Hola. Mi nombre es Abdiel y soy de Puerto Rico. Mis amigos y yo tenemos planificado este fin de semana ir a mi playa favorita que se llama Playa Flamenco en Culebra. Vamos a ir a disfrutar de la playa durante el día y después, vamos y probamos un restaurante local. En aquel restaurante escojamos, me gusta tener dos cosas: mariscos y mofongo. Y de beber, pruebo una piña colada. A mis amigos les gusta probar cosas distintas, como arroz con gandules y tostones. Es bueno pasar un día en playa en Puerto Rico con los amigos, y por supuesto, comer comida buena.

Social Spaces

Going out and about in your community or elsewhere will often involve fun plans with friends. Building on the parts of a city or town that we've previously covered, let's learn a few more vocabulary words related to places people might visit with friends.

el cine	the movie theater
la playa	the beach
el concierto	the concert
el museo	the museum
el gimnasio	the gym

In order to talk about the places we go with our friends, we can use the regular present tense or even the present progressive. We can also use the verb *salir*, which can mean to leave or to go out (with friends in this case). The verb *salir* is a bit irregular, so let's take another look at its conjugation chart (table 8.1).

table 8.1

Remember that the *yo* form of salir is irregular, being *salgo*. The rest of the conjugations follow a regular present-tense conjugation pattern. So, for example, I can use a variety of verb tenses to indicate going out with friends:

Present tense	Yo **salgo** mucho con mi novio al cine.	I go out to the movies a lot with my boyfriend.
Present progressive	**Estoy saliendo** con mis amigas.	I am going out with my friends.
Near future	**Voy a salir** a bailar este fin de semana.	I am going to go out dancing this weekend.

You can see that to communicate when I am going out to do something, I have used a variety of verb tenses we have covered thus far to conjugate the verb *salir*. But before you can actually go out with people, you need to make plans with them, right? An easy way to do this is to simply ask someone, "Do you want to go out?" This requires us to use the verb *querer*, which means "to wish" or "to want." It is an irregular verb because it has an *e*-to-*ie* stem change, which you can see highlighted in table 8.2.

Like many of the stem-changing verbs we have covered, *querer* is a boot verb, because the stem change does not take place in the *nosotros* and *vosotros* forms.

| 8 | Out and About 159

table 8.2

querer (e-ie) = to wish / to want			
yo	**quiero**	nosotros/as	**queremos**
tú	**quieres**	vosotros/as	**queréis**
él ella usted	**quiere**	ellos ellas ustedes	**quieren**

Now that we can conjugate *querer* in the present tense, let's look at how to ask someone to go out.

¿Quieres salir (conmigo)?	Do you (informal) want to go out (with me)?
Sí/No quiero salir (contigo).	I do/don't want to go out (with you).
¿Quiere salir (conmigo)?	Do you (formal) want to go out (with me)?
Sí/No quiero salir (con usted).	I do/don't want to go out (with you - formal).

I do need to clarify that in Spanish, if you ask someone to *salir contigo*, it's not the equivalent of asking them to be your significant other, or even necessarily to go on a date. It is totally normal to ask friends this question in Spanish without any romantic overtones.

Also, I want to point out two words that are likely new to you. The word *conmigo* means "with me," and the word *contigo* is the informal form of "with you." These two words don't follow the pattern of the rest of our pronouns; with *usted*, for example, it is *con usted* (with you formal), *con nosotros* (with us), and so on.

Once you've established some more places to go with friends and how to make those plans with others, it becomes important to know how to navigate in those places you plan to go.

Shopping: Costs and Comparisons

A huge part of going out and about is spending money, whether it's on necessities like groceries or fun stuff like restaurants, drinks, or event tickets. Buying things is something most people do nearly every day, so in this section we will focus on something that can be either an essential or a fun thing: clothing. Keep in mind that shopping for clothing can be done in a formal clothing store you might find at a mall, or at a market. We will discuss what you need to know to navigate a variety of shopping settings. We'll start with some verbs that are essential to communicating about shopping.

comprar	to buy
vender	to sell
preferir (e-ie)	to prefer
pedir (e-i)	to ask (for an object, favor, or action) or to order
preguntar	to ask (a question or ask for information)

In our list of verbs, there are two irregular verbs: *preferir* and *pedir*. Since we are still working on mastering stem-changing verbs, charts for both verbs are provided in tables 8.3 and 8.4.

table 8.3

preferir (e-ie) = to prefer			
yo	**prefiero**	nosotros/as	**preferimos**
tú	**prefieres**	vosotros/as	**preferís**
él ella usted	**prefiere**	ellos ellas ustedes	**prefieren**

table 8.4

pedir (e-i) = to ask			
yo	**pido**	nosotros/as	**pedimos**
tú	**pides**	vosotros/as	**pedís**
él ella usted	**pide**	ellos ellas ustedes	**piden**

As the charts show, both verbs are irregular boot verbs with stem changes. However, the stem changes are different for each verb: *preferir* has an *e*-to-*ie* stem change, and *pedir* has an *e*-to-*i* stem change.

The verb list also contains two verbs that are similar in meaning: *pedir* and *preguntar*. The verb *pedir* means to ask and is used to ask for an object, favor, or action. Here are some examples using *pedir*:

Quiero pedir una talla más grande.	I want to ask for a bigger size.
Necesito pedir un favor.	I need to ask for a favor.
Estoy pidiendo ayuda.	I am asking for help.

The verb *preguntar* also means to ask, but it is used to ask for information, rather than for a specific object or action. Look at the examples using *preguntar*:

Voy a preguntar cuánto cuesta.	I am going to ask how much it costs.
Necesito preguntar dónde está el baño.	I need to ask where the bathroom is.

Now that we have some essential verbs in our vocabulary, let's work on combining them with some shopping terms.

la talla	the clothing size
el número	shoe size

The words *talla* and *número* both refer to sizes, but *talla* is used to describe clothing size and *número* (also meaning number) applies to shoe size. There is another word for size, *el tamaño*, which refers to the dimensions or size of physical objects. If you were shopping for objects such as furniture or cars, you could use the word *el tamaño* to refer to their size.

On the topic of sizes, it's important to know how to ask for a bigger or smaller size when shopping. Below are example sentences that express the need for different sizes.

Necesito un número de zapato más grande/pequeño.	I need a bigger/smaller shoe size.
Prefiero una talla más grande/pequeña.	I prefer a bigger/smaller size.

In the first sentence, the word *pequeño* ends in *o* because the word for "shoe size" is masculine. The word *pequeña* in the second sentence ends in *a* to agree with the feminine word for size, *talla*.

Before we continue to discuss communication when shopping, let's add a few more essential clothing-related vocabulary words to give us more to work with.

los zapatos	the shoes
la ropa	the clothing
los pantalones	the pants
los pantalones cortos	the pants (technically the short pants)
la camisa	the shirt
la camiseta	the T-shirt
el suéter	the sweater
el anillo	the ring
los aretes	the earrings
el collar	the necklace
la bolsa	the bag

I have a quick tip for remembering the difference between *la camisa* and *la camiseta*. The Spanish word for "T-shirt" has the letter *t* in it, and the word for "shirt" (not a T-shirt) does not contain the letter *t*.

The topic of clothing is a great one for further learning and exploration. If you look up more clothing words to learn, be aware that for some there will be regional differences. For example, my friend from Venezuela uses the word *los zarcillos* for earrings, a word I had never heard of when living in Mexico!

Since the clothing-related vocabulary words are pretty straightforward and don't require much explanation, we are going to combine some of them with a new verb, *costar*, meaning "to cost," so we can practice asking the prices of items when shopping.

table 8.5

costar (o-ue) = to cost			
yo	**cuesto**	nosotros/as	**costamos**
tú	**cuestas**	vosotros/as	**costáis**
él ella usted	**cuesta**	ellos ellas ustedes	**cuestan**

| 8 | Out and About

The verb chart in table 8.5 shows the present-tense conjugation of the verb *costar*, which has an *o*-to-*ue* stem change. Because we use *costar* mostly to discuss how much items cost, we will focus on using the third-person singular and plural forms of the verb: *cuesta* and *cuestan*.

The verb *cuesta* is used to discuss the price of something that is singular. For example:

¿Cuánto cuesta la camisa?	How much does the shirt cost?
La camisa cuesta diez dólares.	The shirt costs ten dollars.

The verb *cuestan* is used to discuss the price of something that is plural:

¿Cuánto cuestan los zapatos?	How much do the shoes cost?
Los zapatos cuestan cincuenta dólares.	The shoes cost fifty dollars.

We can also use forms of the verb *costar* to make comparisons between prices of items:

Los zapatos cuestan **más que** las camisas.	The shoes cost more than the shirts.
La camisa cuesta **menos que** el anillo.	The shirt costs less than the ring.
Los zapatos azules cuestan **tanto como** los zapatos negros.	The blue shoes cost as much as the black shoes.

We covered *más* and *menos* in chapter 6, in the context of making comparisons. You may notice that the sentence examples above have an extra word, *que*. The sentence using *más que* is using the phrase to mean "more than," while the sentence using *menos que* is using that phrase to mean "less than." The completely new words here are *tanto como*, which is equivalent to "as much as." The phrases *más que*, *menos que*, and *tanto como* can be followed by a verb (like the verb *costar* in the sentences above) when making comparisons. Here are a few more sentence examples using other verbs with these phrases in a sentence.

Yo compro tanto como mi amiga.	I buy as much as my friend.
Me gusta la camisa más que tú.	I like the shirt more than you. (informal)
Voy de compras menos que mis amigos.	I go shopping less than my friends.

However, if we want to compare with adjectives, such as color, for example, we can still use *más que* and *menos que*, but the adjective goes between the two words. And when it comes to *tanto como*, we use a slightly different set of words. To say an item is as something as something else, we use *tan* (adjective) *como*.

La camisa es **más** grande **que** la blusa.	The shirt is bigger than the blouse.
Los aretes son **menos** caros **que** los anillos.	The earrings are less expensive than the rings.
Los zapatos son **tan** rojos **como** las camisas.	The shoes are as red as the shirts.
Las camisas son **tan** bonitas **como** los suéteres.	The shirts are as pretty as the sweaters.

Being able to make comparisons of prices and characteristics of items can help you better communicate with store employees who are assisting you in finding the best purchase for your needs. Once you have informed yourself of your choices and come to a decision about your purchase, you will be ready to check out. You as the client (*el cliente/la clienta*) will approach the cashier (*el cajero/la cajera*), and they will probably tell you something along the lines of "Son (#) en total," meaning "It's (amount) in total." Most stores will accept cash (*el efectivo*), a credit card (*la tarjeta de crédito*), or a debit card (*la tarjeta de débito*). If you pay with cash, the cashier will likely tell you, "Aquí está su cambio," or "Here is your change." Notice that they will likely use "su," which is the formal possessive adjective, to show respect to you as the client. If you are paying with a card, they may ask you for "su firma" (your signature) on the receipt. You may also be asked something like, "¿Desea su recibo?", which roughly translates to "Would you like your receipt?" Interactions like this can be nerve-wracking at first, but after some practice, they will come more naturally to you.

Grocery Shopping and Going Out to Eat

One of the most common categories of shopping and spending money is food, whether you're talking about grocery shopping or going out to eat. In this section, we will focus mainly on eating out, as that is where most of your conversational skills will be needed. However, we will start with a few basics to get you by when grocery shopping.

Navigating the Grocery Store

¿Dónde está(n) _____?	Where is/are _____?
¿Tienen _____?	Do you have _____?
Estoy buscando _____.	I am looking for _____.
la carne	meat
los mariscos	seafood
las frutas	fruit
las verduras	vegetables
los productos lácteos	dairy products
los huevos	eggs
la comida enlatada	canned food
la comida congelada	frozen food

Navigating the basics of a grocery store is pretty much a matter of knowing your vocabulary. You can communicate a lot of your needs simply by saying the name of the product or food item you are looking for.

For practice, try making your grocery lists in Spanish! You could also seek out an online cooking tutorial video in Spanish and see what words you recognize.

Eating Out

Eating out can definitely be a situation that puts your Spanish comprehension and conversational skills to the test. It can be anxiety-provoking when you're trying to get your order right, especially if there are certain foods you must avoid due to allergies or for other health reasons, or if there's something you just don't like.

We will start with some essential vocabulary needed to communicate in a restaurant setting.

una mesa (para dos)	a table (for two)
la comida	the food / the meal
la cuenta	the bill
el plato	the dish/plate
la taza	the cup
el vaso	the glass
el cuchillo	the knife

la cuchara	the spoon
el tenedor	the fork
la servilleta	the napkin
la botana / el aperitivo	the appetizer
el plato fuerte / la entrada	the main dish/plate
el postre	the dessert
la bebida	the drink
la soda / el refresco / la gaseosa	the soda/pop
el jugo	the juice
el vino	the wine
la cerveza	the beer
el café	the coffee

When you're eating at a restaurant, vocabulary can be one of the biggest challenges, especially because menus are very heavy with vocabulary. The above list is in no way conclusive; there are myriad words to know related to restaurant menus and experiences. A lot of the vocabulary you use will depend on what kind of restaurant you are visiting and what kind of cuisine you are eating.

If you are dining in different parts of Latin America, the types of food you encounter are going to vary by region, as will some of the vocabulary. For example, in the vocabulary list above I included three words for "soda"—if you're from the northern United States, you might refer to it as "pop." The English words *pop* and *soda* are great examples of how food words can vary in a language depending on geographical location. The names of dishes can also be unique to an area.

Now that we have some essential vocabulary to work with, we can combine those words with some related verbs, both regular present-tense conjugations and some irregular conjugations.

Here are some regular present-tense verbs:

añadir	to add
comer	to eat
ordenar	to order
tomar/beber	to drink

Let's look at an example script of a cashier and a client at a restaurant using the verbs we just learned.

Cajero:	¿Lista para **ordenar**?
Cliente:	Sí, estoy lista. Para **comer**, una hamburguesa por favor. ¿Puede **añadir** cebolla?
Cajero:	Claro. Una hamburguesa con cebolla. Y, ¿para **tomar**?
Cliente:	Un vaso de jugo, sin hielo por favor.
Cajero:	¿Es todo?
Cliente:	Sí, es todo.
Cajero:	Son diez dólares con ochenta centavos.
Cliente:	Aquí tiene. Gracias.
Cajero:	¡Gracias a usted! En unos minutos va a estar lista su comida.

In the exchange above, you probably noticed two new vocabulary words that can be quite useful when ordering food: *con* (meaning "with") and *sin* (meaning "without"). You'll need those words to customize and clarify ingredients when ordering.

The script also used the word *para* combined with the verbs *comer* and *tomar*, giving the meaning of "to eat" or "to drink." Using this construction eliminates the need to conjugate the verb into the present tense; therefore, it stays in its infinitive form. There are some other essential verbs related to eating out that are more irregular, and we will cover those in more detail.

table 8.6

venir = to come			GO
yo	**vengo**	nosotros/as	**venimos**
tú	**vienes**	vosotros/as	**venís**
él ella usted	**viene**	ellos ellas ustedes	**vienen**

table 8.7

probar (o-ue) = to try			
yo	**pruebo**	nosotros/as	**probamos**
tú	**pruebas**	vosotros/as	**probáis**
él / ella / usted	**prueba**	ellos / ellas / ustedes	**prueban**

table 8.8

recomendar (e-ie) = to recommend			
yo	**recomiendo**	nosotros/as	**recomendamos**
tú	**recomiendas**	vosotros/as	**recomendáis**
él / ella / usted	**recomienda**	ellos / ellas / ustedes	**recomiendan**

The verbs shown in tabless 8.6, 8.7, and 8.8 are irregular present tense verbs. They will take some time to master, as they have a variety of stem-changing patterns. To start with, the verb *venir* is not only a boot verb but also a go verb, since the *yo* form is *vengo*. The next two verbs, *probar* and *recomendar*, are both boot verbs with different stem changes. Focused conjugation practice can be extremely helpful with getting these irregular verbs memorized. Let's also take a moment to look through a script of a conversation between a waiter (*mesero*) and a woman (*mujer*) using this new set of verbs to order.

Daniel from Mexico speaks as the waiter (mesero) and Arantza, also from Mexico, will speak as the woman client (mujer). Listen carefully as Arantza asks Daniel for recommendations and decides what to order.

To watch the QuickClip, use the camera on your mobile phone to scan the QR code or visit the link below.

www.quickclips.io/spanish-11

Mesero:	¿Lista para **ordenar**?
Mujer:	Todavía no. No sé qué **pedir**. ¿Qué me puede **recomendar**?
Mesero:	La carne aquí es muy buena. Yo **prefiero** el bistec, pero muchos clientes **piden** el pollo también. La carne siempre **viene** con una ensalada, puré de papa y pan.
Mujer:	Gracias por la recomendación. Yo quiero el bistec, por favor.
Mesero:	Muy bien. ¿Y para tomar?
Mujer:	Me gustaría tomar un vino. ¿Qué vino **recomienda**?
Mesero:	Yo **recomiendo** el vino tinto de Argentina. ¿Quiere probar un poco?
Mujer:	Sí, por favor.
Mesero:	En un momento **vengo** con el pan y el vino.
Mujer:	¡Muchas gracias!

In this exchange, the verbs we just learned are bolded. Some of the verbs are conjugated in the present tense, while others are used in their infinitive state.

The Conditional

Ordering food in Spanish often involves using a verb tense known for its polite tone: the conditional tense. Examples of the conditional in English would be "I would like to order a dessert" or "Could you recommend something, please?" The "would" or "could" part is what makes it conditional, and it makes your request seem less direct, less demanding, and therefore more polite. However, the conditional tense in Spanish works differently than in English. Instead of simply putting the word "would" or "could" in front of a verb, we actually change the verb's ending to signal that we are using the conditional tense. For example, "Me gustaría ordenar" means "I would like to order." In other words, the verb conjugation *gustaría* literally means "would like." Take a closer look at the verb chart in table 8.9 with conditional verb endings.

table 8.9

Conditional Verb Endings			
yo	ía	nosotros/as	íamos
tú	ías	vosotros/as	íais
él ella usted	ía	ellos ellas ustedes	ían

Just as we've learned verb endings for the present tense, the conditional tense has its own set of endings: *ía, ías, ía, íamos, íais,* and *ían*. The major difference with this verb tense is that we do not drop the ending of the infinitive verb prior to adding these endings. Normally, when conjugating verbs in Spanish, we drop the -AR, -ER, or -IR and then add the new ending. But with the conditional tense, we simply add this ending onto any infinitive verb. This means we have only one set of endings to memorize, and we simply attach one onto the end of the verb. Here are a few sentence examples of the conditional tense at work.

Me gustaría probar el vino.	I would like to try the wine.
Yo preferiría el bistec.	I would prefer the steak.
¿Qué recomendaría usted?	What would you (formal) recommend?
¿Podría tener más tiempo, por favor?	Could I have more time, please?

You will see that sentence examples 1, 2, and 3 are conjugated just as we already discussed. I simply took the infinitive forms of the verbs *gustar, preferir,* and *recomdendar* and added the appropriate conditional ending for the subject of each sentence.

Sentence example 4, however, uses the verb *poder*, but it clearly doesn't exactly have the word *poder* and the conditional ending added. This is because there are some irregular verbs in the conditional tense, and *poder* is one of them. For *poder*, the stem for the conditional is *podr*, and the appropriate conditional ending is added to get *podría*.

A few other common irregular stems in the conditional tense are *tener*, which becomes *tendr*, the verb *hacer*, which becomes *har*, and *querer*, which becomes *quer*.

If you are ready to get serious about learning the conditional tense in depth, do an internet search for irregular verbs in the conditional tense to memorize the irregular stems. Luckily, there aren't a ton of irregular verbs in the conditional, so if you're not ready to dive into that, you'll still be able to communicate quite well with the conditional tense.

The conditional tense isn't usually taught to beginners, but because the mechanics of it are relatively simple, I think it's actually a good one to at least dip into at this stage. Just knowing the phrase "me gustaría" followed by an infinitive for a two-verb construction can get you a long way in communicating your needs politely!

At this point in the book, you've been introduced to quite a few irregular present-tense verbs in Spanish. Focused conjugation practices can be extremely helpful with mastering these irregular verbs. The book's Digital Asset library includes verb charts for twelve of the high-frequency irregular present-tense verbs in Spanish, as well as conjugation exercises to help you get more comfortable conjugating irregular verbs. Visit go.quickstartguides.com/Spanish

Food is obviously a huge part of any culture; it impacts what you eat, when you eat, with whom, and so on. If you travel to Spanish-speaking countries, you will notice that mealtimes tend to be different than what you typically find in the United States. Many families tend to eat dinner very late at night. You've also likely heard of *la siesta*, meaning "nap," which is common in Spain, where people leave work for a few hours in the middle of the workday to go home, eat, and rest. When I lived in Mexico, I got to be part of *la merienda*, basically the equivalent of "snack time," which is an evening snack often consisting of Mexican sweet bread, or pan dulce, and coffee or tea. There is no way I can explain the culture of food for all Spanish-speaking countries in one paragraph, but if you travel abroad to a Spanish-speaking country, I encourage you to keep an open mind and be ready to experience the culture of food, as it will teach you a lot about the overall culture.

Chapter Recap

This chapter covered vocabulary and grammar concepts related to navigating various situations when you are out and about, which included the following:

» Learning terms for places we frequent with friends as well as how to make plans with someone.

» Introducing some new vocabulary and a wide variety of verbs, both regular and irregular, related to shopping for clothing and food, which gave us a chance to practice how to navigate finding items in a store and paying for them.

» Going over the basics of ordering food in a restaurant, involving an introduction to the conditional tense, which is a way to communicate politeness when shopping, dining, or in other situations where you want to remain cordial.

All these concepts have helped you build a solid foundation for getting out and about, whether it be hitting the mall, trying a new restaurant, or checking out a local market in a Spanish-speaking country. I encourage you to get out and about to practice your Spanish however you can, whether that means traveling abroad, attending a Spanish conversation group, or finding a local business that has Spanish-speaking employees and asking if they will speak with you in Spanish. The more you put yourself out there, the quicker you will master these kinds of situations!

| 9 |
Community Connections

Being able to understand and communicate about the past helps us to better understand and navigate the present moments we find ourselves in. Specifically, the past events of a community can inform a deeper understanding of that culture, whether it's our own or one we're coming in contact with that we want to learn more about. In this chapter, we will focus on the topic of community, and so we will explore building the vocabulary and grammar needed to talk about events that happened in the past, using the past tense. While covering the topic of past events, we will weave in vocabulary related to cultural activities and values, as well as words that can help us express our feelings about the past. As with our understanding of the past, these past-tense skills will inform how we communicate in the present.

Chapter Overview

By the end of this chapter, you will be able to do the following:
» Use vocabulary related to the topic of community.
» Use basic conjugation patterns for the preterite and imperfect tenses in Spanish.
» Use the preterite and imperfect tenses when communicating about the past.
» Learn vocabulary words that will enable you to have conversations about history and culture.
» Express feelings about events.

For an overview of the concepts that we will be working with in this chapter, listen to the QuickClip and follow along with the script below. You will hear the native speaker describe her childhood and cultural background.

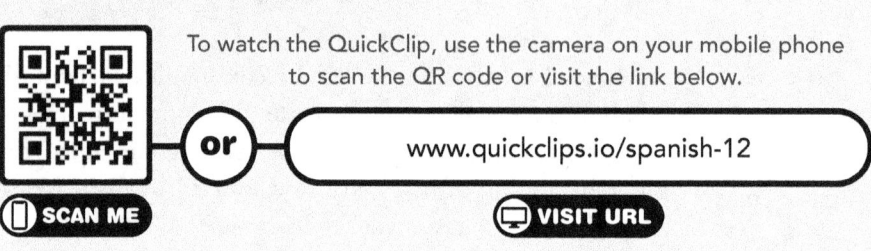

Listen to María from Venezuela describe her childhood and background. She will tell you which language she spoke before Spanish, as she shares about her love for her cultural heritage.

To watch the QuickClip, use the camera on your mobile phone to scan the QR code or visit the link below.

www.quickclips.io/spanish-12

María: Saludos, mi nombre es María y yo soy de Venezuela. Yo nací en Caracas, pero mis ancestros eran de Italia. Cuando era niña, yo solo hablaba italiano, pero cuando entré a la primaria, aprendí el español. Cuando era niña, mis padres siempre me contaban historias sobre nuestra cultura, y eso me ayudó a aprender sobre mis raíces culturales. Siempre participaba en las tradiciones festivas de mi familia y siempre éramos felices celebrando como familia. Yo me sentía muy feliz creciendo con parte de la cultura de mis ancestros. Ahora, enseño las mismas cosas a mi hija, Oriana.

A Sense of Community

In order to talk about our community, it helps to build up a vocabulary capable of describing the things that make a community what it is—the people, the land, and so on. Building this vocabulary will in turn enable us to expand on the topic of community by diving into the past tense in Spanish. Storytelling is a huge part of what gives us a sense of community, because shared stories bring us together, and stories are often told in the past tense. But first, let's take a look at the vocabulary list below.

la comunidad	the community
la sociedad	the society
la ciudad	the city
el pueblo	the town
la tierra	the land

la diversidad	the diversity
la amistad	the friendship
la relación	the relationship
la población	the population
la gente	the people (this is always feminine and singular and is never written in the plural form)
el vecindario	the neighborhood
los vecinos	the neighbors
el evento	the event
el área	the area
apoyar	to support
ayudar	to help
convivir	to coexist
mejorar	to improve

These words should give you a foundation on which to start communicating about your community, or whatever community you may find yourself in. The verbs above are all regular verbs, meaning they do not have irregular conjugation patterns. Now that you have built a foundation of vocabulary, we are ready to start covering the past tense.

A Trip Down Memory Lane: Describing Your Past

Any time you share about your childhood experiences, a favorite memory, or something that happened during your workday, you use verbs in the past tense. Although you are still likely working on mastering present-tense verbs, it is a good time in your Spanish-language journey to begin familiarizing yourself with the past tense too. This will also take some time to master, but it's important to be able to express basic ideas like places you've lived or worked and what you did there. The past is often key to understanding the present, whether in terms of philosophy, history, or your personal biography.

The past tense in Spanish consists of two verb tenses: the preterite tense (*el pretérito*) and the imperfect tense (*el imperfecto*). I personally think these tenses can easily become overcomplicated; it can seem like a lot of information, and the substantial number of irregular verbs in the preterite tense can make it seem like a heavy topic. However, you can rest assured that we'll start out slow and simple, with an explanation that I've found works well with Spanish students.

Before we get into how to conjugate Spanish verbs in the various past tenses, let's start by highlighting the overall differences between the preterite and the imperfect. Both are used to describe the past, but for different types of past events. Let's first look at some examples in English and Spanish so that we can discuss what each tense is used for.

table 9.1

		PRETERITE VS. IMPERFECT TENSE	
			EXAMPLES
PRETERITE		The preterite tense is used to express an event in the past with a clear start and end point.	Yo **nací** el 18 de febrero. (I **was born** on February 18th.) Mi familia y yo **fuimos** a Florida. (My family and I **went** to Florida.)
IMPERFECT		The imperfect tense is used to express an ongoing or repeated action in the past.	Yo siempre **jugaba** con juguetes. (I always **used to play** with toys.) Yo **era** una niña muy tranquila. (I **was** a very calm child.)

Table 9.1 shows some examples of sentences in English with Spanish translations, divided into the preterite and the imperfect. Based on these examples, you can see that, generally, the preterite is used to talk about very specific moments in the past that have clear beginning and ending points. The two sentence examples align with that concept; being born and going to a destination are moments that clearly happened and ended at specific points in the past.

The imperfect examples represent actions in the past that were more ongoing and did not have such cut-and-dried start and end points. For example, if you used to play with a certain toy as a child, that obviously happened in the past, but not at one specific point in time; it likely happened repeatedly in an ongoing way that is now over. The same goes for the example of being a calm child. In this case, it describes a characteristic rather than a specific situation, but there isn't a clear beginning or end point for someone having that trait.

Another way I like to explain the difference between these two verb tenses is in terms of a timeline. Something in the preterite would be easy to pinpoint on a timeline: it happened at this single point. The imperfect, however, would be difficult to put on a timeline as a dot; it would be more like a shaded area that represents a span of time: this was happening for an extended period in the past. Figure 9.1 illustrates what I mean.

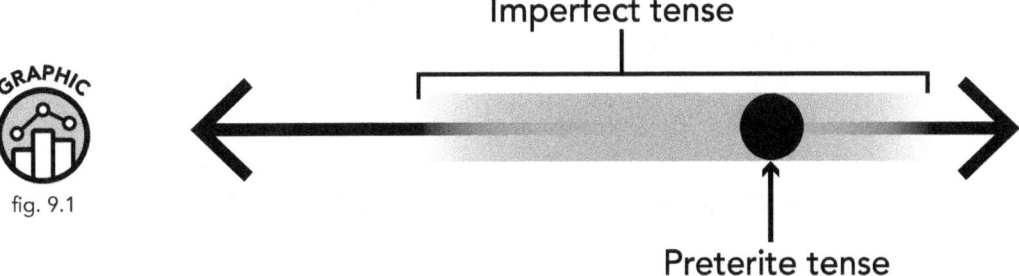

fig. 9.1

Before we get into conjugating these verbs in Spanish, here are some examples I usually start with in English to show how these tenses work together:

» **"While it was raining, the tree fell over."**
The action of rain does not have a clear beginning or ending, which is why the imperfect tense is used to describe it. The tree falling over, however, happened at a very specific moment during the rainstorm, which is why that action uses the preterite tense. See how the rain is the shaded area on the timeline, and the tree falling is the dot on the timeline?

» **"My mom called me when I was in my room listening to music."**
The action of my mom calling me is a specific interruption to my listening of music, which is why "my mom called me" requires the preterite tense. My action of listening to music was for an extended period of time that was ongoing, which is why it requires the imperfect tense.

» **"While I was walking to school, I tripped and fell."**
The action of walking to school is in the imperfect tense; you have a general idea of when that action took place in the past, but nothing specific because it was an ongoing action for an extended period of time. However, the moment when I tripped and fell was a specific point in the whole process of walking to school.

You've seen the basics of how the preterite and imperfect can work together to tell a story about the past, and toward the end of this chapter we will get more into how to use these two tenses together. But first we are going to take it one step at a time.

Figure 9.2 shows an acronym that is often used to teach the uses of the preterite and imperfect. Acronyms can make it easier for learners to remember tricky grammar concepts, and the one I've used in this case is SIMBA CHEATED. Don't ask me where this came from. I know it's strange; I came across it when I first started teaching Spanish and I never found anything better, so here we are. You'll see that SIMBA represents the uses for the preterite tense and CHEATED represents the uses for the imperfect tense.

PRETERITE

S ingle actions
I nterruptions
M ain events
B eginning actions
A rrivals/departures

IMPERFECT

C haracteristics/descriptions
H ealth
E motion
A ge
T ime
E ndless activities
D ate

fig. 9.2

Notice that the items in the SIMBA acronym for the preterite tense do indeed refer to events that have a very clear start and finish and that could be clearly pinpointed on a timeline. Let's look at a sentence example for each letter in SIMBA:

Single actions	**Fui** a la tienda y después **limpié** la casa.	**I went** to the store and afterward **I cleaned** the house.
		This is a series of two single actions that were completed at different times.
Interruptions	Mientras estaba durmiendo, mi amiga **llegó** a mi casa.	While I was sleeping, my friend **arrived** at my house.
		The verb *llegó* is in the preterite tense, and it interrupted the other ongoing action ("I was sleeping"), which is actually in the imperfect tense. Later in this chapter we will learn more about how both tenses can work together.

Main events	El héroe **se murió**.	The hero **died**. This example shows how the preterite tense can be used to sum up main events of a story.
Beginning actions	El maestro **comenzó** a hablar.	The teacher **started** to speak. This example shows the use of the preterite with verbs that give the meaning of a beginning, such as the start of an action.
Arrivals/ departures	Yo **salí** a las ocho ayer.	I **went out** at eight o'clock yesterday. This is an example of a departure, but I could also use it for an arrival, such as "Yo **llegué** a las ocho ayer," or "I **arrived** at eight o'clock yesterday."

Each of the sentences above using the preterite tense has an action with a clear beginning and end that could be pinpointed on a timeline. Now, for the imperfect tense, look at the CHEATED sentence examples below.

Characteristics/ descriptions	Yo **era** una niña tranquila.	I **was** a calm child. Traits or characteristics someone had in the past can't be pinned down to one brief moment; they were ongoing.
Health	Yo **estaba** enferma.	I **was** sick. If you were sick, it was likely for an extended period, and illness doesn't always have a crystal-clear beginning or end. Since you can't quite pin it on a timeline, you the need the imperfect tense.
Emotion	Yo **estaba** triste.	I **was** sad. Similar to sickness, the emotions you felt in the past were typically happening for an ongoing period of time.

| 9 | Community Connections

Age	En esta foto, yo **tenía** ocho años.	In this picture, I **was** eight years old. Although each age lasts for a year, it is an ongoing period in the past, which is why it generally requires the imperfect. You cannot designate your entire year as an eight-year-old with one dot on a timeline.
Time	**Eran** las ocho de la noche.	It **was** eight o'clock at night. When talking about time in the past, the imperfect tense is always used, even for specific times like eight o'clock.

Time is generally an ongoing thing (in the sense that 8:00 p.m. happens every day, for example), and often when we talk about time in the past, it is to set the scene of a story. This is where the imperfect and preterite tenses can work together. For example: *Eran las ocho de la noche cuando mi papá llegó.* This means "It was eight o'clock at night when my dad arrived." The verb *llegó* is in the preterite tense because his arrival interrupts the ongoing action, which in this case is the description of the time that sets the scene. This can be confusing, because we don't think of a particular time as ongoing; it may be easiest to think of this rule about using the imperfect tense for time as an "irregular" rule, because it doesn't completely conform to our ideas about time.

Endless activities	Siempre **jugaba** afuera.	I always **played** outside. This is an example of something I did a lot that doesn't have clear starting and ending points.
Date	**Era** el quince de agosto.	It **was** August 15th. We use the imperfect tense to communicate a past date, because usually we are stating the date to set the scene for a description of events that happened on that day.

Now that we have an overall view of the differences between the preterite and the imperfect, we are ready to start learning the preterite and imperfect conjugation endings, shown on the verb charts in table 9.2.

Conjugating the Preterite and Imperfect Tenses

table 9.2

Preterite -AR

yo	é	nosotros/as	amos
tú	aste	vosotros/as	asteis
él ella usted	ó	ellos ellas ustedes	aron

Imperfect -AR

yo	aba	nosotros/as	ábamos
tú	abas	vosotros/as	abais
él ella usted	aba	ellos ellas ustedes	aban

Preterite -ER/-IR

yo	í	nosotros/as	imos
tú	iste	vosotros/as	isteis
él ella usted	ió	ellos ellas ustedes	ieron

Imperfect -ER/-IR

yo	ía	nosotros/as	íamos
tú	ías	vosotros/as	íais
él ella usted	ía	ellos ellas ustedes	ían

Now that you have the endings for regular verbs in the preterite and imperfect tenses, let's review a few workbook-style exercises to further understand how these tenses work.

Preterite

1. Yo __comí__ (comer) un sandwich ayer.
   (I ate a sandwich yesterday).

This sentence uses the preterite tense because it describes a single action that had a clear beginning and end.

2. Ella __llegó__ (llegar) el sábado.
   (She arrived on Saturday).

This sentence uses the preterite tense because it is communicating an arrival, which can be pinpointed on a timeline.

3. Mi hermano __rompió__ (romper) la ventana.
   (My brother broke the window).

This sentence uses the preterite tense because it describes a single action with a clear beginning and end.

Imperfect

4. Ella siempre __tenía__ (tener) muchos amigos.
   (She always had a lot of friends).

This sentence uses the imperfect tense because having had a lot of friends in the past is not something that can be pinpointed on a timeline.

5. Los niños __jugaban__ (jugar) afuera mucho.
   (The children played outside a lot).

This sentence uses the imperfect because it is an action that happened repeatedly in the past and does not have a clear start or end point.

6. Yo __estaba__ (estar) cansada.
   (I was tired).

This sentence uses the imperfect because it describes a feeling someone had in the past, and it is not clear how long it went on.

There are certain keywords that tend to be accompanied by either the preterite or the imperfect. For the preterite, a few examples would be *entonces* (then), *ayer* (yesterday), *una vez* (one time), and similar words that imply that an event had a specific and clear occurrence in time. For the imperfect, some examples would be *siempre* (always), *cada semana* (every week), *frecuentemente* (frequently), and similar words that imply that an event was ongoing or repeated in the past with less specific points of occurrence.

Irregular Verbs in the Preterite and Imperfect

As is the case with every verb tense we have covered, there are some notable irregular verbs that require our attention. First I'll introduce you to the easier tense in terms of irregular verbs—the imperfect. Luckily, the imperfect tense has only three irregular verbs: *ir* (to go), *ser* (to be), and *ver* (to see). The charts are shown in table 9.3.

IMPERFECT IRREGULAR VERBS

ir = to go			
yo	**iba**	nosotros/as	**íbamos**
tú	**ibas**	vosotros/as	**ibais**
él / ella / usted	**iba**	ellos / ellas / ustedes	**iban**

ser = to be			
yo	**era**	nosotros/as	**éramos**
tú	**eras**	vosotros/as	**erais**
él / ella / usted	**era**	ellos / ellas / ustedes	**eran**

ver = to see			
yo	**vi**	nosotros/as	**vimos**
tú	**viste**	vosotros/as	**visteis**
él / ella / usted	**vio**	ellos / ellas / ustedes	**vieron**

table 9.3

Now let's talk about the preterite tense. I think the preterite tense is one of the most challenging verb tenses to master, because there are many irregular verbs. I am not going to cover every single irregular verb in the preterite tense. Instead, I'll stick with the most high-frequency ones that I think you would need to communicate at a beginner level when talking about the past. The verbs we will cover are presented in table 9.4: *ir* (to go), *ser* (to be), *hacer* (to do/make), *dar* (to give), *ver* (to see), and *decir* (to say/tell). And yes, *ir* and *ser* are the same conjugation in the preterite tense!

table 9.4

PRETERITE IRREGULAR VERBS			
ir/ser = to go / to be			
yo	**fui**	nosotros/as	**fuimos**
tú	**fuiste**	vosotros/as	**fuisteis**
él ella usted	**fue**	ellos ellas ustedes	**fueron**
hacer = to do / to make			
yo	**hice**	nosotros/as	**hicimos**
tú	**hiciste**	vosotros/as	**hicisteis**
él ella usted	**hizo**	ellos ellas ustedes	**hicieron**
dar = to give			
yo	**di**	nosotros/as	**dimos**
tú	**diste**	vosotros/as	**disteis**
él ella usted	**dio**	ellos ellas ustedes	**dieron**

186 SPANISH QUICKSTART GUIDE

PRETERITE IRREGULAR VERBS

ver = to see

yo	**vi**	nosotros/as	**vimos**
tú	**viste**	vosotros/as	**visteis**
él / ella / usted	**vio**	ellos / ellas / ustedes	**vieron**

decir = to say / to tell

yo	**dije**	nosotros/as	**dijimos**
tú	**dijiste**	vosotros/as	**dijisteis**
él / ella / usted	**dijo**	ellos / ellas / ustedes	**dijeron**

With so many irregular conjugations in the preterite tense, the only strategy I have to offer you is memorization. However, you can see in the charts that many of the irregular conjugations have similar conjugation patterns, so hopefully that will help. I definitely recommend that you make time to practice your preterite conjugations outside of this book, because the verbs I have provided are intended to give you a solid foundation on which to get started.

To help you with your mastery of the preterite and imperfect tenses, the book's Digital Asset library includes a practice worksheet to further reinforce everything you've just learned. You may want to refer back to this part of the chapter as you work through the exercises. Visit go.quickstartguides.com/spanish.

Making Sense of the Past

To truly get a deep understanding of the culture and values of a society, we must take a trip to the past. Past events have shaped the world we live in today, and understanding the past can help us better understand why we are who we are. Just as knowing your own history can enhance your understanding of your current situation, taking the time to educate yourself about the history of the people and culture whose language you are learning will help you better understand their worldview. This, in turn, can help you form stronger bonds with those people.

> Although this is not a history book, I feel a responsibility, as a white American author of a Spanish-language instruction book, to shed light on the history of the indigenous peoples of Latin America and to bring attention to the often-overlooked indigenous populations of these countries. That is why I have integrated bits and pieces of information on this topic when it has been relevant to the subject of this book. If you want your mastery of Spanish to be truly well-rounded, I encourage you to take on the responsibility of educating yourself about the history of what are now Spanish-speaking countries, and the issues that impact the people today.

History and Culture

Let's apply the concepts of the preterite and imperfect tenses to the topic of history and culture. In this section, you will get to see how these two tenses can interact with one another to tell a story. Naturally, this involves introducing some more vocabulary words:

Verbs

celebrar/festejar	to celebrate
representar	to represent
contar	to count, to tell (a story)
participar	to participate
valorar	to value
creer	to believe

Vocabulary terms

la reunión	the reunion/gathering
la tradición	the tradition
la cultura	the culture

la creencia	the belief
la religión	the religion
las canciones	the songs
los valores	the values
la ceremonia	the ceremony

Luckily, the verbs above are all regular verbs without any irregular conjugation patterns. This will help us see how the preterite and imperfect can work together without our having to handle the topic of irregular verbs at the same time.

Take a look at a few workbook-style exercises below that reflect the proper use of the preterite and imperfect tenses using the verbs above combined with some of the new vocabulary words we just covered.

1. **Imperfect**: Mi familia siempre __festejaba__ (festejar) la navidad con canciones y comida.

   Preterite: Mi familia __festejó__ (festejar) la navidad la semana pasada.

2. **Imperfect**: Cada domingo, nosotros __participábamos__ (participar) en una ceremonia religiosa.

   Preterite: Yo __participé__ (participar) en la celebración de mi amiga.

In these examples, you can see that the same verb can be used in the preterite or imperfect tense depending on what kind of action is being spoken of. Below, you will see more examples of how the preterite and imperfect tenses can be used on their own or combined in the same sentence depending on the idea that is being communicated. These examples will reference the history of the Aztec people, enabling you to learn a little about this ancient civilization while also studying the uses of the preterite and imperfect tenses.

Preterite Examples

1. Los aztecas (encontraron) un lago y allí (fundaron) la ciudad de Tenochtitlán.

(The Aztecs found a lake and there they founded the city of Tenochtitlán.)

2. Los españoles (mataron) a muchos aztecas.
(The Spanish killed many Aztec people.)

These two sentences show how the preterite tense can be used effectively. Notice that all the verbs that are circled are indeed preterite verb conjugations, as they reflect actions that could be clearly pinpointed on a timeline.

Imperfect Examples

1. Los aztecas **vivían** en las pirámides y **tenían** un sistema de agricultura muy avanzado.
(The Aztecs lived in pyramids and had a very advanced agricultural system).

2. El dios Huitzilopochtli **representaba** el sol, la guerra y el sacrificio.
(The god Huitzilopochtli represented the sun, war, and sacrifice).

The two examples above show how the imperfect tense can be used. The underlined verbs have imperfect verb conjugation endings, and all the verbs reflect actions that were either repeated or that were happening for an extended period in the past.

Preterite and Imperfect Examples

1. Los españoles **buscaban** oro cuando (encontraron) a los aztecas. (The Spanish were searching for gold when they found the Aztecs).

2. Los españoles (aprendieron) palabras en náhuatl, el idioma que **hablaban** los aztecas. (The Spanish learned words in Náhuatl, the language that the Aztec people spoke).

These examples show how the preterite and imperfect tenses can work together in the same sentence. The imperfect verbs (underlined) are actions that were ongoing in the past, and the preterite verbs (circled) describe actions that happened at more specific points in time that interrupt or intersect with the other ongoing (imperfect tense) action.

Mastering the preterite and imperfect can take a lot of effort. However, having a basic grasp of how these verb tenses work is important so that you can start noticing how they are used in the real world, as that will help you understand their uses even more. At the very least, learning a few high-frequency verb conjugations that you'll need to communicate basic ideas about the past will get you a long way in your conversational Spanish, while you continue to work on mastering the preterite and imperfect.

Expressing Emotion

Bringing up the past, whether in terms of personal experience, broader history, or both, often brings up feelings. Being able to express those feelings is important work that we all have to do as humans in order to truly empathize with and understand others. It only makes sense, then, that newcomers to the Spanish language will need to be able to communicate about feelings at some point.

We have already touched on the topic of conveying feelings by learning how to answer the question ¿*Cómo estás?* The ways you have learned to answer, such as "Estoy bien" or "Estoy más o menos," are ways to communicate your feelings in the present. When we covered *ser* versus *estar* in chapter 7, we learned how the verb *estar* is used to express feelings. Now let's learn some more emotions that can be used to communicate how you are feeling.

las emociones	emotions
estar de buen humor	to be in a good mood
estar de mal humor	to be in a bad mood
feliz	happy
triste	sad
enojado(a)	angry
emocionado(a)	excited
aburrido(a)	bored
tranquilo(a)	calm
avergonzado(a)	embarrassed
preocupado(a)	worried
ansioso(a)	anxious
asustado(a)	frightened
decepcionado(a)	disappointed

cansado(a)	tired
confundido(a)	confused
sorprendido(a)	surprised

These vocabulary terms can, of course, be combined with the present tense to answer the question *¿Cómo estás?* For example, you could say "Estoy de mal humor" or "Estoy muy triste." However, these terms can also be combined with other verb tenses, such as the past tense, to describe your feelings in the past.

You may recall from our overview of the preterite and imperfect tenses that the first *E* in SIMBA CHEATED stands for *emotion*. Generally, it will be the imperfect tense that's used to describe emotion in the past, because emotion is an ongoing thing that doesn't have clearly delineated starting and ending times. Therefore, you would say something like "Yo estaba muy preocupada," meaning "I was very worried." Another verb you can use to describe how you are feeling is the reflexive verb *sentirse*, which means "to feel." Take a look at the conjugation chart in table 9.5.

table 9.5

sentirse = to feel			
yo	**me sentía**	nosotros/as	**nos sentíamos**
tú	**te sentías**	vosotros/as	**os sentíais**
él ella usted	**se sentía**	ellos ellas ustedes	**se sentían**

Because we tend to use the imperfect tense for emotion, the reflexive verb *sentirse* is conjugated in the verb chart in the imperfect tense. Therefore, if I was feeling anxious in the past, I would say "Me sentía ansiosa." The verb chart also shows how you would conjugate a reflexive verb in the past tense. Just like with the present tense, you drop the reflexive pronoun *se* off the end of the verb, and it moves to the front of the verb as a reflexive pronoun, followed by the verb, which is conjugated the same as any other regular past-tense imperfect verb.

Now that you are familiar with the preterite and imperfect tenses and have learned more about how to express emotion, you will be able to start communicating with others and expressing yourself about past experiences. This will help you build strong connections with others in Spanish, as being able to share in the telling of stories is something unique to the human experience.

Chapter Recap

In this chapter, our grammar and vocabulary were focused on concepts related to community. These included the following:

» Building a foundation of community-related communication with some new vocabulary terms and verbs.

» Studying the past tense, a major grammatical concept necessary for talking about our own histories as well as the histories of our communities. We learned that there are two verb tenses that make up the past tense in Spanish: the preterite and the imperfect.

» Using the preterite and the imperfect to describe events and ideas from the past, which enhances our ability to communicate about ourselves and our communities.

» Learning more vocabulary words related to culture and history, which alongside new tenses and verbs enable us to learn about the past, and emotion-related vocabulary to better express feelings about current and past events when storytelling.

I hope you recognize how much work you have done to get to this point in the book—learning the past tense is no easy feat. However, I'm confident you'll be able to "overcome the past" in no time because of your dedication to learning Spanish!

PART IV

THE BIGGER PICTURE

The first three parts of this book focused on building your understanding of the basics of the Spanish language. You have learned many of the essential grammatical concepts, building everyday communication skills related to yourself and the familiar and comfortable everyday environments that you find yourself in. With that repertoire of essential vocabulary and grammar established, and with the tools to navigate the basics of everyday life in mind, we are ready to venture out of our comfort zones and into the topic of traveling. Traveling in another language will push you not only linguistically, but personally and culturally. So buckle up, because we are about to take your Spanish to new territories.

| 10 |
Places We Visit

Though much of our daily life can be defined by our routines, there are countless ways to venture out of our comfort zones, whether it's trying a new restaurant, visiting an unfamiliar city or country, or, yes, learning a language. These unknown territories can give life new depth or additional meaning. Entering unknown territory can take many forms, but in this chapter we will focus on travel: learning how to communicate about places we have visited and would like to visit. We will also cover weather, geography, and the clothing we'll need to prepare for those conditions—plus other necessary to-do-list items that come up when we're traveling abroad. So pack your bags and get ready to go!

Chapter Overview

By the end of this chapter, you will be able to do the following:
- » Describe places you have visited and would like to visit.
- » Conjugate the present perfect tense and review the conditional tense to communicate things you have already done as well as things you would like to do in the future.
- » Review essential vocabulary and phrases related to weather, geography, and clothing.
- » Talk about required to-do-list items when traveling abroad, such as passports and foreign currency.
- » Recognize the passive voice when it is used to express requirements.

For an overview of the concepts that we will be working with in this chapter, listen to the QuickClip and follow along with the script below. You will hear the speakers describe where they live as well as other places they have visited and would like to visit in the future.

In this clip, you can hear Valentín from Argentina and Mónica from Colombia describe the typical weather and geographical highlights of their countries, and discuss their travel experiences.

To watch the QuickClip, use the camera on your mobile phone to scan the QR code or visit the link below.

www.quickclips.io/spanish-13

Valentín:	Hola, vos sos de Colombia, ¿verdad?
Mónica:	Sí, yo soy de Colombia.
Valentín:	¡Qué lindo! ¿Y cómo es Colombia?
Mónica:	Pues, es un país muy bonito. Hay muchas montañas y playas, también muchas plantaciones de café. El clima es muy variado. Hay lugares en los que hace mucho calor, y otros en los que hace frío. También hay mucha lluvia. ¿Cómo es tu país, Valentín?
Valentín:	Mi país es hermoso. En Argentina tenemos climas cálidos en el norte, fríos en el sur. Tenemos montañas, sierras, cataratas y lugares con mucha nieve. También tenemos playas muy bonitas para disfrutar. ¿Has viajado a otro país?
Mónica:	Sí, he viajado a Panamá y a Perú. Son países muy bonitos también. ¿Y tú?
Valentín:	No, no he viajado fuera de Argentina. Pero algún día me gustaría conocer Estados Unidos. Espero poder sacar una visa de turista para poder ir a conocer allá.
Mónica:	¡Excelente! Me gustaría ir a los Estados Unidos contigo. ¿Me invitas?
Valentín:	Por supuesto.

Places We've Been and Places We'll Be

Many of us have a bucket list of places we would like to see, and perhaps your interest in learning another language indicates an interest in destinations where you will be able to put your Spanish to the test. Spending time living in a Spanish-speaking country was the best thing for my Spanish, and if you're able to travel abroad, I highly recommend taking that opportunity. But even if you don't have any trips planned, being able to talk about places you've been, and places you'll go in the future, is a major conversational skill. In this section, we'll go over how to utilize the present perfect tense to communicate places you have already visited, and we'll review the conditional tense to communicate places you would like to visit someday.

Before we dive into verb tenses, it is worth mentioning that the names of countries are not always the same in other languages as they are in English. This was something that surprised me when I was learning Spanish—you mean to tell me that the name of a country is not a universal thing? I wish it were, but that's not the case, so below I've provided a list of a few countries that have different names in Spanish. Note that some are spelled the same but pronounced differently, because you would use Spanish pronunciation rules. For instance, China, Argentina, and Cuba are spelled the same in English and Spanish, but vary in pronunciation.

Los Estados Unidos	The United States
Espanã	Spain
La República Dominicana	The Dominican Republic
Alemania	Germany
Brasil	Brazil
Canadá	Canada
Egipto	Egypt
Marruecos	Morocco
Tailandia	Thailand
Francia	France
Irlanda	Ireland
Los Países Bajos	The Netherlands
Polonia	Poland

Obviously, this is not a comprehensive list. For any countries that you want to add to your Spanish vocabulary, do an internet search so you can learn them! The names of continents apply here as well. For example, *Europe* in Spanish is *Europa*.

The Present Perfect

With countries in mind, let's examine how to discuss places you have or haven't visited. For example, you might say "I have traveled to Mexico" or "I haven't visited Colombia." The word "have" combined with a past participle such as "traveled" forms the present perfect. Let's look at how the present perfect is formed in Spanish.

table 10.1

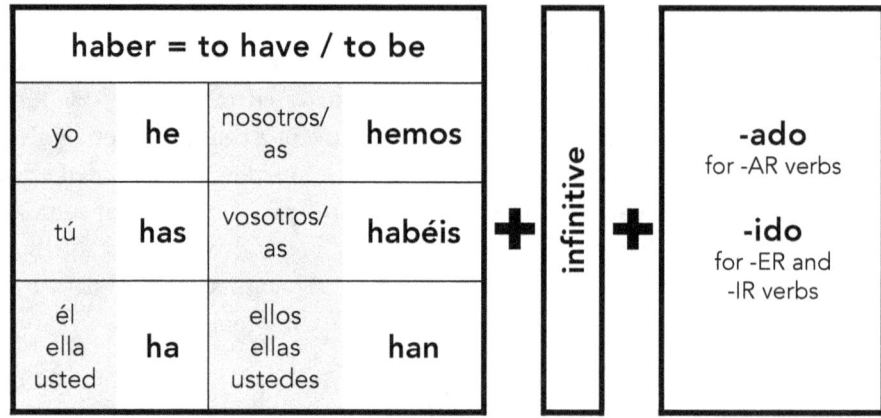

The verb chart in table 10.1 shows the present-tense conjugations for the verb *haber*, which is an auxiliary verb. To form the present perfect, we need a present-tense conjugation of *haber* followed by a verb in its past participle form.

It might seem strange that *haber* is conjugated in the present tense, given that we are using it to communicate about the past. But think about it: we do the same thing in English. In the present tense in English, I can say "I have a dog." *Have* is in the present tense (it's "have," not "had"). If I say in English, "I have traveled to Mexico," the verb *have* is still there. The past participle, "traveled," is what communicates that this action has already happened.

Luckily, those past participles are quite easy to form in Spanish. As you can see in the chart, for -AR verbs you drop the ending off the infinitive form and add *ado*, and for -ER and -IR verbs, you drop those endings off the infinitive and add *ido*. For example, the verb *viajar* would become *viajado* in its past participle form. The verb *comer* would become *comido*, and the verb *vivir* would become *vivido*.

Look at a few workbook-style exercises below showing how to put the present-tense conjugation of the verb *haber* together with a past participle to form the present perfect tense.

1. Yo (viajar) a Madrid. ____Yo he viajado a Madrid.____

2. Ella (visitar) Argentina. ____Ella ha visitado Argentina.____

3. Nosotros no (ir) a España. ____Nosotros no hemos ido a España.____

Keep in mind that there are some irregular past participles in Spanish. There are twelve "main" past participles that are normally taught in a basic Spanish language course. Here are those twelve verbs with their infinitives and the irregular past participle form:

abrir → abierto	to open → opened
cubrir → cubierto	to cover → covered
decir → dicho	to say → said
escribir → escrito	to write → written
hacer → hecho	to (do/make) → (done/made)
morir → muerto	to die → died
poner → puesto	to (put/set/place) → (put/set/placed)
romper → roto	to break → broken
resolver → resuelto	to resolve → resolved
satisfacer → satisfecho	to satisfy → satisfied
ver → visto	to see → seen
volver → vuelto	to return → returned

Although this list is pretty comprehensive, keep in mind that you will see some other irregular past participles of less commonly used verbs that are not in this list. Also, some of these verbs can have a prefix but would still take the irregular past participle listed above. For example, the prefix *des* added to the verb *cubrir* gives us the word *descubrir* (meaning "to discover"), so as a past participle it would become *descubierto*.

Of course, the present perfect isn't only for communicating about where we've traveled. Let's look at a few sentence examples of other ideas we can express using the present perfect.

No **he comido** en el nuevo restaurante.	I haven't eaten at the new restaurant.
¿**Has limpiado** tu cuarto hoy?	Have you cleaned your room today? (informal)
Nosotros **hemos visto** muchas películas.	We have seen a lot of movies.

In each sentence, the present perfect tense is bolded. I also want to point out that example number 3 uses an irregular past participle found in the list above.

The present perfect can be used to describe a lot of things you have and haven't done, so be sure to practice this in other contexts when it's appropriate. Now that you're familiar with this tense and can communicate places you've been to and visited, let's review the conditional tense so we can also communicate our future bucket list wishes.

Places I'd Like to Go and Things I'd Like to Do

Back in part III, we learned how to conjugate the conditional tense, which is used to talk about hypothetical events: things that might happen or that you'd like to happen. Communicating about places you'd like to visit in the future requires use of this tense, so let's briefly revisit this concept. For a review of the conditional conjugation endings, see chapter 8.

To use the conditional to communicate places you'd like to visit and things you'd like to do, you will need to use a two-verb construction. The first verb will be *gustar* conjugated in the conditional tense, and the second verb will be an infinitive. Consider the examples below.

Me gustaría visitar Europa.	I would like to visit Europe.
Nos gustaría viajar por toda Latinoamérica.	We would like to travel through all of Latin America.
A mi amiga le gustaría nadar en el mar.	My friend would like to swim in the ocean.

The verb *gustar* conjugated in the conditional gives the meaning that you would like to do something, and the infinitive clarifies what it is that you would like to do.

Another way to communicate things you want to do is with the phrase *tener ganas de*, which roughly means "to have the desire to" (or not to) do something. To form a sentence this way, conjugate the verb *tener* in the present tense (see chapter 4). You also need an infinitive to communicate the action you desire to perform. For example:

Tengo ganas de ir a México	This basically means "I have a desire to go to Mexico."
Tengo muchas ganas de viajar a todos los países de Latinoamérica.	This roughly means that I *really* want to travel to all the countries in Latin America.

I say "roughly" because the word *ganas* is one of those words that doesn't have a perfect one-to-one translation into English. The word by itself simply means "desire," so if you say "Tengo ganas," you're literally saying you have desire, which in English would more commonly be communicated as wanting to do something, or feeling like doing something. You can use the phrase "tener ganas de" to communicate pretty much anything you feel like doing—or don't feel like doing. For example, one common phrase is "No tengo ganas de hacer nada," meaning "I don't feel like doing anything."

In Spanish we can use double negatives, so it's correct to say you don't want to do nothing.

If you plan to travel to a Spanish-speaking country, you'll want to find the *ganas* to continue to the next section, so you can properly prepare for whatever destination you have in mind!

What to Pack

When making travel plans, it helps to preview the weather conditions and overall geography of your destination. This will help you decide what types of activities you might like to try out and what you'll need to pack to be properly prepared. In this section, we'll cover essential terms related to geography, weather, and clothing so that you can build your communication skills related to these topics.

Geography

Before we can pack our suitcases, we need to take the time to educate ourselves about the geography and weather of our destination. Geography is an important factor informing our clothing choices. For example, is there a beach to swim at, or a mountain to ski down? Is my destination in the northern or southern hemisphere, and what season is that hemisphere in right now? Here are some common geography terms:

el hemisferio	the hemisphere
las montañas	the mountains
el desierto	the desert
el bosque	the forest
el río	the river
el lago	the lake

la playa	the beach
el mar/océano	the sea/ocean

Other geography-related words that are useful to know are the cardinal directions. They help us communicate where these geographical features are (as well as what direction to head in when we're looking for a specific site). For example, are you going to be visiting the southern hemisphere? In Spanish, that would be *el hemisferio sur*. Is the beach located in the northern part of the country, and the mountains in the south? Figure 10.1 shows the cardinal directions in Spanish.

fig. 10.1

Of course, just because there is a beach doesn't mean you'll be able to swim there; you might need to make sure you're visiting at the right time of year to enjoy certain geographical elements, or that the weather is cooperating with your plans once you get there.

Rain or Shine

Becoming familiar with weather terms and phrases in Spanish will not only help you pack your suitcase, but it will help you communicate with the locals. Who doesn't love small talk about the weather? And if weather conditions suddenly change, you'll be able to understand when that news is conveyed to you.

First, let's take a moment to learn the difference between two very similar Spanish words related to weather: *el clima* and *el tiempo*. *El clima* refers to climate, and that's easy to remember, as it's a cognate. The word *tiempo*, however, looks like the word *time*. *Tiempo* can indeed mean "time," but it can also mean "weather." The words *clima* and *tiempo* can be synonymous in certain situations, but usually *clima* refers to the general weather conditions of an area, and *tiempo* refers to temporary or current weather conditions of a specific location.

The vocabulary list below shows some common components of weather.

la lluvia	the rain
la nieve	the snow
el sol	the sun
las nubes	the clouds
el viento	the wind

These terms will help you describe general weather conditions, but there's also the matter of asking and answering questions about the weather. You can see that the question "¿Cómo es el clima?" uses the verb *ser*, which usually indicates more permanent conditions; this accords with the concept that climate isn't as fast-changing as weather. For example, in the southern United States, the climate is generally warm, or "El clima es generalmente cálido."

To address the more immediate question about temporary forms of weather—a cold front moving in, a heavy rainstorm, and so on—the question in Spanish is phrased "¿Qué tiempo hace?" which roughly translates to "What's the weather?" Here are some phrases that can answer that question (or just inform someone of the weather, even if they haven't asked about it):

Hace (sol/frío/calor/viento).	It's (sunny/cold/hot/windy).
Hace (#) grados.	It's (#) degrees.
Está (nublado/lloviendo/nevando).	It's (cloudy/raining/snowing).

It can be confusing that the question "¿Qué tiempo hace?" uses the verb *hacer*, which normally means "to do" or "to make." We have talked about the fact that not everything perfectly translates from one language to another, and this is a great example. In English, we ask, "What is the weather?" and we don't necessarily attach a verb to an adjective like "sunny" or "cold." The phrase *hace sol* in Spanish literally translates to "doing sun" or "making sun," which is an idea that can take some adjustment for English speakers.

The other common phrase, using *está*, might seem more intuitive for describing a current weather condition, as we have established that the verb *estar* is used to describe a temporary condition, and it translates into English more seamlessly to mean "it is"—cloudy, cold, and so on.

To make matters potentially more confusing, some weather conditions can be expressed using either the *hacer* or *estar* phrases. For example, *hace sol* and *está soleado* are interchangeable, as both communicate that the weather is sunny. But one phrase uses the word *sol* and the other *soleado*, because of the differing verbs. Keeping them straight may be tricky at first, but once you start hearing native speakers express weather conditions, these phrases will become more familiar.

Another aspect of weather is temperature, which raises some differences between the United States and other countries. As you are probably aware, the United States uses the Fahrenheit scale to measure temperature, while most other countries use Celsius. If you are great at math, you'll have no trouble figuring out the local temperature in Celsius when you're traveling abroad. But if mental math isn't your strong suit, all you really need to get by is a weather app that will give you the local temperature in Fahrenheit. Just remember that if you're in a country that uses Celsius and you hear someone say "Hace 25 grados hoy" (it's 25 degrees today), it's not as cold as it sounds!

Now that you're familiar with some geographical and weather terminology, you can better analyze the weather of your travel destination and consider what items you'll need to pack for a trip.

Weather-Ready Wardrobe

In chapter 8, we covered some basic clothing vocabulary and applied it to the topic of shopping. Now that we're talking about packing our suitcases, it's a great opportunity to revisit the topic of clothing and add some additional clothing words to our vocabulary. Take some time to go over the list below so that you're ready to pack your suitcase, which in Spanish is *empacar la maleta* or *hacer la maleta*.

la maleta	the suitcase
la mochila	the backpack
las sandalias	the sandals
las botas	the boots
los tenis	the tennis shoes
los calcetines	the socks
el traje de baño	the swimsuit
los guantes	the gloves
el abrigo	the coat
la bufanda	the scarf
las gafas / los lentes (de sol)	the (sun) glasses
el paraguas	the umbrella

The terms above are more specific to traveling and being prepared for certain weather conditions. For example, if you're traveling, you'll likely pack a *maleta*, and you might also bring a *mochila* to carry some personal items. The weather will play a factor in what footwear you'll need, as well as any accessories to keep you either warm or cool. There are many ways to say the word "sunglasses," but two common ones are *gafas de sol* and *lentes de sol*. You may also hear people refer to them simply as *gafas* or *lentes*, even though, technically, *gafas*, *lentes*, and even *anteojos* can also be used to refer to regular prescription eyeglasses. The last word I want to point out is the word for umbrella. Yes, it is correct that it has the masculine definite article *el* followed by *paraguas*, which appears to be feminine plural. This is one of those words that doesn't follow the regular pattern in which everything matches in gender and number. So one umbrella would be *el paraguas*, and multiple umbrellas would be *los paraguas*.

Another item you might want to pack, depending on the weather, is a hat. In Spanish there are several words for "hat," and it can get a bit confusing. Figure 10.2 shows some visual representations of the different words for hat.

fig. 10.2

el sombrero   **el gorro**   **la gorra**

Of the three words in figure 10.2, the easiest to remember is likely *el sombrero*. Most of us are already familiar with that word, as it is often used by English speakers. We might more closely associate the word with the stereotypical Mexican sombrero traditionally worn by members of a mariachi band. However, it can refer to any wide-brimmed hat. The other two words, *el gorro* and *la gorra*, can cause confusion since they are essentially the same word except that one is in the masculine form and the other in the feminine form. *El gorro* is more of a winter hat that is used to keep you warm, whereas *la gorra* is more of a cap, such as a baseball cap, typically used to shield you from the sun. I don't have any amazing tricks for remembering these words, but perhaps this might help: the English word "snow," when pronounced out loud, ends in an *o* sound, just like the word *el gorro*, which is the hat you would want to wear in snowy conditions.

Now that you have a wider vocabulary related to clothing, you can pack your suitcase! However, packing your suitcase is not the only thing you need to do before traveling abroad. We still have a few more action items to cover in the next section.

Traveling To-Do List

Packing isn't the only thing you need to do to prepare for a trip abroad. Planning to travel outside of the country comes with an extra level of responsibility and more to-do-list items. Generally speaking, you cannot just show up in another country and begin your vacation. So in this section we will talk about some of the important things that need to be taken care of prior to your departure.

Identity Check

If you are planning to set foot in a foreign country, you need the proper travel documents. Each country has its own set of required documents that enable you to enter as a tourist. Let's cover the essential vocabulary terms, and then we will discuss this further.

un pasaporte	a passport
una visa	a visa
una identificación nacional	a national ID

We are all familiar with a passport, and if you don't have one and plan to travel abroad, you need to book an appointment well in advance to be sure the passport will be ready in time for your trip. When I have traveled to Mexico, all I needed was my passport, and when I went through customs (*la aduana* in Spanish) the customs officer would stamp my passport, which served as my visa, permitting me to be in Mexico as a tourist for up to six months. Not every country is this easy; each has its own requirements. Some countries require you to obtain a visa before departing your home country, and the application and waiting process can take some time. So be sure to do your research ahead of time so that you don't get sent on the next flight back to your home country after trying to enter a country without the proper documents. It would also be a good idea to carry a form of national ID, such as a driver's license, as additional proof of your identity.

Impersonal *se*

If you were to investigate travel requirements online in Spanish, you would probably see use of the impersonal *se*. For one thing, it conforms to the tendency in Spanish to be less direct. It is also an efficient way to communicate things that everyone needs to do without literally saying "*You* need to do this." In English, an example that illustrates the meaning of the Spanish impersonal *se* would be "One needs a passport to enter the country." That same sentence in Spanish would be "Se necesita un pasaporte para entrar al país." The phrases "one needs" and "se necesita" both imply that anyone coming into the country will need a passport, but it does so without a direct reference or command. This works well for stating requirements that apply to anyone in the given situation.

To get a clearer idea of how the impersonal *se* can be used, take a look at these sentence examples:

Para viajar en avión, **se tiene** que usar una maleta.	To travel on a plane, one must use a suitcase.
Para ir a Europa, **se necesita** una visa.	To go to Europe, one needs a visa.
No **se puede** entrar al país sin un pasaporte.	One cannot enter the country without a passport.

The three examples above all use *se* accompanied by a third person singular present-tense conjugation. (For a review on conjugating verbs in the present tense, see chapter 4.) To further enforce this process of combining *se* and a third person singular conjugation, look at the workbook-style examples below.

1. Tener que usar un pasaporte: <u>Se tiene que usar un pasaporte.</u>

2. Necesitar empacar la maleta: <u>Se necesita empacar la maleta.</u>

The impersonal *se* is quite simple to form, and even if you aren't ready to put it into practice, I think it's important to be aware of its existence. *Se* can have a lot of meanings (remember, it is also a reflexive pronoun, as we learned in chapter 5), and that can be confusing for someone who is learning Spanish. I know it took me a while to get comfortable with it. But now that you are aware of the impersonal *se*, you can be on the lookout for its use in the real world, which will definitely help you assimilate it.

You're getting close to finally being ready to go on your trip, but you're missing one important thing. As we would say using the impersonal *se*, "¡Se necesita *dinero* para viajar!"

Keeping Up on Currency

If you're traveling abroad, I definitely recommend that you do some research ahead of time on what currency you'll need to use. A few Spanish-speaking countries have adopted the US dollar, but many others use their own form of currency. Also, exchange rates can change daily, so it's up to you to research and decide whether you should exchange some money at your local bank prior to traveling or wait until you get to your destination. This brings us to a variety of money-related vocabulary words:

la tarjeta de crédito	the credit card
el efectivo	the cash
la tasa de cambio	the exchange rate
la casa de cambio	the exchange house

First, if you plan to use your *tarjeta de crédito* abroad, make sure to find out whether there are extra fees involved, and keep in mind that some places (such as local markets) will not accept credit cards, so it's best to have some *efectivo* on hand. I personally recommend having some of the local money in pocket before you land at your destination. I tried to be very cautious as a foreigner living in Mexico; I felt I might draw a lot of attention to myself if I exchanged money at the airport upon arriving, so I always made sure I had some money already exchanged beforehand. Later I would go to a *casa de cambio* in the city to exchange more of my money, typically in smaller amounts to lower the risk. I was living on my own in Mexico at age eighteen, so everything I did was out of an abundance of caution.

Now let's talk about how to have a conversation with someone at a bank (*el banco*) or an exchange house so that you can express that you want to exchange your money. Take a look at the sentences below.

Me gustaría cambiar mis dólares a (insert name of foreign currency).	I would like to exchange my dollars for (foreign currency).
Quiero billetes de (amount).	I want bills of (amount).
Quiero monedas de (amount).	I want coins of (amount).

These phrases are really all you need to be able to exchange your money. If you wanted certain denominations or amounts of bills and coins, you could request that, but I usually just took whatever bills were given to me.

I think the most challenging thing for me to get used to was constantly having to do mental math to figure out how much things cost. When I lived in Mexico in 2012, one US dollar would get me about twelve Mexican pesos. So everywhere I went, I had to remind myself that something with a price of 150 pesos was not as expensive as it seemed.

If there is a foreign destination of high interest to you, I suggest researching the currency and the exchange rate, and I'd even recommend that you venture onto some online stores from that particular country so you can get used to seeing prices in its currency.

Now that you've checked all the boxes for traveling abroad, you are ready for takeoff … to the next chapter, at least!

Chapter Recap

In this chapter, we learned the essentials of travel planning in Spanish. This included the following:

» Introducing vocabulary related to geography, weather, identification, clothing, and money exchange.

» Using the past perfect verb tense to communicate about places we have already been and things we have already done.

» Reviewing the conditional tense to express things we would like to do in the future.

» Learning how the impersonal *se* can be used to state general requirements in a more indirect way that doesn't require a specific person as the object.

You are now prepared to make travel plans in Spanish! Your next step is to get ready to navigate and communicate in common traveling scenarios once you reach your chosen destination. I wish you a *buen viaje* (good trip)!

| 11 |
Navigating the Unknown

Visiting a new place as a tourist, whether you're relatively close to home or thousands of miles away, engages a different set of communication skills than those you need when spending time in your home environment. When you've lived in a place long enough to be familiar with it, there are plenty of things you take for granted; you tend to know where things are, how to get there, what resources are available, and so on. You probably aren't stopping to ask for directions very frequently in your day-to-day life, for example. But when you're visiting another place, all of that changes; you may be without your typical resources, whether it's your accumulated knowledge about the layout of a neighborhood, a dependable mode of transportation, or your ability to know what to look up on your smartphone when you need more information.

This chapter ventures further outside the realm of your everyday experience to build up those communication skills you need when you visit somewhere new—in this case, presumably a Spanish-speaking country where you haven't spent a lot of time. We'll look at navigating modes of transportation; the basics of giving and receiving directions, including the verb tense for commands; and some more vocabulary-building related to activities you might indulge in while traveling. Altogether, this chapter will help you get ready to start exploring the Spanish-speaking world and put your language skills to the test!

Chapter Overview

By the end of this chapter, you will be able to do the following:
» Review transportation vocabulary needed to navigate taking a taxi and other forms of public transportation.
» Give and receive basic directions, and understand how commands and two-verb constructions can be used to do so.
» Expand your vocabulary related to common travel activities.

» Use indirect object pronouns with the present tense to communicate recommendations.

For an overview of the concepts we will be working with in this chapter, listen to the QuickClip and follow along with the script below. You will hear the native speaker give basic directions to her favorite place in her city as well as what modes of transportation you will need to get there. She will make additional recommendations about what you shouldn't miss out on when visiting her city.

Listen to Luisa from Colombia describe how to get around her city. She will give you directions from her home to one of her favorite parks in town, as well as share recommendations about public transportation and food.

To watch the QuickClip, use the camera on your mobile phone to scan the QR code or visit the link below.

www.quickclips.io/spanish-14

Luisa: Hola, mi nombre es Luisa y soy de Bucaramanga, también conocida como la ciudad de los parques, así que les voy a indicar cómo llegar desde mi casa hasta el Parque Chicamocha. Es muy fácil. Lo primero que deben hacer es caminar dos cuadras desde mi casa hasta la estación colonial "Papi Quiero Piña." Ahí van a tomar un bus que los va a llevar hasta San Gil, pero le deben decir al chofer que se van a bajar en el Parque Chicamocha. Es muy importante que lleven dinero en efectivo ya que en Colombia no reciben tarjetas de débito o tarjetas de crédito para pagar el bus, deben pagarlo en efectivo. En el Parque Chicamocha les recomiendo comer arepas de choclo o arepas de maíz, que es una de las más populares de Bucaramanga, y también desde ahí van a poder apreciar el hermoso cañón de Chicamocha que es uno de los más bellos de Colombia y de los más grandes de Sudamérica.

Moving from Place to Place

I grew up in a small town that didn't have any type of public transportation or taxi service, so when I first started living in Mexico, one of my greatest anxieties was learning how to navigate the world of public transportation. Not only was I doing this on my own for the first time, but I was learning how to do it in my second language! Whether this territory is completely new to you or familiar from your everyday life, you can prepare for this topic by covering some verbs related to transportation in the vocabulary list below.

llegar	to arrive
*salir	to leave/depart
tomar (un taxi)	to take (a taxi)
subir (al autobús)	to get on (the bus)
bajarse (del taxi)	to get out of (the taxi)
caminar	to walk
parar	to stop
*estar lleno(a)	to be full
*estar retrasado(a)	to be delayed
manejar/*conducir	to drive

*These are irregular verbs. We covered *salir* in chapter 5 and *estar* in chapters 4 and 7. *Conducir* is addressed below.

Most of the verbs listed above are considered regular; the exceptions are *salir* and *estar*, which we have already learned. First I want to draw attention to two verb phrases on the list. *Estar lleno(a)* and *estar retrasado(a)* are both verbs that are followed by an adjective that can take the masculine or feminine form (as well as the singular or plural form). For example, if I was describing a bus that was delayed, I would say, "El autobús está retrasado." Since *autobús* is masculine, so is my adjective, *retrasado*. To describe the streets being full, I would say, "Las calles están llenas." You can see that because I used the feminine plural word *calles*, I needed the feminine plural word *llenas*. Although we covered the concept of gender agreement early in this book (see chapter 2), it is something that requires frequent review and practice to truly master.

While we're discussing transportation terms, let me draw your attention to the verbs that can mean "to drive." There are two verbs in Spanish that carry this meaning: *manejar* and *conducir*. The verb *manejar* can mean many things, such as "to drive," "to manage," "to handle," and so on, but when *manejar* is combined with something like *el carro*, it takes on the meaning of "to drive a car." It is a verb that follows a regular present-tense conjugation pattern. The second verb, *conducir*, is considered an irregular verb. You can see that *conducir* looks a lot like the English verb "to conduct," so it's obvious why this verb might make more sense to an English speaker. Because *conducir* is an irregular verb, I have provided the present-tense verb conjugation chart in table 11.1.

table 11.1

conducir = to drive			
yo	**conduzco**	nosotros/as	**conducimos**
tú	**conduces**	vosotros/as	**conducís**
él ella usted	**conduce**	ellos ellas ustedes	**conducen**

Now that you have a set of verbs to work with, we can add some additional words to our vocabulary related to the topic of transportation:

el auto/coche/carro	the car
el barco	the boat
la bicicleta	the bicycle
la parada (de autobús)	the (bus) stop
la estación (de tren)	the (train) station
el horario	the schedule
el boleto	the ticket
el mapa	the map
la ruta	the route

As you can see, there are several words for "car." I avoided using the word *carro* for years, until I finally figured out how to roll my *r*'s (which took literally years of practice). Preference for *auto*, *coche*, or *carro* can depend on the region, but don't sweat the differences too much; if you're still struggling to roll your *r*'s, you can use one of the others without sacrificing understanding.

MY TAKE

If you weren't feeling up to facing the double *r* when it was first introduced in chapter 1, now might be a good time to revisit this. You can find many helpful videos on YouTube that explain the proper placement of the tongue as well as the airflow needed to produce this sound. After watching some videos, I used to spend my morning drive to work trying to produce this sound on its own as well as in words like *carro* and *perro*. I eventually moved on to pronouncing those words in complete sentences. After lots of patience and practice, I have mostly mastered this sound. Remember, your tongue is a muscle, and it has practiced making the sounds of your native language for years; you can't expect this muscle to instantly learn a new movement.

Note that there are also some variances related to the word *autobús*. Clearly this is the Spanish word for "bus," but I want to warn you that not every Spanish speaker uses this word. For example, in the Caribbean, a common word for bus is *la guagua* (and there's a really fun song on YouTube called "La Guagua"). When I lived in Cuernavaca (in the Mexican state of Morelos), people referred to the bus as *la ruta*. Our vocabulary list above shows that *la ruta* means "route." However, it made sense to me that the bus was called *la ruta*, since buses have specific routes that they take. Also, it's worth mentioning that the word *tren* can refer to a traditional train or to some sort of subway. I've also seen a subway referred to as *el metro* in Spanish. However, if you simply use the words *autobús* or *tren*, you'll have no problem being understood by Spanish speakers. This is just another reminder that you should be prepared to learn completely different words for things depending on what area of the Spanish-speaking world you find yourself in.

Travel Talk: Communicating Transportation Needs

Let's build on those vocabulary words and go over some common phrases you might need in order to indicate your needs when taking transportation. This can be one of the most challenging topics to navigate in another language, because there is a lot at stake. After all, whether you're close to home or many miles away, you don't want to have a miscommunication and end up in the wrong destination (as I've done many times). The phrases below should be helpful in clarifying your travel options.

¿A qué hora sale (el tren)?	At what time does the (train) leave?
¿A qué hora llega (el tren)?	At what time does the (train) arrive?
¿Cuánto tiempo dura el viaje?	How long is the trip?

Quiero dos boletos para ir a _____.	I want two tickets to go to (destination).
¿Cuánto cuesta la tarifa / el pasaje?	How much is the fare?
Creo que este es mi asiento.	I believe this is my seat.
Estoy perdido(a).	I am lost.
Perdí mi boleto / el autobús.	I lost my ticket. / I missed the bus.
¿Cómo llego a _____?	How do I get to (destination)?

Always make sure to double-check that you are on the right route when getting on a bus, train, etc., in another country (or even, frankly, in your own!), or you can get very lost very quickly. This happened to me a few times, and it was not fun trying to figure out how to get back home when I had no idea where I had ended up. Do what I didn't do: always double-check by asking the driver, "¿Este (autobús/tren/etc.) llega a (destination)?"

For some practice with understanding public transportation information, check out the website metromadrid.es, where you can see real metro routes and information, all in Spanish. This is a great way to challenge your Spanish with a real-world resource!

The benefit of using public transportation is that even if you're alone, you're usually not completely isolated, as you tend to be surrounded by other people. However, there is one mode of transportation in which you may feel a lot more alone when trying to get to your destination, and for that reason it's one of the more intimidating forms of transportation, in my opinion: taxis.

Taxi Tips

If you're traveling in Latin America, you may decide a taxi is the best form of transportation for certain situations or destinations. If you choose to take a taxi, I caution you to put safety first. Always trust your gut, and never put yourself in an uncomfortable situation. If you are staying at a hotel, see if the hotel staff can call a taxi for you. If that's not possible, consider using an app like Uber. Or if you hail a taxi on your own, make sure it is radio-equipped, as that adds a level of security. My intention is not to scare anyone off from taking a taxi in Latin America; these practices are recommended anywhere you go, including your home country.

Some taxis in Latin America use a meter to calculate the cost of your ride. If your taxi does not have a meter, the driver will verbally give you a price. In these situations, you may want to negotiate, as some drivers try to overcharge—and if you do negotiate, do so *before* getting in the cab.

The taxi driver should pull up on the side of the road and roll down their window. You can then ask something like, "¿Cuánto cuesta para ir a _____?" ("How much does it cost to go to (destination)?") They will quote you a price. If you don't like the price, you can try saying, "¿Aceptaría menos?" ("Would you accept less?") or "¿Aceptaría (#)?" ("Would you accept (price)?"). Once you agree on a price, you can get into the taxi and be on your way! If you don't like the price they give you, or if they won't negotiate, I recommend saying "Gracias" and walking away. You can keep asking taxis until you get the price you're looking for. I don't recommend arguing to prove that you know what price they should actually be charging you (yet again, this was not my best moment). Also, remember that, as with any taxi ride, you don't necessarily need to provide your exact destination. If you want to be extra cautious, have them drop you off a block or two away from your hotel or house, or at a nearby store. If you want to tell your taxi driver to stop, just say, "Puede parar aquí, por favor," which means "You can stop here, please."

Need Directions?

When we are out and about in an area that primarily speaks another language, it's easy to run into major barriers when it comes to understanding directions. (Unfortunately, I have too many real-life experiences in this area.) Though map apps have immeasurably improved this situation, there are still times when you need to ask someone for extra assistance; maps, whether digital or old-fashioned paper, can be confusing or incomplete, or may refer to information that's not readily accessible where you are. (For that matter, even digital maps aren't always accessible, depending on your cell service.) This is all to say that it's best to have the basic language tools you need to ask for directions, just as you would when speaking your native language. Below is a list of some common direction words that I think will get you pretty far, no pun intended.

derecho / recto	straight
a la derecha (de)	to the right (of)
a la izquierda (de)	to the left (of)

en frente (de) / delante (de)	in front (of)
detrás (de)	behind (the de is for when something is behind something else)
al lado de	next to
al fondo	at the back
cerca (de)	close (to)
lejos (de)	far (from)
al otro lado	to/on the other side

For me, two of the most confusing and anxiety-causing words on this list have been *derecho*, meaning "straight," and *derecha*, meaning the directional word "right." When I was first learning Spanish, I did not appreciate the one-letter difference between these two completely different direction words! And to make matters worse, the ending of *derecha* can change if something masculine is being described. For example, *el lado derecho* would be "the right side." You can see that the *-a* changes to an *-o* to agree with the masculine word *lado*. The same applies to the word "left," *izquierda*. When combined with a masculine word, such as in *el lado izquierdo* ("the left side"), it can take on the masculine ending. I wish I had a really innovative way to help you remember these endings, but it's one of those things you'll just have to memorize—and, in the case of confusion between *derecho* and *derecha*, rely on context to clue you in or use the word *recto* instead (or simply rely on body language by pointing).

I also want to call attention to the word *al fondo*, which I learned when I was first living in Mexico and was still developing my Spanish abilities. I was in a store in downtown Cuernavaca, Morelos, and I needed to find a restroom. The first person I asked about the location of the restroom responded with "Al fondo." I was too embarrassed to tell them I didn't understand, so I said thank you and figured that if I asked someone else, I might get a response different enough for me to understand. The second person also responded with "Al fondo." Finally I approached a third person, and when he also said "Al fondo," I said, "Pero, ¿qué significa al fondo? ¡Todos me dicen al fondo!" You might be able to figure out my frustration: "But what does *al fondo* mean? Everyone tells me *al fondo*!" Luckily this man spoke English, and he explained that *al fondo* meant "to the back." I couldn't believe how thrown off I was in this situation because of one word I didn't know!

Basically, learning direction words is a lot of pure memorization and practice, and may involve some trial and error. But the more you use these words and phrases, the more naturally they will come. Here are some more words that can come in handy when giving or receiving directions:

una milla	a mile
un kilómetro	a kilometer
una cuadra	a block
una calle	a street
una avenida	an avenue

Keep in mind that the metric system is used in Spanish-speaking countries, so distances will be given in kilometers. Also, the words in the list with *una* in front of them, such as *una cuadra*, can be combined with other numbers to say things like "tres cuadras" ("three blocks") to communicate distance.

Now, if you haven't had enough fun with directions yet, things are about to get even more interesting. I am going to introduce some verbs that would commonly be used when giving directions.

doblar/hacer una vuelta	to turn
seguir	to follow / to keep going
parar	to stop
cruzar	to cross

Naturally, some of these verbs have irregular conjugation patterns. For example, *hacer* is a "go" verb, and seguir is a "go verb" and also a boot verb that has an *e*-to-*i* stem change. So far in this book we have mostly focused on the present tense. And although learning these verbs in the present tense is important, for this section you're going to see a few examples of a new verb tense: commands, also known as the imperative tense. When we give directions in English, we typically use a command. For example, in English we would say something like "Turn left. Keep going for three blocks. Then turn to the right." In English, commands use the infinitive form of the verb, such as "go" or "stop," which imply that I am telling "you" (or a group of people; whoever is receiving the command) to do that particular action. Spanish, on the other hand, has a separate set of conjugations for command verbs. Let's take a look.

Commands

In table 11.2, you can see there are two categories. The first, informal *tú* commands, consists of commands you would use with someone that you can address informally using *tú*. The second category, formal *usted* commands, consists of commands used with someone you need to address formally with *usted*. Most of the verb conjugations look pretty similar in each category, with slight variations in the verb endings: the *tú* commands are conjugated as if it were a third person singular present-tense conjugation, and the *usted* commands have the opposite ending than they would in present tense (meaning -AR verbs would take on the -ER/-IR endings, and -ER/-IR verbs would take on the -AR endings).

table 11.2

INFORMAL "TÚ" COMMANDS	FORMAL "USTED" COMMANDS
dobla a la derecha **turn** to the right	**doble** a la derecha **turn** to the right
haz una vuelta a la izquierda **make** a turn to the left	**haga** una vuelta a la izquierda **make** a turn to the left
sigue por dos cuadras **keep going** for two blocks	**siga** por dos cuadras **keep going** for two blocks
para en frente de la casa **stop** in front of the house	**pare** en frente de la casa **stop** in front of the house
cruza la avenida **cross** the avenue	**cruce** la avenida **cross** the avenue

The commands we've gone over so far are affirmative commands, which mean someone wants you to do that action. There are also negative commands, which tell you not to do something. To make *usted* commands negative, you simply need the word "no" in front of the verb conjugation that was shown in the previous chart. However, negative *tú* commands take on the opposite present tense *tú* endings. See some common examples in table 11.3.

table 11.3

NEGATIVE INFORMAL "TÚ" COMMANDS	NEGATIVE FORMAL "USTED" COMMANDS
no hables do not speak	**no hable** do not speak
no digas eso don't say that	**no diga eso** don't say that
no fumes do not smoke	**no fume** do not smoke

Admittedly, commands are not the easiest verb tense to use; that's why I'm only giving you a few examples with brief explanation. My goal is to expose you to these conjugations, with a deeper dive better suited to a more intermediate-level book. However, you will see and hear commands being used, especially when giving or receiving directions, so it's worth introducing their unique conjugation pattern. For now, it might be helpful just to familiarize yourself with the commands in table 11.3.

Even if you're not an expert at commands, learning the verbs in their infinitive state will probably help you understand the general idea of what someone is communicating when they use a command. For example, if someone were to say "Limpia la mesa," knowing the verb *limpiar*—to clean—would help you recognize the similar-sounding *limpia*, so you could gather that you're being asked to clean the *mesa* (table). There are also ways to completely avoid using the command form, something I learned when I was first learning and struggling with commands. For example, I would say things like "Necesitas limpiar la mesa," or "You need to clean the table," because that two-verb construction would enable me to use the present tense and the infinitive *limpiar* to convey my instructions.

Two-Verb Constructions

The concept of two-verb constructions is something we have already covered, but now is a good opportunity to briefly revisit this topic; it's a helpful workaround to rely on before you've mastered command/imperative conjugations. Even when I was at a level where I was ready to learn the command conjugation patterns, I was still nervous about using them, specifically because sometimes a formal and an informal command will have a one-letter difference. For example, "pasa" (the informal command for *pasar*, meaning "to pass," which can be used to tell someone to go ahead of you) is only one letter away from "pase" (the formal *usted* command for *pasar*), and I didn't want to be seen as informal or impolite because of a simple mistake. Two-verb constructions helped me avoid this sort of situation until I was ready to fully embrace using commands.

Let's look at some examples of how a two-verb construction can be used to tell someone to do something without using the command form.

table 11.4

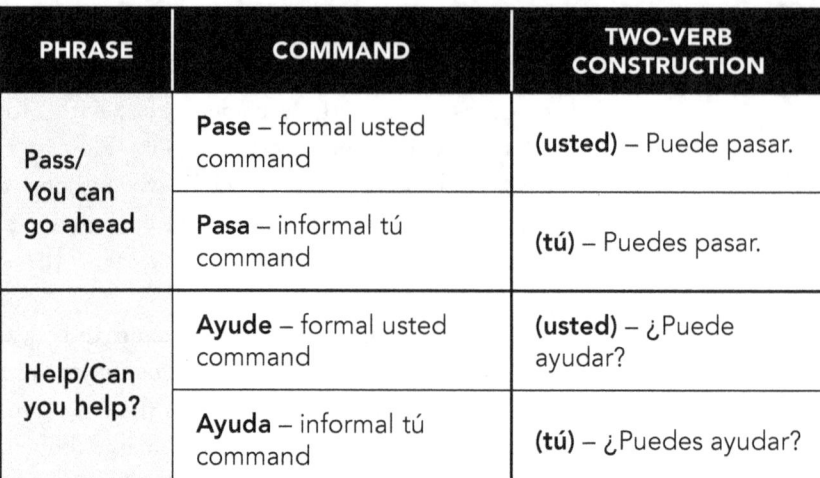

PHRASE	COMMAND	TWO-VERB CONSTRUCTION
Pass/ You can go ahead	**Pase** – formal usted command	**(usted)** – Puede pasar.
	Pasa – informal tú command	**(tú)** – Puedes pasar.
Help/Can you help?	**Ayude** – formal usted command	**(usted)** – ¿Puede ayudar?
	Ayuda – informal tú command	**(tú)** – ¿Puedes ayudar?

As you can see in table 11.4, there is a one-letter difference between the formal *usted* forms and the informal *tú* forms. If you wanted to avoid using a command, you could use a two-verb construction like the examples on the right side of the chart to communicate essentially the same idea. The two-verb constructions use the regular present-tense conjugation for the first verb, and the second verb is an infinitive. This is a great way to communicate your needs, give directions, etc., without having to use the command form. I offer this as an option that may be more compatible with this level of Spanish, especially for anyone who is using the language while traveling.

Insider Tips: Travel Recommendations

Traveling to other places doesn't consist only of the ins and outs of the travel process, of course. There are plenty of leisure and travel activities for you to communicate about, so let's go over some vocabulary words related to common travel activities, and then we'll explore how to ask for and give travel recommendations. This will help you engage in conversations with the locals, learning about your travel destination from those who know it best, and perhaps being able to discuss past trips with Spanish speakers.

el itinerario	the itinerary
tomar/sacar fotos	to take photos
nadar	to swim
acampar	to camp
bucear	to snorkel

tomar el sol	to sunbathe
visitar (el museo)	to visit (the museum)
*estar de vacaciones	to be on vacation
*dar una caminata	to go hiking
*hacer una reservación	to make a reservation
comprar recuerdos	to buy souvenirs
*ir a un parque de diversiones	to go to an amusement park
*hacer una excursión	to go on a day trip
*ver las atracciones	to see the attractions

*The irregular verb estar was covered in chapters 4 and 7, and the verbs *dar*, *ver*, *ir*, and *hacer* were covered in chapter 5.

All the above phrases are verbs except for *el itinerario*, which is what you would create to keep track of all the activities you have planned during your travels. All the verbs are considered regular verbs, except for those indicated by an asterisk. However, if you were discussing your travel activities with others, you would likely find yourself using the following:

» the near future tense (introduced in chapter 7) to describe the activities you will be doing

» the present progressive (introduced in chapter 7) to describe what you're doing right now

» the past tense (introduced in chapter 9) or the present perfect (introduced in chapter 10) to describe activities you did in the past

Also, you could use some transition words to more clearly explain the sequential order of your plans in your *itinerario*. For a review of transition words, see chapter 6. Now that you have some ideas for how to communicate about your travel plans, let's move on to the next step: giving and receiving recommendations.

Indirect Object Pronouns

Giving recommendations in Spanish requires the use of an indirect object pronoun. To help you understand the purpose of indirect object pronouns, I'll use the English verb "to give" as an example. When someone *gives* something, they are giving it to someone, and that someone is the indirect object (the direct object is the thing they are giving). When they use a pronoun (e.g., her) instead of a name (e.g., Mary) then "her" is the indirect object pronoun. So, for example, if you say, "I gave a gift to Mary," you could instead say you gave a gift to *her*. In either sentence, *Mary* or *her* would be the indirect object of the sentence. However, if I leave Mary's name out of the sentence and instead use *her*, I am referring to Mary with an indirect object pronoun.

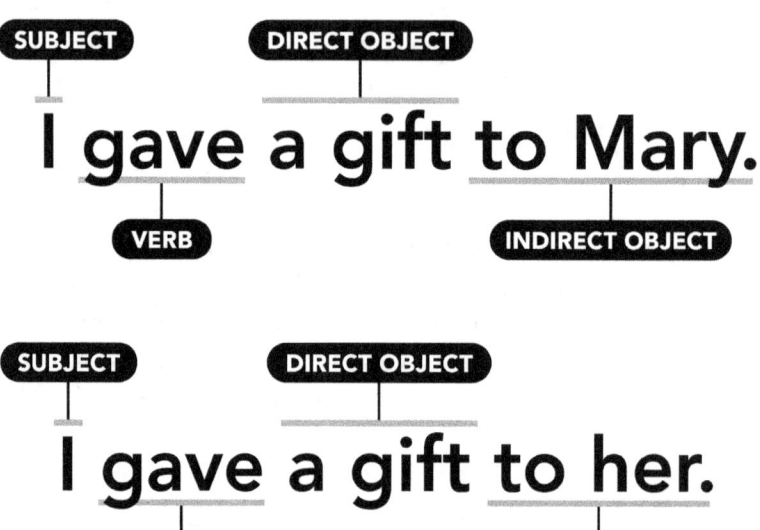

fig. 11.1

As you can see in figure 11.1, an indirect object pronoun refers to the person to whom or for whom an action is being done. If you are buying something *for* someone, giving something *to* someone, or recommending something *to* someone in Spanish, you will need an indirect object pronoun to communicate who your action is intended for (rather than the thing that's being bought, given, or recommended, which is the direct object). There are many verbs in Spanish that take an indirect object pronoun. Let's start by looking at the list of examples below, and then we will get more into how to use indirect object pronouns effectively.

*dar(le) algo	to give someone something
*decir(le) algo	to tell someone something
*recomendar(le) algo	to recommend something to someone
regalar(le) algo	to gift something to someone

dar (see chapter 5) and *recomendar* (see chapter 8) are considered irregular

Notice that all these verbs, when written in their infinitive form, are followed by the word *le* in parentheses. This implies that the verb can be combined with an indirect object pronoun so that someone can be on the receiving end of these actions.

But before we talk more about indirect object pronouns, let's first learn a new verb conjugation: the verb *decir*. *Decir* is also a "go verb," first covered in chapter 5; you can see in table 11.5 that the *yo* conjugation is *digo*. However, there is something else irregular about this verb. You can see by looking closely at the conjugations in table 11.5 that the verb *decir* also has an *e*-to-*i* stem change in the "boot" of the conjugation chart.

table 11.5

decir = to say/tell			GO 🥾
yo	digo	nosotros/as	**decimos**
tú	dices	vosotros/as	**decís**
él ella usted	dice	ellos ellas ustedes	dicen

Now that you have seen how to conjugate the verb *decir*, let's return to indirect object pronouns. In the vocabulary list at the beginning of the chapter, all of the verbs, when written in their infinitive form, were followed by the word *le* in parentheses. This implies that the verbs can be combined with an indirect object pronoun so that someone can be on the receiving end of these actions. Here are a few sentence examples in English and Spanish (figures 11.2, 11.3, and 11.4).

fig. 11.2

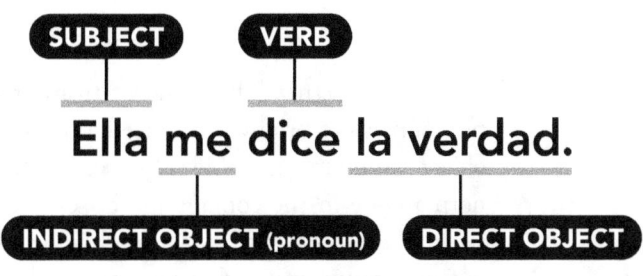

She tells me the truth.

| 11 | Navigating the Unknown   227

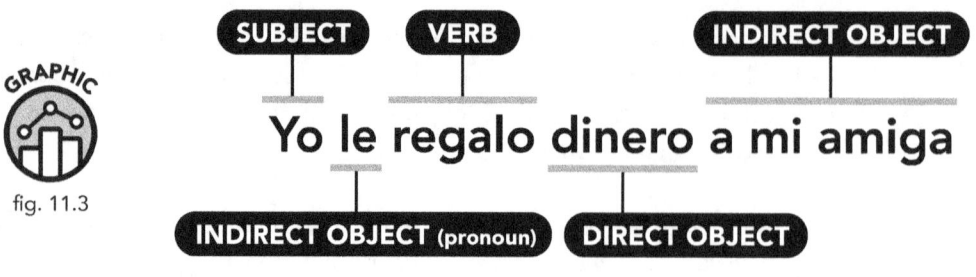

fig. 11.3

I gift money to my friend.

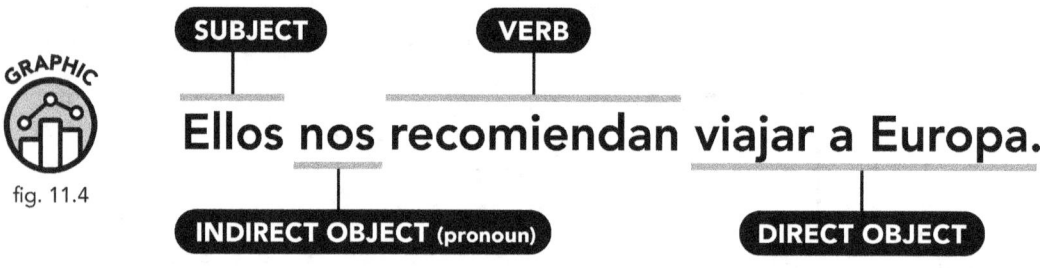

fig. 11.4

They recommend that we travel to Europe.

In these examples, all the sentences contain present-tense verb conjugations: *dice*, *regalo*, and *recomiendan*. The indirect object pronouns are telling us who is receiving those actions. Note also that the first and third sentence examples (figures 11.2 and 11.4) used only an indirect object pronoun, but the second sentence example (figure 11.3) also used an indirect object. In Spanish, when you use an indirect object pronoun, it is sometimes not enough information about who you are talking about. For example, the indirect object pronoun *le* can mean "he," "she," or "you" (formal). So, if I haven't already made it clear who I was talking about in a previous sentence, it is important that I provide more information—in this case, *mi amiga*—to let you know who I am talking about when I say *le*. Table 11.6 shows all the indirect object pronouns, and you can see that the indirect object pronouns *le* and *les* might need extra clarification at times.

You may recognize this concept from chapter 6, where indirect object pronouns were briefly introduced alongside the verb *gustar*. The indirect object pronouns in table 11.6 correspond with pronouns that would normally be in the conjugation boxes: *yo*, *tú*, *él*, *ella*, and *usted*, *nosotros*, *vosotros*, *ellos*, *ellas*, and *ustedes*. Where *yo* would normally be, we have *me*, which communicates that an action is being done to or for me. Where *tú* would normally be, we have *te*, which is the informal way to say that something is being done to or for you. In the bottom left box where we normally have *él, ella,* and *usted,* we have *le. Le* can mean that an action is being done to or for him, her, or you formal (or for an object that is singular). In the top right box where *nosotros* normally goes, we have *nos,* which means something is being done to or for us. Next, we have *os* where the *vosotros* form usually is, and in some areas it would be used to communicate to or for you plural in an informal way. However, in many areas of Latin America, you won't hear *os* being used, only *les.* Finally, where we normally have *ellos, ellas,* and *ustedes,* we have *les. Les* expresses that something is being done to or for you plural or them (or plural objects). In areas that use the *vosotros* form *os, les* would work as the formal version of you plural.

table 11.6

	Indirect Object Pronouns		
me	to/for me	nos	to/for us
te	to/for you (informal)	os	to/for you all (informal)
le	to/for it/him/her/you (formal)	les	to/for you all/them (formal)

To correctly structure a sentence using an indirect object pronoun, the pronoun must be placed before the verb. Take another look at these sentences, where the indirect object pronouns are now bolded and the verbs are now underlined.

» (Ella) **me** <u>dice</u> la verdad.
  (She tells me the truth).

» (Yo) **le** <u>regalo</u> dinero a mi amiga.
  (I gift money to my friend).

» (Ellos) **nos** <u>recomiendan</u> viajar a Europa.
  (They recommend that we travel to Europe).

These sentences show the proper placement: the indirect object goes before the verb. You can also see that I put the subjects of the sentences in parentheses. This aligns with the present-tense verb conjugations that are underlined, because the subject of the sentence is the person doing that action, and the person receiving the action—the indirect object pronoun—is still in bold. I also put the subjects in parentheses because I could leave them out in a conversation where I have already established who I'm talking about. For example, if you already knew I was talking about my friends, and I said, "Nos recomiendan viajar a Europa," then you'd know the verb *recomiendan* is the action of my friends.

I don't expect you to be an expert in indirect object pronouns; this is just a brief introduction. As you advance your language skills, you'll want to start incorporating indirect object pronouns into your speech to communicate in more detail. Before we finish this chapter, though, I want to give you a few sentence examples you can easily incorporate into your repertoire so that you can give and receive travel recommendations using indirect object pronouns.

¿Qué me recomienda hacer aquí?	What do you recommend for me to do here? [formal]
Yo (no) le recomiendo (probar los mollettes).	I (don't) recommend that you (action). [formal]
¿Qué me recomiendas hacer aquí?	What do you recommend for me to do here? [informal]
Yo (no) te recomiendo (visitar el museo)	I (don't) recommend (action). [informal]

Simply memorizing the few sentences above can get you a long way! Once you master these, you'll be ready to start replacing the verb *recomendar* with other verbs to experiment more with indirect object pronouns.

Chapter Recap

In this chapter, we covered all things related to finding your way around your travel destination so you can complete the activities on your *itinerario*. This included the following:

» Learning vocabulary related to the common modes of transportation and how to communicate when navigating transportation.

» Using the command or imperative verb tense to give or receive directions—and, until you've mastered that tense, using two-verb constructions that offer other ways to communicate similar ideas.

» Expanding vocabulary to be able to communicate about the various activities you might discuss related to a vacation or a trip abroad. These activities often require use of indirect object pronouns, to indicate that actions are being received by another person—such as giving and receiving recommendations during your travels.

Put together, these vocabulary words, new verb tenses, and indirect object pronouns will set you up for success when you're navigating the basics of traveling abroad in Spanish. And the more practicing you do in Spanish, whether abroad or at home, the further you'll advance in your language fluency!

| 12 |
Celebrating Cultural Diversity

You've made it to chapter 12, which is no small accomplishment! Throughout the past eleven chapters, your commitment and dedication have helped you build your knowledge of Spanish concepts that will set you up for success as you continue your studies or use of the language. Because part IV has been focused on branching out of our comfort zones and the small circles of our everyday lives, this final chapter will center around experiencing the Spanish-speaking world and its diversity. We will celebrate the beauty of the large, diverse, and ever-evolving cultures of Spanish speakers. Even if you do not plan to travel outside of the United States, you will still be able to experience this culture right where you are. We will learn about some celebrations that many Spanish speakers in the US practice today, we will gain some appreciation of the cultural influence Spanish speakers have had on the entertainment industry, and we'll embrace the rich cultural diversity that Spanish speakers contribute to the United States.

Chapter Overview

By the end of this chapter, you will know more about the following:
» Celebrations commonly observed by Spanish speakers and key vocabulary related to these celebrations
» The cultural influence of Spanish speakers on the entertainment industry, along with related vocabulary
» The unique cultures of Spanish speakers and the contributions they make to our society in the United States

For an overview of the concepts that we will be working with in this chapter, listen to the QuickClip and follow along. The speaker will describe the influence of Spanish speakers in the United States and the contributions they make to their communities.

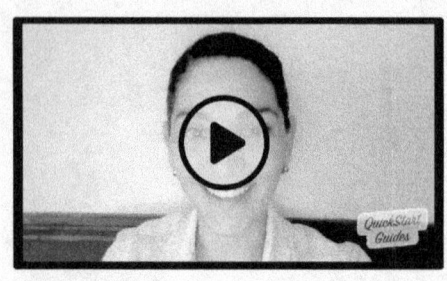

Sunciree from Guatemala describes living in Houston, Texas. She will share about the diverse Spanish-speaking culture, the festivities she participates in, and the Hispanic influence that can be seen in popular US sports.

#15

To watch the QuickClip, use the camera on your mobile phone to scan the QR code or visit the link below.

www.quickclips.io/spanish-15

Sunciree: ¡Hola! Mi nombre es Sunciree. Soy de Guatemala y tengo más de veinte años viviendo en Houston, Texas. Hoy voy a hablar sobre la diversidad cultural de los hispanohablantes aquí en los Estados Unidos. Houston es la cuarta ciudad más grande de Estados Unidos y existe una gran diversidad cultural en esta ciudad. Los hispanos tienen una influencia enorme en la cultura de Houston, ya que hay una población muy numerosa de hispanos y sus contribuciones se pueden apreciar en diferentes maneras y en diferentes ámbitos. Aquí es muy común tener celebraciones donde los hispanos se reúnen a celebrar y a comer. Por ejemplo, aquí en Houston celebramos la independencia durante el mes de septiembre en un parque muy famoso en el centro de la ciudad. Y los guatemaltecos en particular celebramos las Navidades en un festival llamado Navidad guatemalteca, donde puedes escuchar música de marimba y comer muchos platillos de comida 100% guatemalteca. La influencia hispana en mi comunidad también se puede ver en los deportes como el fútbol y el béisbol. Es muy común escuchar nombres de jugadores famosos hispanos como José Altuve a Humberto Castellanos cuando vas a un partido de béisbol. Y si te gusta el fútbol, puedes ver jugadores de alto rendimiento como Héctor Herrera y Carlos Ferreira. Es muy bonito vivir en una ciudad que tiene mucha diversidad. Hay hispanohablantes de muchos países y todos convivimos y compartimos nuestras culturas. También convivimos con la cultura estadounidense.

Celebrations of Spanish Language and Culture

Given that the United States has such a large population of Spanish speakers, it makes sense that many of its holidays and celebrations have been influenced by Spanish-speaking cultures. The various cultures in the melting pot of the United States borrow things from one another, forming something new that draws from diverse sources. Before we dive into some common celebrations and holidays, let's cover essential vocabulary related to the topic of holidays and celebrations.

el día festivo/feriado	the holiday
la fiesta/celebración	the party/celebration
la costumbre	the custom
celebrar/festejar	to celebrate
invitar a (mis amigos)	to invite (my friends)
asistir	to attend

These verbs are all regular in the present tense, so there are no irregular conjugation patterns. Just like in English, a party can also be referred to as a celebration. If you plan to invite someone to a party, you will need to use the "*a* personal" that I mentioned in chapter 5, because inviting is an action performed on others. For example, if I want to invite my friends over to my house, I say, "Voy *a* invitar a mis amigos a mi casa."

Now we're ready to talk about some celebrations commonly practiced by Spanish speakers. You will get to put your Spanish to the test by reading a short paragraph about each celebration. Keep in mind that these paragraphs are simplified explanations of these cultural events; there is much more to the celebrations, but the readings were written with your level of Spanish in mind. However, I highly encourage you to educate yourself more about these holidays by talking to Spanish speakers, watching documentaries, or reading articles.

In this chapter, I will use the term *Spanish speakers* often. Because this book is about learning Spanish and the cultures that speak it, that term is my way of acknowledging the variety of those cultures. However, there are other, more specific terms you may hear more often, such as Hispanic or Latino. Technically, the term *Hispanic* refers to people who have ancestry in a country whose primary language is Spanish. But there are many indigenous populations in predominantly Spanish-speaking areas that do not speak Spanish, or speak it as their second language, because Spanish was the language of colonizers. Another common term is *Latino(a)*. This is used to refer to people whose origin is somewhere in Latin America. There are variations of that term, such as *Latine* and *Latinx*, that are more gender-inclusive. How individuals prefer to identify themselves varies greatly, and the way they use the terms doesn't always coincide with the technical definition—and that's okay! I use the term

| 12 | Celebrating Cultural Diversity

Spanish speaker in this book to clarify that I am speaking about the large, diverse group of people who speak Spanish—without trying to imply that the words I prefer are what others should prefer.

La celebración de los quince años

You may have heard the term *quinceañera*. Some English speakers are familiar with this term referring to a girl's fifteenth birthday party in many Spanish-speaking cultures. However, the word *quinceañera* actually refers to the girl who is turning fifteen, not the party, although in the United States it is common to hear people refer to the celebration itself as the *quinceañera*. Technically, the celebration is known as *la celebración de los quince años* (or, for short, *los quince años*), meaning "the celebration of fifteen years." A somewhat similar celebration in the United States is the "sweet sixteen" birthday party. However, the celebration for *los quince años* has deep cultural meaning—it's not just a big birthday bash. Before we learn more about the history of this celebration, let's look at some essential vocabulary related to it.

mis quince	my fifteen (similar to how someone would say "my sweet sixteen")
la quinceañera	a term used to refer to the girl who is turning fifteen
el vals	the waltz
el brindis	the toast
la misa	the mass

Now that we have covered some essential vocabulary terms related to this celebration, it's time to put to the test everything you've learned in this book by reading the paragraph below. Remember to look for cognates, and focus on understanding the overall ideas from the reading rather than fixating on trying to literally translate every single word.

La celebración de los quince años es una combinación de tradiciones indígenas y católicas. Muchas familias hispanas tienen la costumbre de celebrar los quince años de las hijas para celebrar su entrada a la adolescencia. Muchas veces, la fiesta incluye una misa en la iglesia. Después, hay una celebración en donde la quinceañera baila el vals con su padre. También hay una cena con los invitados, un brindis con la quinceañera y sus padres, y un baile con música. Normalmente, la quinceañera lleva un vestido elegante. Muchas familias gastan mucho dinero para esta celebración que es una costumbre tan importante en la cultura de muchos hispanohablantes.

Now that you've read the paragraph about *los quince años*, you have a basic understanding of this celebration, and you acquired that understanding entirely in Spanish! Let's put your comprehension to the test with some questions about the reading.

1. Where do many of the traditions for *los quince años* originate?

2. What is so important about a girl turning fifteen?

3. What are some common ways that families celebrate *los quince años*?

4. What verb tense is primarily used in the paragraph, and what are some examples of that verb tense from the reading?

Hopefully you felt comfortable answering these comprehension questions. Even though your first instinct is probably to translate word for word as you read, you'll be surprised by how much you understand when you focus on reading for overall meaning. This will get your brain more used to thinking in Spanish, because in the real world, language will move too quickly for you to always rely on translating.

El Cinco de Mayo

I would guess that almost everyone living in the United States has heard of Cinco de Mayo, and many people celebrate this day by going to a local Mexican restaurant. Who doesn't love a good excuse to go out for nachos and margaritas? I decided to include this holiday in this section because, with as much Spanish as you know at this point, I would be doing you a disservice if I didn't tell you the truth about Cinco de Mayo. Namely, that it is *not* Mexico's Independence Day, and that the majority of Spanish speakers do not celebrate this holiday. But before we learn a bit about the real history behind Cinco de Mayo, let's cover a few essential vocabulary words.

conmemorar	to commemorate
una batalla	a battle
el ejército	the army
ganar	to win
contra	against

Here's a short passage about the history of the holiday:

El Cinco de Mayo conmemora una batalla que ocurrió en Puebla, México, en 1862. El ejército mexicano ganó una batalla contra el ejército francés. El Cinco de Mayo no se celebra por todo México, pero sí se celebra en algunas partes de Puebla, México. El Cinco de Mayo no es el día de la independencia de México. El día de la independencia de México se celebra el 16 de septiembre. En los Estados Unidos, el Cinco de Mayo se convirtió en un día de celebración de la cultura mexicana.

Once you have read through the paragraph above, take some time to review the reading with the following comprehension questions:

1. What is the purpose of Cinco de Mayo?

2. When is Mexico's Independence Day?

3. Did you see the preterite tense or the imperfect tense being used when expressing past events? What are some examples of verbs in that particular form of the past tense that were used, and why?

Now that you know that Cinco de Mayo is not Mexican Independence Day, you can mindfully celebrate this holiday if you choose to. In some ways, Cinco de Mayo is a great example of the strong influence Spanish-speaking culture has had on the culture of the United States. That said, some of these holidays have become sensationalized and caused misunderstandings and stereotypes. Hopefully this book has taught you a little about how the nationalities and cultural practices of Spanish speakers are much more diverse than what we've commonly been led to believe. So if you want to celebrate Mexican culture by observing Cinco de Mayo, you can now do so with the true roots of this day in mind, and educate those around you on what this holiday is really about.

El Día de los Muertos

Another Hispanic holiday commonly heard of in the United States is *el Día de los Muertos*, or the Day of the Dead. Many Day of the Dead–style costumes and decorations are seen in stores throughout the United States during the Halloween season. Although the Day of the Dead is celebrated close to when the United States celebrates Halloween, the two holidays are not synonymous with one another. As much as I love seeing Spanish-speaking cultural influences mix with the culture here in the United States, this is another example of how commercialization of elements of a holiday have led people to mistakenly believe they understand the holiday's significance. Many in the US do not realize the deep cultural importance that Day of the Dead has for many Spanish speakers. Before you read about this holiday, familiarize yourself with the vocabulary terms below that are specific to el Día de los Muertos.

la ofrenda	the offering
el altar	the altar
los muertos/difuntos	the dead/deceased
las velas	the candles
el disfraz	the costume
el cementerio/panteón	the cemetery
el cempasúchil	the marigold (the iconic flower of Día de los Muertos)
la tumba	the tomb
el pan de muerto	the bread of the dead (a type of bread made specifically during this time of the year)
la calavera (de azúcar)	the (sugar) skull

With those words in mind, read the following passage and answer the questions that follow.

El Día de los Muertos es una celebración para recordar y honrar a los difuntos y principalmente se celebra en partes de México, Centroamérica y América del Sur. Esta celebración es una mezcla de la cultura indígena de los aztecas y el catolicismo. Generalmente, el Día de los Muertos es celebrado el 1 y 2 de noviembre, pero las fechas pueden variar dependiendo del lugar. Para celebrar el Día de los Muertos, muchas familias ponen un altar en su casa, con una ofrenda para los familiares muertos. Muchas veces decoran el altar con fotos, velas, comida, calaveras de azúcar, pan de muerto y cempasúchiles. A veces, las familias también decoran la tumba del difunto y pasan tiempo en el cementerio. Muchas veces hay personas que se visten con disfraz y se pintan sus caras como calaveras.

1. What is the purpose of Día de los Muertos?

2. What are some ways that families celebrate Día de los Muertos?

3. What is an example of a reflexive verb that was used in the reading?

Clearly, this holiday is about much more than just dressing up. I was lucky enough to witness some of the festivities while I was living in Mexico. The celebration was beautiful and made me rethink my perspective on death, tying it to the process of honoring one's family and one's roots. Not every Mexican or Spanish speaker celebrates this holiday, but pieces of the tradition have spread to the United States. If you live in an area with a Spanish-speaking population, you might be able to take part in some local Día de los Muertos festivities. If there is a Mexican bakery (panadería) in your area, I highly recommend trying the *pan de muerto* that is typically sold during this holiday.

El Mes de la Herencia Hispana

El Mes de la Herencia Hispana, or Hispanic Heritage Month, is a lot more self-explanatory than the previously mentioned celebrations and holidays. But it's still worth mentioning in the context of celebrations often found in the United States. Below are a few vocabulary terms you'll need to prepare to read about this holiday in Spanish.

el logro	the achievement
la influencia	the influence
las contribuciones	the contributions
reconocer	to recognize (go verb)

Take a moment to read the following paragraph to learn more about this holiday, and then try to answer the comprehension questions that follow.

El gobierno de los Estados Unidos reconoce el 15 de septiembre hasta el 15 de octubre como el Mes de la Herencia Hispana. Este mes festivo es para reconocer y celebrar la influencia y los logros que las personas hispanas han contribuido al país. Las contribuciones de las personas hispanas al gobierno, la cultura y la economía de los Estados Unidos han sido significativas por muchas generaciones. El Mes de la Herencia Hispana es un buen momento para informarse sobre la historia de los hispanos en los Estados Unidos.

1. When is Hispanic Heritage Month celebrated?

2. What is the purpose of Hispanic Heritage Month?

3. What are some examples of the present perfect tense that were used in the reading?

It is clear that the impact of Spanish speakers on the United States cannot go unnoticed. If you take the time to educate yourself, you will uncover Spanish speakers and their impact in almost every aspect of the history of this country. The holidays and celebrations that we covered in this section are not even close to being a conclusive list—we only scratched the surface. But I hope this section has encouraged you to continue learning about and appreciating the diverse cultures of Spanish speakers.

Cultural Crossroads

Spanish speakers have certainly impacted the history of the United States and how we celebrate many traditions, but the influence doesn't stop there. Spanish speakers' passion, creativity, and diversity have made an indelible mark on the world of entertainment and art. In this section, we will cover some of the fundamentals of these industries as we work on building vocabulary in Spanish.

el entretenimiento	the entertainment
la industria musical	the music industry
los deportes	the sports
el fútbol	the soccer
el cine	the cinema
la película	the movie
la literatura	the literature
el arte	the art
la obra (de arte, teatro)	the work (of art, theatre, etc.)
impactar	to impact (regular verb)

After reviewing the vocabulary, read the following Spanish passage about Spanish-speaking culture in entertainment and the arts. Remember that when you're reading, it's important to focus on the overall ideas being communicated and to try not to depend on translating the sentences word by word. Once you have read through the passage, I recommend that you take the time to go back through it and pay attention to grammatical concepts we have covered throughout this book, to review and reinforce what you've learned.

Los hispanohablantes han tenido un gran impacto en las formas de entretenimiento en los Estados Unidos.

Hay muchas películas increíbles gracias a los hispanohablantes en el cine; como Javier Bardem, Penélope Cruz, Guillermo del Toro, y Alejandro González Iñárritu. También hay muchas películas que muestran la cultura de los hispanohablantes que viven en los Estados Unidos como *McFarland, USA* y *Flamin' Hot*.

Los hispanohablantes también han impactado la industria musical. El reggaetón es un estilo de música muy popular en Latinoamérica y los Estados Unidos. La salsa, la bachata, el flamenco y el merengue son tipos de música y baile creados por los hispanohablantes.

Uno de los deportes más populares en Latinoamérica es el fútbol. Algunos jugadores famosos son Lionel Messi, Diego Maradona y Cristiano Ronaldo. Cada día el fútbol es más popular aquí en los Estados Unidos. El béisbol es otro deporte popular con muchos jugadores hispanohablantes como Roberto Clemente.

Si estudias la literatura en español, vas a aprender que hay muchos escritores hispanohablantes muy impactantes como Isabel Allende y Gabriel García Márquez. Muchas obras de arte clásicas fueron creadas por artistas hispanohablantes como Frida Kahlo y Pablo Picasso.

Here are some questions to test your comprehension:

1. Give an example of a Spanish speaker who has been influential in the film industry.

2. What is "reggaetón"?

3. What two sports are very popular in many Spanish-speaking countries?

4. In what industries are Frida Kahlo and Gabriel Garcia Márquez well known?

The information in the passage above hardly scratches the surface regarding the contributions of Spanish speakers to the world of arts and entertainment, but hopefully it made you aware (or reminded you) of some connections while also making you realize how much more there is to uncover and learn. As you continue your Spanish-learning journey, build community, and connect with Spanish speakers around you, your appreciation for these contributions will only increase.

Unity in Diversity: Embracing Our Differences

Throughout this book, I've tried to highlight the fact that Spanish speakers are extremely diverse, and that's why I think it's important for us to end this chapter by celebrating the rich diversity that exists in the Spanish-speaking world. For this final section, let's focus in on communicating about cultural differences—and doing so in a way that enables us to embrace those differences and thus celebrate cultural diversity. Earlier in this chapter, I discussed how even some basic, familiar terminology like "Hispanic," "Latino," and so on can have different meanings for different people. So it's important to build inclusive vocabulary in Spanish in order to be able to discuss our differences in a respectful way. Here are some words and phrases that can be helpful in that regard:

la diversidad (lingüística)	the (linguistic) diversity
la diferencia	the difference
el respeto	the respect
aunque	although
la discriminación	the discrimination
enriquecer	to enrich (irregular verb, conjugated like the verb *conocer* in chapter 7)
apreciar	to appreciate (regular verb)
el multiculturalismo	the multiculturalism

With these words in mind, you should be ready to read the paragraph below. Remember to read for overall comprehension. One potentially helpful strategy is to underline or highlight the words in a reading that you *do* understand, to help you focus on the overall meaning rather than getting hung up on any words you don't know.

El mundo hispanohablante es muy diverso. El español es el idioma oficial de 21 países, y por eso existe tanta diversidad cultural y lingüística. Aunque el español no es un idioma oficial en los Estados Unidos, hay una población muy grande de hispanohablantes. La población hispanohablante

> en los Estados Unidos es muy diversa, pero desafortunadamente existe mucha discriminación lingüística y cultural. Es importante aprender a apreciar a todas las culturas que contribuyen tanto a los Estados Unidos. Los hispanohablantes enriquecen la cultura de los Estados Unidos. ¡El multiculturalismo es algo que necesitamos celebrar!

Now that you've read about the importance of embracing the cultural diversity of Spanish speakers, I recommend that you take some time to review the above paragraph. Think back on the concepts we have learned throughout this book, and see which ones you notice in the paragraph above in this real-life working example. I also encourage you to take a moment to appreciate diversity itself. One of my favorite things about Spanish is that I will never run out of things to learn. Each place that Spanish speakers inhabit is unique and comes with new vocabulary and new cultural practices to learn about. Each person I have encountered has enabled me to continue to blossom into a better version of myself. And as we celebrate cultural diversity, we must also celebrate your completion of this book!

Chapter Recap

In this final chapter, we celebrated the cultural diversity of Spanish speakers and their significant influence on the world around us. This included the following:

» Learning vocabulary related to cultural events that are commonly celebrated by Spanish speakers.

» Challenging our Spanish comprehension by reading about these celebrations completely in Spanish.

» Acquiring some new vocabulary related to the arts, sports, and entertainment industries while reading in Spanish about the contributions that many incredibly talented Spanish speakers have made to these industries.

» Further enriching our vocabulary related to communicating inclusively about cultural differences, and revisiting one of the most important takeaways: that there is vast cultural diversity among Spanish speakers.

All of this together will enable you to have meaningful conversations with Spanish speakers as you open yourself to learning more about the unique cultural perspectives and practices that form a part of each individual you encounter. Know that I am cheering you on in your completion of this book as you embark on your Spanish-speaking journey beyond these pages!

Conclusion

Throughout this book, I have led you on a journey through the basics of the Spanish language. Chapter by chapter, step by step, we've built up your language skills with the goal of helping you venture further and further out into the Spanish-speaking world. This is nothing new; the Spanish language has existed far longer than you or I have. But while there have been many books written with the same goal of helping people learn Spanish, my goal in writing this one was to create the book that I needed when I was learning Spanish, in hopes that it could help others. For me, Spanish really started to click when I was able to understand how the language worked in real-life contexts. I also learned best when complicated grammatical concepts were taught in steps that didn't seem overwhelming and that could be accompanied with visual learning aids when possible. Throughout my years of studying the language and teaching it to students, I have found that I am far from being the only one who needs to learn language in this way.

Besides learning essential vocabulary and key grammar concepts and being exposed to reading and listening in Spanish, there are even greater things that I hope you take away from this book. First of all, I hope you've come away with an even deeper appreciation for people who learn another language—it's not easy to do, especially if you are an immigrant who is navigating not only a new language but a new culture. I hope that scratching the surface of the topic of how diverse the Spanish-speaking world truly is will leave you wanting to learn more about all of its incredible cultures. Lastly, I hope I've imparted the sense that beyond the Spanish language, there are thousands of other languages and cultures out there, all with their own unique history. Although I'm grateful to have been able to teach you more about this language that I love so much, imagine all the beautiful languages that exist in this incredibly diverse planet that we all inhabit. Despite our differences, we are all the same in that we would not be able to thrive as a species if it were not for the gift of language.

Of course, this one book is not enough to teach you everything I know about Spanish—or everything you might need or want to know. But I hope that I have helped you start out on the right foot, and that you will be motivated to continue exploring and learning the Spanish language. I am incredibly grateful that you have trusted me to help you on your journey. You will certainly encounter many incredible teachers as you continue, and your learning will only expand if you move ahead in your journey. All you have to do is decide to take the next step. What are you waiting for?

DON'T FORGET TO DOWNLOAD YOUR FREE DIGITAL ASSETS!

- Preterite vs. Imperfect Workbook
- Gender Agreement Workbook
- 12 Irregular Present Tense Verbs Workbook
- Ser vs. Estar Workbook

TWO WAYS TO ACCESS YOUR FREE DIGITAL ASSETS

Use the camera app on your mobile phone to scan the QR code or visit the link below and instantly access your Digital Assets.

go.quickstartguides.com/spanish

Appendix

More on the Cultural Experience of Traveling

The overall goal of this book is not to be a travel guide. However, I recognize that many of you reading it might be doing so to learn the basics of Spanish in preparation for some kind of trip abroad, which is why a few of the chapters focus on the topic of traveling. This appendix is meant to provide additional information on that topic for those who are planning a trip to a Spanish-speaking country. And even if you're not planning or able to travel abroad any time soon, this appendix can offer some insight into the Spanish-speaking world(s) from the comfort of wherever you are at this moment. We will discuss a few cultural differences that may arise when traveling, and we'll revisit the concept of linguistic diversity, which you will certainly encounter in different Spanish-speaking countries as well as when interacting with Spanish speakers of different origins in your community. This appendix includes a variety of QuickClip audio recordings of native speakers sharing about where they are from, as well as allowing you to hear their different accents. So whether you're planning a specific trip or just want to learn more about the language, this appendix will provide some additional context.

Navigating Cultural Differences While Traveling

Throughout this book, I've highlighted some general cultural differences that are common to the various Spanish-speaking cultures, many of which I have personally experienced as someone who learned Spanish as a second language. But there are plenty more cultural differences to be aware of, especially if you plan to travel abroad. So in this section I'm going to break down some major differences, supplemented by an audio recording of a native speaker describing what these cultural touchstones mean to them personally.

Navigating a Market

If you travel to a Spanish-speaking country, you will likely come across a market, or *mercado*, at some point. These markets are akin to a farmer's market or artisan's market in the United States, but they are far more common in Spanish-speaking countries than they are here, and the way of shopping at a market in those countries can be noticeably different. When shopping in a market in a Spanish-speaking country, it is normal to barter, or *regatear*. Prices are typically not set in stone, so it's not seen as rude to try to negotiate the price, especially if you're buying a large amount or quantity of something. On the other hand, if you are in a regular brick-and-mortar store, prices are set in stone just like they are here in the United States.

There are many types of markets in Spanish-speaking countries; some markets sell food exclusively, for example. Others will have a mixture of items such as household goods, artwork, and so on. If you're interested in a product at a market, you'll first need to ask the seller for a price: "¿Cuánto cuesta?" If you don't like the price and decide you'd like to barter in hopes of talking down the price, you can try saying something like "Está caro," meaning "It's expensive" or "Es mucho dinero," meaning "It's a lot of money." Then the seller may offer you a lower price.

Another way to barter is to respond to the price quote by saying something like "Solo puedo pagar diez dólares," or "I can only pay ten dollars," and see if the seller will accept your price. Bargaining isn't my favorite thing to do in any language, as it doesn't come naturally to me. Also, I know it's pretty obvious that I am a foreigner in these settings, and many times sellers aren't as willing to barter with someone who clearly has the money to travel to another country. I personally don't mind paying a fair price for items at a market, because operating a market is hard work and I like supporting local businesses when possible.

At markets, you will often find beautiful pieces of art handmade by locals. In Spanish, these pieces are called *las artesanías*, the English equivalent of the word "handicrafts." They make great souvenirs, which in Spanish would be *un recuerdo*, which means "a souvenir" but also "a memory." It makes a lot of sense that the words for *memory* and *souvenir* are the same, since souvenirs are purchased to remember your travels. Shopping at a market was certainly an unforgettable experience for me, and thinking back on all the smells, colors, and beautiful chaos of the markets in Mexico gives me a feeling of nostalgia.

Here's an excerpt of a native Spanish speaker describing their typical experience at a local market; you can hear this QuickClip audio recording of this passage in your Digital Assets. Take this opportunity to test your Spanish comprehension and also to hear from someone who gets to experience this type of shopping firsthand!

Natalia: ¡Hola! Mi nombre es Natalia y soy de Costa Rica. En mi pueblo, hay muchos mercados, pero mi mercado favorito se llama el Mercado Verde. Está abierto todos los fines de semana, y normalmente visito este mercado una vez a la semana. Siempre voy a comprar carne, fruta, y verdura porque es más económico comprar en el mercado. A veces compramos otras cosas para la casa, pero la mayoría del tiempo compramos los ingredientes para preparar nuestras comidas.

Cultural Importance of Meals

For many people, food and meals are a central part of their culture; what we eat can symbolize our cultural heritage and traditions. In the United States, many families have taken on busy lifestyles that don't allow for this kind of collective meal-sharing, and while similar trends are certainly happening in urban areas of Spanish-speaking countries, there is still a strong presence of people who deeply value and prioritize meals with their loved ones.

The specific cultural differences regarding meals will vary depending on what area you're visiting. In general, though, the most important difference is that many countries do not follow the mealtimes traditionally practiced here in the United States. My experience when living in Mexico was that lunchtime took place much later than I was used to—around one or two o'clock. Dinner was usually a lighter meal that came much later in the evening. I found myself supplementing with snacks in the late morning as I adjusted to this meal schedule. The foods people eat, as well as what time they eat them and with whom, are heavily influenced by local culture.

Isaac from Spain talks about the Spanish culture surrounding food customs. He will share some popular Spanish dishes with you, as well as explain the typical mealtimes and their cultural significance.

To watch the QuickClip, use the camera on your mobile phone to scan the QR code or visit the link below.

www.quickclips.io/spanish-17

Isaac: Hola. Me llamo Isaac y soy de Madrid, España. En España, la comida principal del día, o el almuerzo, se conoce como "la comida." Durante esta comida, es común comer platos tradicionales como la tortilla española, el gazpacho en verano o el cocido en invierno. También, es común tomarse un tiempo para descansar después de comer, conocido como "la siesta." Muchas tiendas cierran por unas dos horas para la siesta, y después, todos regresan a trabajar. Por la noche, cenamos. Normalmente, la cena se come muy tarde, como a las nueve de la noche, y es una comida más ligera. Las comidas son muy importantes porque también son momentos sociales. Es común hacer "la sobremesa" después de comer. Es un tiempo en el que charlamos, contamos historias y disfrutamos de la compañía de nuestros amigos y familiares.

Social Life in Spanish-Speaking Countries

Meals and markets offer glimpses into a broader subject that can come up when traveling to a Spanish-speaking country: the differences in social life. Many social differences you'll notice come down to urban planning; in many Spanish-speaking countries, cities are designed much differently than they typically are in the United States. Many neighborhoods have small businesses that families operate out of their own home, so you can often be within walking distance of a hot meal, a fresh haircut, or a market where you can buy some ingredients for dinner. This typically means that people are out and about more, which makes their social life noticeably different from that in the United States.

I have often heard Mexico described as a country full of happy and welcoming people, and from my experience, I'd say that characterization is accurate. I think the reason has a lot to do with the fact that people tend to be less isolated than we are in the United States. Here in Texas, I depend on my car to get me everywhere, so every place I go is very intentionally planned. I don't run into people in my neighborhood as I walk to the nearest store, because it's too far to walk to, and I barely even know any of my neighbors. In many Spanish-speaking countries, including Mexico, people typically don't have to go as far or make as much of an effort to get out of the house, and so they naturally connect with others frequently. For example, a family can easily walk down the street to a local restaurant and will likely see other families they know while doing so. And they end up hanging around the area to socialize with others before returning home.

Daniel from Mexico shares how the Mexican culture can be experienced through food, festivities, and music. You'll also learn about how all of these elements reflect the cultural value of social interaction.

To watch the QuickClip, use the camera on your mobile phone to scan the QR code or visit the link below.

www.quickclips.io/spanish-18

Daniel: Hola, yo soy Daniel y vivo en la Ciudad de México. Aquí en la ciudad la vida social se vive con intensidad y color, en un ambiente que invita a la convivencia y la celebración.

La gastronomía es un pilar de la vida social. La comida no es solo un alimento, sino un pretexto para reunirse y compartir momentos con amigos y familia. Desde los tacos en una esquina hasta los sofisticados restaurantes, las comidas aquí son largas y llenas de conversación, creando lazos profundos entre las personas.

Los festivales son otro elemento clave de la vida social. Celebraciones como el Día de Muertos o las fiestas patrias no solo son espectáculos visuales llenos de color, música, y danza, sino también momentos en los que las personas se unen para reafirmar su identidad y compartir en comunidad.

La fiesta y la música también juegan un papel central. Desde las tradicionales "fiestas de barrio" hasta las noches en plazas como Garibaldi, donde el mariachi y el baile toman protagonismo. Los bailes como la salsa, la cumbia, o el danzón no solo se disfrutan en fiestas, sino en espacios públicos donde la gente se anima a participar.

La cultura mexicana se vive en las calles, en los mercados, en los bailes, y en las festividades, generando un ambiente de cercanía que promueve la interacción cara a cara.

The Challenge of Accents in Spanish

If you have the opportunity to travel to different Spanish-speaking areas, you will quickly realize that not every Spanish speaker sounds the same. Although accents can be found anywhere, in any language, I think the fact that Spanish is spoken in so many areas can make accents particularly challenging. For example, I am originally from South Dakota, and I now live in Texas. The southern accent is quite different from what I was used to in the northern part of the US, and if I were to go to the UK, the range of accents would be even greater. There are twenty-one official Spanish-speaking countries, and you could hear innumerable accents in just one of those countries—so imagine how many Spanish accents are actually out there in the world. It can be overwhelming to think about!

Because I learned Spanish in Mexico, I am forever influenced by that experience, and I have an easier time with that accent than those from Central America or the Caribbean. It is not uncommon for someone with an advanced proficiency in Spanish to meet someone with an accent they're not used to and to feel as if they are speaking a completely different language. It's a humbling experience, but it's not one that is unique to non-native speakers of Spanish. Native speakers also can find it difficult to comprehend accents they are not accustomed to. If you run into a situation like this, try not to be too hard on yourself. When a language is as global as Spanish is, it's going to have many variations, and it's not realistic to expect to be prepared for every accent that exists.

That said, I do have some advice for how to deal with this difficult aspect of the Spanish language. One of the most helpful strategies I have discovered is to find audio recordings of Spanish speakers with an accent that I am not accustomed to and to listen to that audio with subtitles, or a script when possible. For example, if you're watching a movie in Spanish, turn on the subtitles *in Spanish*. This will help your brain associate the words on the screen with the pronunciation you are hearing, and it will eventually start to sound more familiar to you.

Unfortunately, you cannot turn on subtitles when speaking with people in the real world, so those situations can be difficult. Asking someone to speak slowly can help a lot. Luckily, you've been exposed to many different accents throughout this book via the audio recordings, and I did that intentionally in hopes that you wouldn't get too used to one specific speaker or accent in Spanish.

I want to provide you with some practice to help you train your brain to stretch outside of its comfort zone and get familiar with new accents. The following QuickClip contains a script written in Spanish about the Spanish language. In each section that follows, you will be able to listen to a different native speaker read this script. I encourage you to focus on one accent at a time and listen a couple of times as you read along with the script. Then move to the next accent and repeat the process so that you can really focus on paying attention to the differences you hear.

Please keep in mind that each audio recording is of a native speaker from the country indicated. But remember that there can be many different accents within one country, so just because you listen to a native speaker from Spain, it doesn't mean that all Spanish speakers from Spain will have the same accent.

The following is the script for all recordings in QuickClip #19:

Script: El español es el idioma oficial de veintiún países en el mundo, pero se habla en muchos países más. El español nació en España y se origina del latín. Es un idioma muy diverso; existen muchos acentos y variedades lingüísticas. A veces, es difícil para un hispanohablante de un país entender a otro hispanohablante de otro país porque las palabras que usan pueden ser muy diferentes. La pronunciación también varía mucho dependiendo del lugar. Todas las personas que hablan español siempre pueden aprender algo nuevo.

Isaac: Spanish Accent
1. Did you notice anything in particular about this accent?
2. Were any words in the script especially hard for you to understand?

Abdiel: Puerto Rican Accent
1. How was the pronunciation different from what you were expecting, or compared to the previous speaker in this section?
2. What did you find particularly challenging about this accent?

Valentín: Argentinian Accent
1. What about this accent stood out to you?
2. Were there certain words that were easier to understand than others?

Luisa: Colombian Accent
1. How was the accent of this speaker different from or similar to those of the other speakers in this section?
2. Was this accent easier or more difficult to understand than the other examples in this section?

Hopefully you have found the listening exercises to be helpful in drawing your attention to various accents in the Spanish language. Please keep in mind that this is not an easy thing to do and is something that can take a long time to get comfortable with. If you plan to travel to a certain country or are going to be around Spanish speakers from a certain country, I suggest you do some preparation by finding YouTube videos, movies, or podcasts of speakers from that area, and turn on the subtitles in Spanish when possible so you can start training your ear. If you get frustrated, just remember that it will get easier with time, and that even many native Spanish speakers can relate to this struggle!

Places to Visit

I am the type of person who would love to see every inch of the earth if I could. I find the world fascinating, and I hope to see as much of it as I can. Unfortunately, the only Spanish-speaking country I have been able to visit so far is Mexico, and because of that, I have referenced my personal experiences in Mexico frequently throughout this book. I am fortunate enough to have learned a lot about other countries, thanks to the Spanish speakers I have met here in the United States who have shared with me about their countries, but they are not experiences I have had firsthand. I have also learned a lot from watching documentaries and videos about other Spanish-speaking countries that I hope to see in person someday.

If you are like me, you'll likely never run out of places you'd like to travel to. This section focuses on native speakers describing something in their country that they think is worthy of being on your travel list—so you can think about where you might want to travel, or have those learning experiences virtually, from home.

España

To showcase Spanish speakers in Europe, the following is the transcript of QuickClip #20 of a native speaker from Spain. Isaac will be sharing a little bit about his country and highlighting what he thinks is worth visiting as a tourist in his country.

Hear Isaac from Spain share about his top must-see in Spain: La Alhambra, an impressive palace of historical and architectural importance.

To watch the QuickClip, use the camera on your mobile phone to scan the QR code or visit the link below.

www.quickclips.io/spanish-20

Isaac: Hola, me llamo Isaac y hoy quiero contarles sobre mi lugar favorito de España. Se llama la Alhambra y está en Granada, una ciudad en el sur de España, en la región de Andalucía. La Alhambra es un palacio muy antiguo y hermoso, con jardines, fuentes y decoraciones en las paredes. La Alhambra tiene una historia muy interesante y me encanta caminar por sus pasillos. Además, las vistas desde la Alhambra son increíbles y puedes ver las montañas con nieve. Si algún día visitas España, no dudes en visitar la Alhambra. Es increíble y te encantará.

México

To showcase Spanish speakers in North America, the following is the transcript of QuickClip #21 of a native speaker from Mexico. Arantza will be sharing a little bit about her country and highlighting what she thinks is worth visiting as a tourist.

Hear Arantza share about her favorite place in all of Mexico: Xcaret, a natural water park and so much more!

To watch the QuickClip, use the camera on your mobile phone to scan the QR code or visit the link below.

www.quickclips.io/spanish-21

Arantza: Hola, mi nombre es Arantza y quiero hablarles de Xcaret, mi lugar favorito en México. Situado en la Riviera Maya, este increíble parque eco-arqueológico te ofrece una experiencia inigualable donde la naturaleza, la cultura y la historia se unen.

En Xcaret, podrás nadar en ríos subterráneos, disfrutar de playas de arena blanca, y explorar un asombroso acuario de arrecifes de coral. Además, podrás aprender sobre la fascinante historia y tradiciones de México a través de sus espectáculos culturales, como el famoso show nocturno "Xcaret México Espectacular."

Ya sea que te guste la aventura o prefieras relajarte rodeado de belleza natural, Xcaret tiene algo para todos. Es un lugar ideal para familias, amigos, o parejas que quieran vivir la esencia de México.

¡No te pierdas la oportunidad de descubrir Xcaret! Será una experiencia que recordarás para siempre.

Costa Rica

To showcase Spanish speakers in Central America, the following is the transcript of QuickClip #22 of a native speaker from Costa Rica. Natalia will be sharing a little bit about her country and highlighting what she thinks is worth visiting as a tourist.

Hear Natalia from Costa Rica share about her favorite place in her home country: Parque Nacional Manuel Antonio, a national park with both rainforest and beach.

Natalia: Hola, soy Natalia, y quiero contarles sobre mi lugar favorito en Costa Rica. Se llama el Parque Nacional Manuel Antonio, y está en la costa del Pacífico. Es un parque lleno de playas hermosas, selvas tropicales, y una increíble variedad de animales, como monos y perezosos. Me encanta caminar por los senderos del parque y disfrutar de la naturaleza. También, las vistas al océano desde allí son espectaculares. Si alguna vez visitas Costa Rica, te recomiendo mucho ir al Parque Nacional Manuel Antonio. En mi opinión, es el mejor lugar en Costa Rica.

Colombia

To showcase Spanish speakers in South America, the following is the transcript of QuickClip #23 of a native speaker from Colombia. Luisa will be sharing a little bit about her country and highlighting what she thinks is worth visiting as a tourist.

Luisa from Colombia shares about her favorite city in Colombia, Salento, which inspired the popular Disney movie *Encanto*. She also shares about a valley nearby filled with the national tree of Colombia.

To watch the QuickClip, use the camera on your mobile phone to scan the QR code or visit the link below.

www.quickclips.io/spanish-23

Luisa: Hola, me llamo Luisa, y quiero hablarles de mi ciudad favorita en Colombia. Se llama Salento, y es muy conocida por ser la inspiración para la película "Encanto." Me gusta mucho caminar por el centro, ver sus casas de colores y sentir la cultura del lugar. También, me gusta mucho ir al "Valle del Cocora," para ver sus grandes palmas de cera, que es el árbol nacional de Colombia. Si alguna vez vas a Colombia, te recomiendo mucho visitar Salento.

Puerto Rico

To showcase Spanish speakers in the Caribbean, here is the transcript of QuickClip #24 of a native speaker from Puerto Rico. Abdiel will be sharing a little bit about his country and highlighting what he thinks is worth visiting as a tourist.

Abdiel from Puerto Rico shares his favorite place on the island in the recording "Visit Puerto Rico." He will tell you all about the beautiful sights and nature you can see in the El Yunque rainforest.

To watch the QuickClip, use the camera on your mobile phone to scan the QR code or visit the link below.

www.quickclips.io/spanish-24

Abdiel: Hola. Me llamo Abdiel, y mi lugar favorito en Puerto Rico es El Yunque. Es un bosque tropical en el noreste de la isla. El Yunque es un lugar lleno de árboles, ríos, y cascadas. Me gusta mucho caminar por los senderos y ver la naturaleza, especialmente las aves y las plantas. También, las vistas de las montañas son muy hermosas. Si alguna vez visitas Puerto Rico, te recomiendo mucho ir a El Yunque.

Perú

To showcase Spanish speakers in South America, here is the transcript of QuickClip #25 of a native speaker from Peru. Pepe will be sharing a little bit about his country and highlighting what he thinks is worth visiting as a tourist.

Pepe: ¡Hola! Soy Pepe. Yo soy de Perú y hoy quiero hablarles de mi lugar favorito en todo Perú. Se llama Machu Picchu. Machu Picchu es una ciudad inca muy antigua y está en las montañas de los Andes. Machu Picchu es conocida por su impresionante arquitectura. Yo voy a Machu Picchu cada 2 o 3 años, porque me encanta explorar las ruinas, los caminos, y sentirme conectado con la historia y la cultura de los antiguos incas que vivían en Perú. Además, las vistas desde la ciudad son espectaculares. Puedes ver las montañas que tocan el cielo y puedes ver también los valles con los ríos y los animales, caminando muy lejos. Cuando vayas a Perú, si alguna vez visitas Perú, te recomiendo mucho que vayas a Machu Picchu; es una experiencia inolvidable. Vas a estar muy arriba. Casi puedes tocar el cielo.

I am so grateful for all the Spanish speakers that we were able to feature in this book. They have helped us go on this journey together. Even if visiting a Spanish-speaking country is not something you plan to do, I hope you have enjoyed getting to know bits and pieces of these beautiful countries through listening to the people who have been kind enough to share their countries and cultures with us.

Glossary

Basic Grammar Terms

adjectives
Words used to describe nouns.

cognates
Words that appear to be similar across two different languages.

definite articles
Words used to identify a noun or group of nouns—in English, "the."

indefinite articles
Words used to identify words with less singular specificity than a definite article—words like "a," "an," or "some," rather than "the."

infinitives
Verbs in their original state before conjugation. For example, English infinitives include to walk, to eat, to read, etc.

nouns
Words representing a person, place, or thing.

subject pronouns
Words used to communicate who we are talking about (or directly addressing) when we speak. In English, these are words like "I," "he," "she," "we," "they," and both plural and singular forms of "you."

verbs
Words that represent an action.

verb conjugation
The process of changing the form of a verb to show a change in person, number, tense, and so on. (For example, the difference between "I was" and "I am," or "I walk" and "she walks.")

Glossary of Spanish Words and Phrases

ESSENTIAL WORDS

after
después

and
y/e

bathroom
baño

before
antes

bless you / cheers
salud

date
fecha

day
día (m.)

English
inglés

he
él

hour/time
hora

I
yo

job/work
trabajo

late / the afternoon
tarde

less
menos

like (or as)
como

money
dinero

month
mes

more
más

my
mi(s)

never
nunca

night
noche

or
o/u

school
escuela

she
ella

Spanish
español

that
ese/esa

that (far away)
aquel/aquella

the
el/la/los/las

these
estos/estas

those
esos/esas

those (far away)
aquellos/aquellas

then
entonces

there is/are
hay

they
ellos/ellas

this
este/esta

time/weather
tiempo

tomorrow
mañana

we
nosotros/nosotras

week
semana

with
con

without
sin

yesterday
ayer

you (formal)
usted

you (informal)
tú

you (plural)
ustedes

QUESTION WORDS

how much/many
cuánto/a/os/as

how/what
cómo

what
qué

when
cuándo

where
dónde

which one(s)
cuál(es)

who
quién(es)

why
por qué

ESSENTIAL PHRASES AND QUESTIONS

Can you help me?
¿Puede ayudarme? (formal)
¿Puedes ayudarme? (informal)

Congratulations
Felicidades

Do you speak _____?
¿Habla (usted) _____? (formal)
¿Hablas (tú) _____? (informal)

How do you say _____?
¿Cómo se dice _____?

I'm allergic to _____
Soy alérgico(a) a _____

I'm hungry
Tengo hambre

I'm sick
Estoy enfermo(a)

I'm sorry
Lo siento

I'm thirsty
Tengo sed

I need help
Necesito ayuda

I speak (a little bit of) _____
Hablo (un poco de) _____

I don't know
No sé

I don't understand
No entiendo

It's an emergency
Es una emergencia

It's okay
Está bien

Maybe
Tal vez

Me too
Yo también

Me neither
Yo tampoco

No
No

Please
Por favor

Repeat, please
Repita por favor (formal)
Repite por favor (informal)

Slower, please
Más lento / despacio, por favor

That's great!
¡Qué bueno!

Thank you
Gracias

What does _____ mean?
¿Qué significa _____?

What is this?
¿Qué es esto?

What time is it?
¿Qué hora es/son?

Yes
Sí

You're welcome
De nada

WORDS FOR FAMILY AND FRIENDS

aunt
tía

brother
hermano

boyfriend
novio

brother-in-law
cuñado

cat
gato

child
niño(a)

children/sons
hijos

cousin (female)
prima

cousin (male)
primo

couple
pareja

daughter
hija

daughter-in-law
nuera

dog
perro

family
familia

father/dad
padre/papá

father-in-law
suegro

friend
amigo(a)

girlfriend
novia

goddaughter
ahijada

godfather
padrino

godmother
madrina

godson
ahijado

granddaughter
nieta

grandfather
abuelo

grandmother
abuela

grandchildren/grandsons
nietos

great-grandfather
bisabuelo

great-grandmother
bisabuela

half-brother
medio hermano

half-sister
media hermana

husband
esposo

man
hombre

mother/mom
madre/mamá

mother-in-law
suegra

nephew
sobrino

niece
sobrina

pet
mascota

siblings/brothers
hermanos

sister
hermana

sister-in-law
cuñada

son
hijo

son-in-law
yerno

stepbrother
hermanastro

stepdaughter
hijastra

stepfather
padrastro

stepmother
madrastra

stepsister
hermanastra

stepson
hijastro

uncle
tío

wife
esposa

woman
mujer

BASIC ADJECTIVES

good-looking
guapo(a)

happy
feliz

kind
amable

mischievous
travieso(a)

nice
simpático(a)

pretty
bonito(a)

serious
serio(a)

short
bajo(a)

strong
fuerte

tall
alto(a)

NUMBERS

one
uno

two
dos

three
tres

four
cuatro

five
cinco

six
seis

seven
siete

eight
ocho

nine
nueve

ten
diez

eleven
once

twelve
doce

thirteen
trece

fourteen
catorce

fifteen
quince

sixteen
dieciséis

seventeen
diecisiete

eighteen
dieciocho

nineteen
diecinueve

twenty
veinte

thirty
treinta

forty
cuarenta

fifty
cincuenta

sixty
sesenta

seventy
setenta

eighty
ochenta

ninety
noventa

one hundred
cien

WORDS FOR SHOPPING AND DINING

box
caja

bread
pan

butter
mantequilla

cashier
cajero(a)

chair
silla

cheese
queso

chicken
pollo

clothing
ropa

clothing store
tienda de ropa

coffee
café

discount
descuento

drink
bebida

fish
pescado

food
comida

fruit
fruta

furniture
muebles

glass
vaso

hat
sombrero

market
mercado

meat
carne

milk
leche

money
dinero

pants
pantalones

pepper
pimienta

plate
plato

price
precio

receipt
factura/recibo

rice
arroz

salt
sal

shirt
camisa

shoes
zapatos

soap
jabón

soup
sopa

store
tienda

supermarket
supermercado

toilet paper
papel higiénico

vegetable
verdura

water
agua

PHRASES FOR SHOPPING AND DINING

Are there vegetarian options?
¿Hay opciones vegetarianas?

Can I pay with a card?
¿Puedo pagar con tarjeta?

Can I pay with cash?
¿Puedo pagar con efectivo?

Can I try this on?
¿Puedo probarme esto?

Can you bring me the menu?
¿Me puede traer el menú?

Can you bring me more water, please?
¿Me puede traer más agua, por favor?

Can you give me a bag?
¿Me puede dar una bolsa?

Can you give me a receipt?
¿Me puede dar un recibo?

Can you bring me the bill?
¿Me puede traer la cuenta?

Do you accept credit/debit cards?
¿Aceptan tarjetas de crédito/débito?

Do you have any special offers?
¿Tienen alguna oferta especial?

Do you have change?
¿Tiene cambio?

Do you have gluten-free products?
¿Tienen productos sin gluten?

Do you have to-go boxes?
¿Tienen cajas para llevar?

How much does it cost?
¿Cuánto cuesta?

I would like a table for two, please.
Quisiera una mesa para dos, por favor.

Is the fruit fresh?
¿Está fresca la fruta?

Is there a discount?
¿Hay algún descuento?

Is there a supermarket nearby?
¿Hay algún supermercado cerca?

What do you recommend?
¿Qué recomienda?

What time does the store close?
¿A qué hora cierra la tienda?

What time does the supermarket open?
¿A qué hora abre el supermercado?

What's on the daily menu?
¿Qué tiene el menú del día?

Where can I pay?
¿Dónde puedo pagar?

Where is the bathroom?
¿Dónde está el baño?

BASIC VERBS

to ask (a question or ask for information)
preguntar

to ask (for an object, favor, or action) or to order
pedir

to bathe oneself
bañarse

to be (permanent)
ser

to be (temporary)
estar

to be able to
poder

to buy
comprar

to call (oneself)
llamar(se)

to close
cerrar

to come
venir

to decide
decidir

to drink
tomar/beber

to do/make
hacer

to eat
comer

to arrive
llegar

to find
encontrar

to follow/continue
seguir

to get dressed
vestirse

to get up
levantarse

to give
dar

to go
ir

to hope/wait
esperar

to jump
saltar

to know
saber

to leave/allow
dejar

to leave/go out
salir

to like
gustar

to listen
escuchar

to live
vivir

to look
mirar

to make/do
hacer

to play
jugar

to prefer
preferir

to put/place
poner

to read
leer

to run
correr

to say/tell
decir

to see
ver

to sleep
dormir

to start/begin
empezar

to stop
parar

to study
estudiar

to take
tomar

to take/to drink
tomar

to touch/play (an instrument)
tocar

to wait
esperar

to walk
caminar

to want/love
querer

to work
trabajar

to write
escribir

to return
regresar

to return
volver

to wake up
despertarse

WORDS FOR TRAVEL AND GETTING AROUND

aisle/hallway
pasillo

airplane
avión

airport
aeropuerto

arrival time
hora de llegada

backpack
mochila

beach
playa

baggage claim
reclamo de equipaje

bicycle
bicicleta

boarding area
zona de embarque

boarding pass
pase de abordar

boat
barco

bridge
puente

bus
autobús

car
coche/carro/auto

city
ciudad

cruise
crucero

departure time
hora de salida

destination
destino

directions
direcciones

driver
conductor(a)

excursion
excursión

exit
salida

flight
vuelo

gas station
gasolinera

hotel
hotel

itinerary
itinerario

luggage
equipaje

map
mapa

market
mercado

monument
monumento

museum
museo

park
parque

passport
pasaporte

police
policía

port
puerto

reservation
reservación

restaurant
restaurante

sidewalk
acera

station
estación

stoplight
semáforo

street
calle

subway
metro

suitcase
maleta

taxi
taxi

ticket (for bus, train, etc.)
boleto

tour guide
guía turística

town
pueblo

train
tren

train station
estación de tren

trip
viaje

truck
camión

waiting area
zona de espera

PHRASES FOR TRAVEL AND GETTING AROUND

Can I walk there?
¿Puedo caminar hasta allí?

Can you give me directions to get to _____?
¿Me puede dar direcciones para llegar a _____?

Continue straight.
Siga recto/derecho.

Does this train/bus/subway go to _____?
¿Este tren/autobús/metro va a _____?

How do I get to _____?
¿Cómo llego a _____?

I need to get off of the bus.
Necesito bajarme del autobús.

I will find it on the map.
Lo encontraré en el mapa.

I'm lost.
Estoy perdido(a).

Is it close to here?
¿Está cerca de aquí?

Is it far from here?
¿Está lejos de aquí?

Is there a bus that goes to _____?
¿Hay un autobús que va a _____?

Is there a city map?
¿Hay un mapa de la ciudad?

Is there a taxi available?
¿Hay un taxi disponible?

Is there somewhere nearby to buy food?
¿Hay algún lugar cerca para comprar comida?

It's about a ten-minute walk.
Está a unos diez minutos caminando

It's close to here.
Está cerca de aquí

It's far from here.
Está lejos de aquí

To the left
A la izquierda

To the right
A la derecha

Turn left at the corner.
Gire a la izquierda en la esquina.

Turn right at the next street.
Gire a la derecha en la próxima calle.

What route do I need to take to get to _____?
¿Qué ruta necesito tomar para llegar a _____?

Where is _____?
¿Dónde está _____?

Where is my seat?
¿Dónde está mi asiento?

Where is the bus stop?
¿Dónde está la parada de autobús?

Where is the nearest bathroom?
¿Dónde está el baño más cercano?

Where is the train station?
¿Dónde está la estación de tren?

About the Author

MARIA BLOCK, M.A.

With over ten years of experience in language education, Maria Block has taught Spanish in both public K-12 schools and at the college level, as well as in private tutoring. She has also taught curriculum design. She earned her BA in Spanish education from South Dakota State University and her MA in Spanish from Sam Houston State University.

Maria developed a love for Spanish during a trip to Mexico while she was in high school. She continued to nurture this interest while working at a local Mexican restaurant and the multicultural center in her hometown. Following her high school graduation, she moved to Mexico to continue learning the language. While there, she taught English and discovered her passion for working with students and language education, and subsequently pursued a Bachelor of Arts in Spanish education. She also used her Spanish as an intern with social services, and volunteered with the CARA Pro Bono Project at an immigration detention center.

After college, Maria spent eight years teaching middle and high school Spanish in Houston-area public schools, including courses such as Spanish for Spanish Speakers, Spanish for Non-Spanish Speakers, and AP Spanish Language and Culture. Today, she works as an instructional designer and adjunct professor of Spanish at Lone Star College. She has also developed appliedspanish.com, a website offering resources to support learners on their Spanish language journey.

About QuickStart Guides

QuickStart Guides are books for beginners, written by experts.

QuickStart Guides® are comprehensive learning companions tailored for the beginner experience. Our books are written by experts, subject matter authorities, and thought leaders within their respective areas of study.

For nearly a decade more than a million readers have trusted QuickStart Guides® to help them get a handle on their finances, start their own business, invest in the stock market, find a new hobby, get a new job—the list is virtually endless.

The QuickStart Guides® series of books is published by ClydeBank Media, an independent publisher based in Albany, New York.

Connect with QuickStart Guides online at www.quickstartguides.com or follow us on Facebook, Instagram, and LinkedIn.

Follow us @quickstartguides

Index

A
a, 19, 40, 45, 47, 79
Accent(s), 16–17, 256–259
Accent marks, 19
ACTFL. *See* American Council on the Teaching of Foreign Languages
Activities. *See* Daily activities
adiós, 56, 59
Adjectives
　comparisons with, 165
　definition of, 46
　demonstrative, 49–53
　estar with, 154
　gender agreement of, 44, 46–47
　gender-neutral, 48–49
　noun and, 38
　possessive, 117–121, 123, 134
　for self-descriptions, 79
　ser with, 154
Affirmative commands, 222
Ages, 83–84
al fondo, 220
Allergies, 66
almohada, 36
Alphabet, 14–20, 15*t*–16*t*
alta, 123
alto, 123
amable, 78
American Council on the Teaching of Foreign Languages, 4
amiga, 40, 91
amigo, 40
-*ando*, 146
Apostrophes, 120–121
Appearance, 81–82
aquel, 50
aquella, 52
aquello, 51–52
Argentinian accent, 258
Articles
　definite, 41–42
　indefinite, 43–44
Arts, 241–243
-ar verbs
　conjugating of, 86–88, 89*t*, 105
　description of, 32
autobús, 65, 215, 217
Auxiliary verb, 113
ayuda, 224*t*
ayude, 224*t*

azúcar, 36

B
b, 19
bañarse, 105*t*
barter, 252
Basic conversation, 60–62, 67
beber, 88
bien, 68
bienvenido(a)(s), 57–58
Birthdates, 83–84
buenas, 57
buenas noches, 57
buena suerte, 67
bueno, 68
buen provecho, 67

C
caminan, 91
camisa, 163
camiseta, 69, 163
carro, 42, 46, 52*t*, 215–216
casa, 52, 120, 140–141
casa de cambio, 211
Catholicism, 122
Celebrations
　description of, 234–235
　El Cinco de Mayo, 237–238
　El Día de los Muertos, 238–240
　El Mes de la Herencia Hispana, 240–241
　quinceañera, 236–237
　vocabulary for, 235
Celsius scale, 206
ch, 17
chau, 59
Checking out at stores, 165
Chores, 144–145
Cinco de Mayo, 237–238
Clarifying words, 66–68
clima, 204–205
Clothing
　shopping for, 160–161, 163
　weather-ready, 206–208
coger, 69
Cognates, 37–38, 54
Colombia, 263
Colombian accent, 259
comadre, 122
comer, 87*t*, 168

Commands, 221–223, 224*t*
commigo, 160
Communicating languages and understanding, 63–64
Community
    errands in, 147
    social spaces in, 158–160
    vocabulary for describing, 176–177
como, 164
compadre, 122
Comparisons, 124–125, 164–165
compartir, 126
Condition, 153
Conditional tense
    for hypothetical events, 170–173
    for places we'd like to visit, 202–203
conducir, 215, 216*t*
Conjugation, verb
    -ar verbs, 86–88, 89*t*, 105
    definition of, 24, 77
    description of, 32, 60
    -er verbs, 87, 90*t*
    -ir verbs, 88–89, 90*t*, 109, 185*t*
    practicing of, 92
    present-tense verbs, 89–93, 102, 125
    reflexive verbs, 106, 192
    ser, 80, 99, 123, 152, 185*t*
    tener, 81*t*, 113, 123
Connecting words, 135
conocer, 150–151, 151*t*
con permiso, 62
Consonants, 42
contigo, 160
Conversation
    basic, 60–62, 67
    description of, 55
    formal, 61*f*
    goodbyes, 59–60
    greetings, 55–60
    informal, 61*f*
    introductions, 60–62
costar, 163*t*, 163–164
Costa Rica, 262
Countries, 199
cubrir, 201
cuesta, 164
cuídate, 59
cuídese, 59
Cultural diversity
    celebrations, 234–241
    unity in, 243–244
Culture
    celebrations, 234–241
    food and, 172–173, 253–254
    time and, 100
    vocabulary words for, 188
Currency, 210–211

D

Daily activities
    present-tense verbs for, 84–93, 102–103
    reflexive verbs for, 103–106
    time applied to, 101
dar, 109–110, 110*t*, 186*t*, 226
Dates, 23–24, 83–84, 153
Day of the Dead. *See El Día de los Muertos*
Days of the week, 22
de, 144
decir, 108, 187*t*, 227, 227*t*
Definite articles
    gender agreement of, 41–42, 44, 47
    plural version of, 42
del, 144
Demonstrative adjectives, 49–53
derecha, 220
derecho, 220
descubierto, 201
descubrir, 201
Diaeresis, 17
Dialogue, 66–71
dieci, 20
Differences, embracing of, 243–244
digo, 227
Directions, 219–220
Direct speech, 113–114
disculpa, 62–63
disculpe, 62–63
discutir, 126
Dislikes, 128–136
dormir, 147
Double negatives, 133, 203

E

e, 19
Eating out, 64–65, 165–170
el, 25, 28, 40–41, 45–46, 123
el banco, 211
el baño, 65
el carro, 38–39, 41*t*, 92, 215
el centro, 148
El Cinco de Mayo, 237–238
el clima, 204–205
El Día de los Muertos, 238–240
el gorro, 207*f*, 208
el imperfecto, 177
el itinerario, 225
ella, 25, 91
ellas, 26, 129
elle, 28
ellos, 26, 92, 129
el mercado, 148, 251
El Mes de la Herencia Hispana, 240–241
el metro, 217
el pretérito, 177
el tamaño, 162

el tiempo, 204–205
Emergencies, 65–66
Emotion, 153, 191–193
encantado(a), 60
encantan, 134
encantar, 133–134
encontrar a mi media naranja, 70*t*
Entertainment, 241–243
Errands, 147–148
-er verbs
   conjugation of, 87, 90*t*
   description of, 32
es, 42, 99–100
esa, 52
escribir, 89
eso, 51–52
España, 260
está, 52, 206
estar
   adjectives that change meaning with, 154
   conjugation of, 143*t*
   description of, 76, 143
   expressing feelings using, 191
   ser versus, 151–154
   transportation uses of, 215
   uses of, 152–153
   weather descriptions and, 206
estar lleno(a), 215
estar retrasado(a), 215
este, 50, 68
esto, 51–52
estudiante, 80
estudiar, 85, 86*t*
Europa, 199
éxito, 67

F

Fahrenheit scale, 206
False cognates, 37–38
Family
   activities of, 125–128
   extended, 141
   possessive adjectives for describing, 117–121
   reflexive verbs for, 126–127
   relatives and relationships, 121–125
   stepfamily, 117–118
   vocabulary for describing, 117–121
Family members, 117–120
Feelings, expressing of, 191–193
felicidades, 67
Feminine gender, 40–41, 44, 54, 118
Filler words, 66–68
Food
   conditional tense, 170–173
   cultural importance of, 253–254
   eating out, 64–65, 165–170
   ordering, 168
   regional variations in, 167
   shopping for, 165–166
   in Spanish-speaking countries/cultures, 172–173
Formal conversation, 61*f*
Formal questions, 31, 58, 60
franela, 69
Friends, 158–160

G

g, 20
gafas, 207
ganas, 202–203
Gender
   feminine, 40–41, 44, 47
   masculine, 40–41, 44
Gender agreement
   adjectives, 44, 46–47
   definite articles and, 41–42, 47
   indefinite articles and, 43–44
   irregulars, 44–46
Gender-neutral adjectives, 48–49
Geography, 203–204
Gerunds, irregular, 146–147
Godparents, 122
Goodbyes, 59–60
"Go" verbs, 107–109
Grandparents, 117
Greetings, 55–60
Grocery shopping, 165–166
gustan, 129*t*, 129–130, 132
gustar, 130, 171, 202, 228
   uses of, 128–133
   verbs similar to, 133–136
gustaría, 171

H

h, 20
haber, 200
hablar, 85
hacer, 107, 108*t*, 109, 172, 186*t*, 205, 221
hasta, 59
hasta luego/pronto/mañana, 59
Hat, 207–208
hay que, 112*t*, 113
Hispania, 36
Hispanic, 235, 243
Hispanic Heritage Month, 240–241
History
   imperfect examples, 189–190
   preterite examples, 189–190
   vocabulary words for, 188
Hobbies, 107
hola, 56–57
Holidays, 234–241
hombre, 47, 52*t*
Home. *See* House
hora, 97

Hospitality, 140
House
    chores around, 144–145
    cultural importance of, 141
    errands outside, 147–148
    layout of, 141*f*
    living arrangements in, 141
    location of rooms and objects in, prepositions for describing, 143–144
    possessive adjectives for describing, 117–121
    present progressive tense, 145
    vocabulary for describing, 140–141

I

i, 19
Iberian Peninsula, 36
Identity documents, 208–209
Idioms, 68–71
-iendo, 146
igualmente, 61
Imperfect tense
    conjugation of, 183*t*
    description of, 177
    examples of, 178, 178*t*
    history examples, 189–190
    irregular verbs in, 184, 185*t*
    preterite tense and, 190
    regular verbs in, 183–184
    on timeline, 178–179, 179*f*
    uses for, 180–181
Impersonal *se*, 209–210
Indefinite articles, gender agreement and, 43–44
Indigenous languages, 36
Indigenous peoples, 188
Indirect object pronouns, 130*t*, 130–131, 225–230, 226*f*
Indirect speech, 113
Individualistic value, 141
Infinitives
    action communicated using, 202
    description of, 32–33, 102
    reflexive verbs as, 103
Informal conversation, 61*f*
Informal questions, 31, 58, 60, 120
Introductions, 60–62
Irregular gerunds, 146–147
Irregular past participles, 201
Irregulars, 44–46
Irregular verbs
    in conditional tense, 172
    conducir, 216, 216*t*
    estar, 143
    "go," 107–109
    hacer, 108*t*, 109
    for hobbies, 107
    pedir, 161
    preferir, 161
    in preterite tense, 184–187, 186*t*–187*t*
    salir, 108*t*, 109
    tener, 81
-ir verbs
    conjugation of, 88–89, 90*t*, 109*t*, 185*t*
    description of, 32, 109–110
    imperfect tense, 185*t*
    as irregular gerund, 146
    present-tense conjugation of, 149
    preterite tense, 186*t*
izquierda, 220

J

j, 20
jugar, 110–112

L

la, 40–41, 45–46, 123
la camisa, 163
la camiseta, 163
la celebración de los quince años, 236–237
la gorra, 207*f*, 208
la guagua, 217
la lavandería, 148
la merienda, 172
Languages, 36–37, 63–64
la panadería, 148
la ruta, 217
las, 41
las fechas, 23–24
la siesta, 172
las vocales, 18–20
Latin, 36
Latin America. *See also specific country*
    dining in, 167
    indigenous languages/peoples of, 36, 188
    markets in, 148
    taxis in, 218–219
    time concept in, 100
Latine, 235
Latino(a), 235, 243
Latinx, 235
la tortillería, 148
le, 229
les, 229
Letters
    alphabet, 14–20, 15*t*–16*t*
    sounds of, 17–18
levantarse, 103
Likes, 128–136
limpia, 223
limpiar, 223
Linguistic variations, 68–71
ll, 17
los, 41
los carros, 41*t*, 42
los días de la semana, 22
lo siento, 62

los meses y las estaciones, 22–23
los padres, 117
los papás, 117
los primos, 122
los quehaceres, 144
los tíos, 122
Loved ones, 121–125

M
maleta, 207
manejar, 215
Manners, 62–63
Maps, 219
Markets, 148, 251–253
más, 64, 124, 164–165
Masculine gender, 40–41, 44, 54, 118
mayor, 83
Meals, cultural importance of, 253–254
menos, 124, 164
mesero, 169–170
Metric system, 221
México, 113, 172, 209, 211, 217, 237–238, 255, 259, 261
mi hermano, 118
Military time, 98
mis padres, 118
mochila, 207
Money-related vocabulary, 210–211
Months, 22–23
mucho gusto, 60
mujer, 47, 52*t*, 169–170

N
ñ, 20
Náhuatl, 36
National ID, 208–209
Near future tense, 148–150
necesitar, 112, 112*t*
Negative commands, 222
no entiendo, 64
nosotras, 25
nosotros, 25, 88, 111, 126, 132, 159
nos vemos, 59
Nouns
  adjectives and, 38
  feminine, 47, 54
  gender of, 41, 47
  masculine, 54
  plural, 48, 129
nuestro abuelo, 118
Numbers, 20–22
numero, 162

O
o, 40, 45, 47, 79
Object-subject-verb format, 39
Obligation, 112–114
Ordering food, 168, 170–173

O-S-V format. *See* Object-subject-verb format
Ownership, 120–121

P
padrinos, 122
pan de muerto, 240
para, 149–150, 168
paraguas, 207
pasa, 224*t*
pasada, 24
pasado, 24
pasar, 85, 223
pase, 224*t*
Passport, 208–209
Past
  describing of, 177–187
  making sense of, 188–193
Past participles, 200–201
Past tense, 177
pedir, 161*t*, 161–162
People
  appearance of, 123
  comparisons of, 124–125
  talking to and describing, 150–155
pequeña, 162
pequeño, 162
perdón, 62–63
perro, 217
Personal space, 56
Perú, 265
Phrases, 55
Physical features, 82, 123
Places
  communication about, 202
  conditional tense applied to, 202–203
  countries, 199
  present perfect used to describe, 200–202
  we'll be, 198–199
  we've been to, 198–199
playera, 69
Plural nouns, 48, 129
Plural words, 42–44
poder, 172
podr, 172
podría, 172
policía, 80
Politeness, 170–171
por, 149–150
Portugal, 36
Possession, 120–121
Possessive adjectives, 117–121, 123, 134
practicar, 85, 129
preferir, 161, 161*t*, 171
preguntar, 162
Prepositional pronoun, 132
Prepositions, 143–144
Present perfect tense, 200–202

Present progressive tense, 145–146, 153
Present-tense verbs
    activities using, 84–86
    -ar verbs, 86–88
    conjugation of, 89–93, 102, 125
    for daily activities, 102–103
    for eating out, 167
    -er verbs, 87
    for hobbies, 107
    -ir verbs, 88–89
    reflexive verbs, 106
    regular, 84–93, 106
Preterite tense
    conjugation of, 183*t*
    description of, 177
    examples of, 178, 178*t*
    history examples, 189–190
    imperfect tense and, 190
    irregular verbs in, 184–187, 186*t*–187*t*
    regular verbs in, 183–184
    on timeline, 178–179, 179*f*
    uses for, 180–181
probar, 169, 169*t*
Proficiency levels, 4–5
Pronouns
    demonstrative, 49–53
    indirect object, 130*t*, 130–131, 225–230, 226*f*
    order of, 77
    prepositional, 132
    reflexive, 103–105, 104*t*, 210
    subject. *See* Subject pronouns
Pronunciation
    of alphabet, 14*t*–16*t*
    differences in, 258
    of vowels, 18*t*
próxima, 24
próximo, 24
Public transportation, 215–218
Puerto Rican accent, 258
Puerto Rico, 264
pues, 68

Q
qu, 20
que, 30, 58, 68*f*, 69, 71, 164
Quechua, 36
querer, 159, 160*t*, 172
Question words, 29–31
quinceañera, 236–237

R
recomendan, 230
recomendar, 169, 169*t*, 171, 226
Reflexive pronouns, 103–105, 104*t*, 210
Reflexive verbs
    conjugation of, 106, 192
    for daily activities, 103–106

    for family, 126–127
    present-tense, 106
regar, 145–146
regatear, 252
Regular present-tense verbs, 84–93
Relationships
    family, 121–125
    non-familial, 150
Relatives, 121–125
Restaurants, 166
retrasado, 215
reunirse, 126, 126*t*
roja, 46
rojo, 46
Rolling your tongue, 17–18, 217
rr, 17, 217

S
S, 20
saber, 150–151, 151*t*
salgo, 159
salir, 107, 108*t*, 159*t*, 215
salud, 67
se
    impersonal, 209–210
    with reflexive verbs, 104
Seasons, 22–23
seguir, 221
Self
    adjectives used in describing, 79
    defining of, 75–76
    ser for describing, 78–80
    tener for describing, 80–82
Sentences, 39
sentirse, 127, 192*t*
ser
    adjectives that change meaning with, 154
    ages using, 83–84
    birthdates using, 83–84
    conjugation of, 80, 99, 123, 152, 185*t*
    dates and, 153
    describing yourself with, 78–80
    estar versus, 151–154
    introduction to, 76–77
    tener versus, 82
    time and, 96–101, 153
    uses of, 78
ser pan comido, 70*t*
Shopping
    checking out, 165
    for clothing, 160–161, 163
    costs and comparisons, 160–165
    for food, 165–166
    grocery, 165–166
    questions for, 64–65
Slang, 68–71
Snacks, 172

Social life, 255–256
Social spaces, 158–160
sombrero, 207*f*, 208
son, 99–100
S-O-V format. *See* Subject-object-verb format
soy, 78, 80
Spain, 36
Spanglish, 37
Spanish accent, 258
Spanish–English comparisons
   cognates, 37–38, 54
   gender agreement. *See* Gender agreement
   greetings, 56
   overview of, 35
   plural words, 42, 44
   word order, 38–40
Spanish language
   celebrations of, 234–241
   history of, 36–37
   linguistic variations in, 68–70
Spanish-speaking countries/cultures
   accents, 16–17
   currency in, 210
   description of, 16
   extended family in homes, 141
   food in, 172–173
   indirect speech in, 114
   individualistic value in, 141
   metric system in, 221
   number of, 16, 256
   punctuality in, 101
   social life in, 255–256
   time concept in, 101
Spring, 23
Stem-changing verbs, 110–112, 147
Stepfamily, 117–118
Storytelling, 176
Subject-object-verb format, 39
Subject pronouns
   abbreviations, 27–28
   application of, 28–29
   list of, 25*t*
   tú, 26–28, 31, 58, 60
   uses of, 24
   usted, 26–27, 31, 58, 60
   variations of, 27–28
Subject-verb-object pattern, 39
Sunglasses, 207
S-V-O pattern. *See* Subject-verb-object pattern

T

talla, 162
tan como, 165
tanto como, 165
tarjeta de crédito, 210
Taxi, 218–219
te, 228

Temperature, 206
tendr, 172
tener
   ages using, 83–84
   birthdates using, 83–84
   conjugation of, 81*t*, 113, 123
   describing yourself with, 80–82
   physical appearance descriptions using, 81–82
   ser versus, 82
tener ganas de, 202
tener que, 112*t*, 113
Tenses
   conditional, 170–173
   imperfect. *See* Imperfect tense
   near future, 148–150
   present perfect, 200–202
   present progressive, 145–146, 153
   preterite. *See* Preterite tense
tiempo, 204–205
tiendas, 52*t*
Tilde, 120
Time
   cultural views on, 100
   daily activities and, 101
   in past, 182
   ser for describing, 96–101
tomar, 168
Tongue, rolling your, 17–18, 217
trabajar, 85, 87*f*
Transportation
   needs for, 217–218
   public, 215–218
   taxi, 218–219
   verbs related to, 215–216
Traveling
   activities during, 224–230
   to Colombia, 263
   to Costa Rica, 262
   cultural differences while, 251–256
   to España, 260
   geography, 203–204
   identity documents for, 208–209
   indirect object pronouns applied to, 225–231
   to México, 261
   to Perú, 265
   present perfect used to describe, 200–202
   to Puerto Rico, 264
   questions to ask, 64–65
   recommendations for, 224–230
   to-do list for, 208–211
   transportation needs, 217–218
   weather, 204–206
tú, 25–28, 58, 60
   for informal commands, 221, 222*t*, 224*t*
   for informal questions, 31, 58, 60, 120
   negative commands, 222*t*
Two-verb constructions, 223–224

U

ü, 17–18
Ud, 28
Uds, 28
un, 43, 43*t*, 80
una, 43, 43*t*, 80
unas, 43*t*
unos, 43*t*
un placer, 61
usted, 25–27, 58, 60
    for formal commands, 221, 224*t*
    for formal questions, 31, 58, 60
    negative commands, 222*t*
ustedes, 26–28, 129

V

v, 19
veinte, 21
venir, 168*t*, 169
ver, 185*t*, 187*t*
Verb(s). *See also specific verbs*
    auxiliary, 113
    chore, 144–145
    conditional, 171*t*
    "go," 107–109
    infinitive, 32, 32*t*, 102
    irregular. *See* Irregular verbs
    present progressive, 145–146
    present-tense. *See* Present-tense verbs
    reflexive. *See* Reflexive verbs
    stem-changing, 110–112
Verb conjugations
    definition of, 24, 77
    description of, 32, 60
    -er verbs, 87, 90*t*
    -ir verbs, 88–89, 90*t*, 109, 185*t*
    practicing of, 92
    present-tense verbs, 89–93, 102, 125
    reflexive verbs, 106, 192
    ser, 80, 99, 123, 152, 185*t*
    tener, 81*t*, 113, 123
Verb-subject-object format, 39
vestido, 40
viejo(a), 83
Visa, 208–209
vivir, 88*t*
vosotras, 25, 27
vosotros, 25, 27, 88, 111, 127, 159, 229
Vowels
    description of, 18–20
    plural form of, 42
voy, 109
V-S-O format. *See* Verb-subject-object format

W

Weather
    clothing for, 206–208
    terminology for, 204–206
Week, days of, 22
Well-wishing words, 66–68
Words
    connecting, 135
    order of, 38–40
    plural, 42–44
    question, 29–31

Y

"y'all," 27
Yes-or-no type questions, 39
yo, 108, 110
Yourself. *See* Self

Z

z, 20, 43

WHAT DID YOU THINK?

We rely on reviews and reader feedback to help our authors reach more people, improve our books, and grow our business. We would really appreciate it if you took the time to help us out by providing feedback on your recent purchase.

It's really easy, it only takes a second, and it's a tremendous help!

NOT SURE WHAT TO SHARE?
Here are some ideas to get your review started...

- *What did you learn?*
- *Have you been able to put anything you learned into action?*
- *Would you recommend the book to other readers?*
- *Is the author clear and easy to understand?*

TWO WAYS TO LEAVE AN AMAZON REVIEW

Use the camera app on your mobile phone to scan the QR code or visit the link below to leave an Amazon review.

www.quickstartguides.review/spanish

SCAN ME   or   VISIT URL

GET YOUR NEXT
QuickStart Guide®
FOR FREE

Leave us a quick video testimonial on our website and we will give you a **FREE *QuickStart Guide*** of your choice!

RECORD TESTIMONIAL   **SUBMIT TO OUR WEBSITE**   **GET A FREE BOOK**

TWO WAYS TO LEAVE A VIDEO TESTIMONIAL

Use the camera app on your mobile phone to scan the QR code or visit the link below to record your testimonial and get your free book.

 or go.quickstartguides.com/free

SAVE 10% ON YOUR NEXT QuickStart Guide®

USE CODE: QSG10

www.quickstartguides.shop/business

www.quickstartguides.shop/rungrow

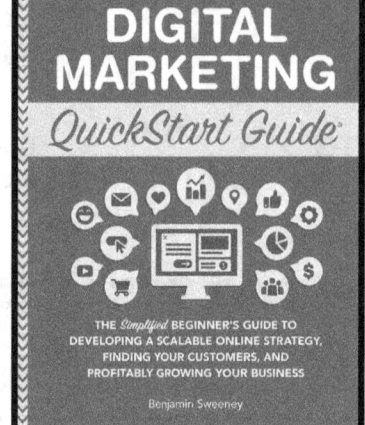

https://quickstartguides.shop/dmarketing

www.quickstartguides.shop/accounting

Use the camera app on your mobile phone to scan the QR code or visit the link below the cover to shop. Get 10% off your entire order when you use code 'QSG10' at checkout at www.quickstartguides.com

CLYDEBANK MEDIA

QuickStart Guides®

PROUDLY SUPPORT ONE TREE PLANTED

One Tree Planted is a 501(c)(3) nonprofit organization focused on global reforestation, with millions of trees planted every year. ClydeBank Media is proud to support One Tree Planted as a reforestation partner.

Every dollar donated plants one tree and every tree makes a difference!

Learn more at www.clydebankmedia.com/charitable-giving or make a contribution at onetreeplanted.org.

www.ingramcontent.com/pod-product-compliance
Lightning Source LLC
Chambersburg PA
CBHW082200070526
44585CB00020B/2210